"This lovely, sensitive account o
intractable behavioral problems c
is a treasure for parents and clinici
not only to describe what she doe. ...p.... .... ..ougnt processes and the science behind her interventions. Clinicians interested in
her approach will find the latter part of the book especially helpful, with
detailed instructions on how they can incorporate into their own practice
the techniques Dr. Lovett uses so adroitly. Parents will treasure her message of hope and find many valuable gems they can use to enhance their
daily efforts to express their love and caring for even the most difficult
children."

—*Glen R. Elliott, PhD, MD, Chief Psychiatrist,*
Children's Health Council; Clinical Professor (Affiliated) in
Child and Adolescent Psychiatry, Department of Psychiatry
and Behavioral Sciences, Stanford School of Medicine

"Dr. Joan Lovett has written a remarkable book that will appeal to parents, teachers, mental health clinicians, daycare workers, doctors, and
nurses—basically, anyone who interacts with children. Readers will be
guided to understand children's behaviors and how to resolve inappropriate behavior though the heartwarming and comprehensive case stories, which describe an array of challenges, including attachment issues,
early medical traumas and hospitalization, vicarious traumatization, loss
of a parent, extreme neglect, and developmental delays. With sensitivity
and skillful artistry, Dr. Lovett models how to help children feel safe and
form positive and loving relationships through the use of EMDR therapy,
engaging games, healing narratives, and other practical, easily imple-
mented tools."

—*Robbie Dunton, MS, MA, EMDR Institute Coordinator*

"This is a fascinating book on the integration of play therapy, narratives,
and EMDR to heal children who have suffered complex traumatization
very early in their development. It focuses on rebuilding trust, resolving
trauma, and repairing attachment. Lovett works from an empathic and
sensitive understanding of the child's world and the child's perspective.
Rich in wonderful clinical case material, this gifted therapist gives detailed
insights into her thinking and offers a variety of very helpful creative
clinical tools and strategies and how to use these to guide parents and
children. It is a must-read for all clinicians working in this complex field."

—*Joanne Morris-Smith, CPsychol, AFBPsS,*
EMDR Europe Accredited Child and Adolescent Trainer;
Co-author of EMDR for the Next Generation:
Healing Children and Families

TRAUMA-ATTACHMENT TANGLE

Trauma-Attachment Tangle offers informative and inspiring clinical stories of children who have complex trauma and attachment issues from experiences such as adoption, hospitalization, or the death of a parent. Some of these children display puzzling or extreme symptoms such as prolonged tantrums, self-hatred, attacking their parents, or being fearful of common things like lights, solid foods, or clothing. Dr. Lovett presents strategies for unraveling the traumatic origins of children's symptoms and gives a variety of tools for treating complex trauma and for promoting attunement and attachment.

Joan Lovett, MD, is a behavioral pediatrician practicing in the San Francisco Bay Area. She is a Fellow of the American Academy of Pediatrics and an EMDRIA Approved Consultant. She has given presentations and trainings about treating childhood trauma in the US, Canada, Central America, Europe, and Asia. Dr. Lovett is also the author of *Small Wonders: Healing Childhood Trauma with EMDR.*

TRAUMA-ATTACHMENT TANGLE

Modifying EMDR to Help Children Resolve Trauma and Develop Loving Relationships

Joan Lovett, MD

Routledge
Taylor & Francis Group

NEW YORK AND LONDON

First published 2015
by Routledge
711 Third Avenue, New York, NY 10017

and by Routledge
27 Church Road, Hove, East Sussex BN3 2FA

Routledge is an imprint of the Taylor & Francis Group, an informa business

Library of Congress Cataloging-in-Publication Data
Lovett, Joan, author.
   Trauma-attachment tangle: Modifying EMDR to help children resolve trauma and develop loving relationships / Joan Lovett.
      p. ; cm.
   Includes bibliographical references.
 I. Title.
[DNLM: 1. Child Behavior Disorders—therapy—Case Reports.
2. Eye Movement Desensitization Reprocessing—methods—Case Reports.   3. Parent-Child Relations—Case Reports.   4. Stress Disorders, Post-Traumatic—therapy—Case Reports. WS 350.6]
   RJ507.A77
   618.9285'88—dc23
   2014026029

ISBN: 978-1-138-78994-4 (hbk)
ISBN: 978-1-138-78996-8 (pbk)
ISBN: 978-1-315-76453-5 (ebk)

Typeset in Sabon
by Apex CoVantage, LLC

For John

I love your kindness, generosity, and fun-loving spirit!

.

CONTENTS

ACKNOWLEDGMENTS

It has been a privilege to know the families described in *Trauma-Attachment Tangle*. I have been inspired by their courage and determination, and I appreciate their willingness to share their stories in the hope that others will benefit.

I appreciate Francine Shapiro, PhD, originator of EMDR, whose therapeutic contribution has relieved suffering around the globe. Without her work, mine would not have been possible.

My colleague and friend Deb Wesselmann, MS, LIMHP, informed me that I was doing attachment work when we both gave presentations at the Menninger Clinic in 2000. Since that time we have collaborated to develop ways to work effectively with children and families struggling with trauma and attachment issues, and we have given numerous presentations together. Many of the ideas in this book originated from her work and our collaboration. Her generosity, humor, knowledge, and commitment to helping children have inspired me.

I am thankful for the assistance of Sheryl Fullerton, my literary agent, who has had faith in this endeavor and who connected me with Routledge, a member of the Taylor and Francis Group. George Zimmar, Routledge publisher, has made the publication of this book possible. Naomi Lucks helped in the preparation of the book proposal.

I am grateful for the assistance of Sasha Harris-Lovett, John Harris, Susan Klee, Ruth Phillips, and Maria Adams, who read my manuscript at various stages in its development and offered comments that improved the organization, readability, and grammar. Many thanks!

I also appreciate Jim Adams, who helped with formatting.

Others who have contributed to this book and supported me in writing it, either directly or indirectly, include John Harris, Karen Harber, Hilda Pastor, Phil Manfield, Jeffrey Olgin, Landry Wildwind, Vivian Mazur, members of my EMDR consultation group, Molly Selvin, Barbara Bloomer, Evan Lovett-Harris, Felix Ratcliff, Zoe Chafe, Chaloha, and Sugar. Thank you all!

INTRODUCTION

Trauma-Attachment Tangle represents the culmination of my decades of work helping children and their parents overcome traumatic experiences. Over and over, I have seen that resolving children's trauma helped them trust that they are lovable, good, and worthy of care and protection. This confidence allows them to blossom emotionally and socially and to enjoy loving relationships with their parents and others, sometimes for the first time. I have observed that attachment issues stem from traumatic experiences. Untangling the trauma-attachment knot through trauma resolution, attachment enhancement, and even "detachment therapy" (detaching the parent from the child's memory of a painful event) has been a deeply satisfying part of my work as a behavioral pediatrician.

When trauma goes untreated, it often emerges later in life, sometimes in unexpected ways, as it did with Tom and Kelly, young parents who were beside themselves with fatigue, frustration, and worry. "I'm terribly afraid to let my baby cry at all," said Kelly. Kelly kept her five-month-old son Andrew with her every moment because she didn't want him to ever be alone. She felt she needed to watch him all the time—even at night—to be able to respond to his every whimper before it became a cry. Because of this, Kelly hadn't gotten much sleep since her baby was born. Baby Andrew had slept fitfully, stretched out in the middle of his parents' double bed, with Tom and Kelly clinging to opposite sides of the bed.

While it is normal for a mother to want to soothe her crying baby, Kelly's reaction was extreme. Whenever she heard Andrew cry, she became sweaty and flushed with fear, her heart pounding furiously. The more fearful she was when she responded to her baby, the more upset the baby became. Tom and his mother had been urging Kelly to put the baby in his own room at night so they could all sleep better. She had refused their advice for five months because she panicked at the thought of her baby wailing alone in another room.

Kelly's extreme fear in response to her baby's crying was a red flag for me: I suspected that trauma was fueling her anxiety. The frequency, amplitude, and inappropriateness of Kelly's anxiety alerted me that her response might stem from an earlier traumatic experience. I was concerned that Andrew was picking up his mother's anxiety, further exacerbating the situation.

I asked Kelly to picture her baby's crying, to pay attention to her emotional response, and to tell me of any earlier memories that seemed connected. After hesitating for a few moments, Kelly said thoughtfully, "Yes, I do have a memory that sometimes flashes through my mind when I hear Andrew cry. When I was a little girl I shared a bedroom with my sister. One night an intruder came into our room through a window, and he tried to molest my sister. She screamed at the top of her lungs. When I heard her cry out, I froze. I felt helpless. The intruder left in a hurry, but I still feel scared when I think of my sister's blood-curdling cries."

Trauma such as Kelly experienced generates a sense of confusion that persists long after the traumatic event is over. As a child, Kelly had felt helpless and terrified when her sister had cried out. As a new mother, Kelly had confused her Andrew's cries with the cries of her sister, who had been attacked years earlier, and responded fearfully, as if her infant were being attacked. While Kelly hadn't consciously connected her baby's cries with the molestation, the thread of terror generated by her sister's cries of distress had entered her subconscious, resurfacing years later to interfere with her relationship with her child.

In response to what Kelly told me, I suggested that Eye Movement Desensitization and Reprocessing (EMDR) therapy could help her resolve the memory of her sister's terrifying scream. EMDR therapy, originated by Francine Shapiro, PhD, in 1989, activates the information processing system that is innate in each of us. It utilizes eye movement or another form of alternating bilateral stimulation (ABS) to desensitize or take the charge off of an old memory and to reprocess the distorted negative beliefs that got stuck at the time of the trauma.[1] Kelly agreed to try EMDR, and during the first session she was able to change the distorted belief about herself from "I'm helpless and in danger when I hear crying" to "I'm safe and can respond calmly when my baby cries."

The next week, Kelly came back to my office smiling and immediately told me, "My baby is sleeping down the hall in his own room now, and we're all sleeping better." One session of EMDR took the distressing charge off the traumatic childhood memory, changed Kelly's belief about herself as a parent, and restored her sense of calm and confidence in taking care of her baby. A parent who believes "I'm safe and can take care of my child calmly" behaves very differently from a parent who is afraid that she and her child are in danger.

I have extensive experience working with children and adults whose daily lives reflect shadows of earlier traumatic events. Kelly's story reminds me that sometimes a small change can make a big difference, and I hope to make that difference in the lives of the children I see. Many of the children in my practice lived through a traumatic experience that happened before they were mature enough to effectively process what was happening to them, whether they experienced trauma resulting from medical procedures or hospitalization, trauma resulting from ruptured attachment with a caregiver, or other traumatic experiences that interfered with their well-being and primary relationships. Integrating EMDR into the treatment of these children has been highly effective.

In my first book, *Small Wonders: Healing Childhood Trauma with EMDR*, I investigate the mysteries of disturbing childhood behaviors, their origins in single traumatic events, and the effectiveness of EMDR therapy in resolving critical incident trauma. In *Trauma-Attachment Tangle*, I have extended my focus to include issues related primarily to the entanglement between early trauma and subsequent attachment problems.

The clinical stories in *Trauma-Attachment Tangle* demonstrate a variety of successful strategies for helping children and families overcome the effects of complex trauma. The people whose stories are presented come from a range of ethnic, cultural, and financial backgrounds. They are Caucasians, African Americans, Asians, and Latin Americans. They are single-parent and two-parent families. They are wealthy families and families who are financially distressed. All identifying information has been changed to preserve confidentiality.

In the section following the clinical stories, I have described valuable tools specifically designed for treating posttraumatic symptoms in children and for strengthening family and social relationships. These include calming exercises, parenting suggestions, cooperation games, and attachment-enhancing activities. The third section includes instructions for developing healing narratives and sample stories. All of the activities were developed to foster effective communication, cooperation, and intimacy. Additional information about EMDR with children is collected in the Appendix.

I have been deeply moved by the children who have come to me for care and by their parents who have been determined to help them maximize their potential and to have a full life. It has been my privilege to know these families. It is their struggles and stories, and the belief that stories are powerful teaching tools, that motivated me to write *Trauma-Attachment Tangle*. It is my hope that the stories and activities in this book will help others untangle the legacy and effects of early trauma.

Note

1 For those unfamiliar with EMDR, the entry on this therapy in the Glossary provides a summary of relevant terminology that may be useful while reading the vignettes in the following chapters.

Part I

THE CLINICAL STORIES

.

1

AMY

Violent Behavior in an Adopted Toddler

It is not unusual for parents of an adopted child to come to me and say, "Is there any hope? We wouldn't really send him back, but the thought has crossed our minds. We have done everything we can, and he just doesn't love us. He hits and kicks and screams and makes our lives miserable."

Parents who adopt are motivated to share their love, care, time, money, and other resources for a child in need of a loving home and family. However, few of these parents have been educated about the challenges and demands of raising an adopted child. They have no experience or perspective from which to understand or approach the complexities of adopting a child whose early months were spent with little opportunity for consistent, attuned care or adequate developmental stimulation. The child they adopt comes with a history: a history that may include trauma in the form of neglect or abuse. Without the proper guidance, resources or preparation, the adoptive families may not fully comprehend the effects of the trauma their child experienced or the resulting attachment issues that await them. Fortunately, there is hope and help for children who have experienced early trauma: Issues stemming from traumatic experiences can be resolved with therapeutic treatment and specific parenting strategies designed to enhance attachment between the parents and child.

Amy

Emily and Peter had no idea what to do with their two-year-old daughter, Amy. They had adopted Amy from an orphanage in China when she was 19 months old. Emily explained, "We fell in love with her when we saw her picture. She was just a year old then. She had shiny black hair, a dimple in her cheek, a twinkle in her eye, and that charming smile." Peter added, "I already had a grown son by a previous marriage, and we wanted a daughter. I was in favor of adopting a toddler because I've already been through the infant stage, and it's intense—all that crying and those night feedings." Peter smiled ruefully, "I thought a girl—and especially a girl who was not an infant—would be easier." What he didn't know was that he and Emily would spend years focusing intensively on Amy's emotional and developmental needs and giving her the nurturing she had missed as an infant.

Their first eight months together as a family were stressful because of Amy's extremely difficult behavior. Amy didn't seem to care about anything—she threw toys, tore up books, tortured the family kittens by twisting their bodies, and attacked her parents and other children with unprovoked biting, hitting, and scratching. When she came close to babies, she tried to jab their eyes with her finger.

Amy also hoarded food by keeping it stuffed in her cheeks, and she sometimes refused to swallow for half an hour. She seemed to have no attention span at all, and she wouldn't listen to a page of a book or play with any toys in an organized way. She just pulled things off the shelves and left them in a jumble on the floor. She slept deeply but appeared to have unhappy dreams and often screamed while asleep.

Peter described the miserable drama he witnessed several times daily: "When Emily or I say 'no,' Amy pitches a world-class fit. I mean she flings herself on the floor and launches this prolonged hissy fit with screaming and kicking and spitting and sobbing. I know that toddlers are opposi- tional, but I've never seen anything like this—she goes into attack mode and sometimes goes on for an hour." Emily looked defeated: "We've tried everything—time out only makes things worse. We've tried talking to her nicely, but it's like she's having a seizure and doesn't hear us. We've tried rewards and punishments. We have a whole closet full of toys we've taken away. There's nothing she cares about enough to motivate her." Peter added, "I feel really sorry for Emily. I work a lot and travel a lot for work, but she's stuck at home with Amy. Emily's exhausted."

Then there was the other side of Amy. Emily and Peter told me that when Amy wasn't being difficult, she was pleasant, and she was outgoing around strangers. They said that she smiled a lot and even wanted strang- ers to pick her up. Toddlers don't usually want strangers to pick them up, unless they have had to rely on acting charming in order to get basic care from anyone they could attract. Amy's history of institutionalization and multiple caregivers, her emotional dysregulation, her inability to relate to her parents, her destructive behaviors, and her indiscriminate willingness to go with strangers were red flags for trauma and attachment issues.

While Amy's early history was a mystery, we did know that Amy was found on the steps of a police station in a remote part of China when she was seven months old. She was small for her age but appeared healthy. She was taken to an orphanage, but we don't know anything about her life there. Amy stayed in the orphanage until she was 19 months old.

The 19-month-old toddler Peter and Emily met seemed to understand Mandarin but didn't speak a word. Her motor development was slightly delayed, and she had only seven teeth. (Most babies have more than that when they are a year old.) She was a little clumsy and frequently ran into things. Peter observed, "She looked like a deer in the headlights when the director of the orphanage handed her to us at the hotel where we met."

When Emily and Peter brought Amy home to the US, they had her examined by a pediatrician. Amy was a little behind developmentally, but the pediatrician thought she would catch up quickly. Emily and Peter were sure that love and healthy food were all she needed to thrive.

Emily worked at home and had a Peruvian babysitter take care of Amy. Imagine Amy's shock at being brought to a home in which no one spoke the language she already understood and two totally foreign languages were spoken. In fact, everything was unfamiliar, scary, and overwhelming for Amy—caregivers, language, smells, food, customs, and expectations.

When I finished taking the history during our first appointment together, Peter had one pressing question: "What should we do about her tantrums? They happen so fast that we can't prevent them. She suddenly goes crazy. Sometimes we don't even know what upset her." I explained to Peter and Emily that Amy's prolonged tantrums were not their fault or Amy's fault. I further explained that optimally, during the first year of a baby's life, a special kind of dance takes place between a baby and his or her most intimate caregiver. The attuned caregiver responds to the baby's expressions and helps to regulate the baby's fluctuating states of arousal through touch, voice, facial expressions, and gestures. In response, the baby's autonomic nervous system becomes regulated and organized to respond to a wide range of internal and external stimuli.

During her first 19 months of life, Amy had not had a sustained relationship with one reliable, attuned caregiver. Amy had become chronically stressed and unable to regulate her strong emotions of fear, frustration, or disappointment. Her sympathetic nervous system, primed to respond to threat, was in overdrive.

Amy's parents were relieved to learn that they hadn't caused Amy's tantrums, and now they had an explanation for how early trauma had affected her ability to regulate her moods. Understanding the cause of her behavior was the first step. Now they needed the tools for dealing with her tantrums.

I advised Emily and Peter that a parent should stay in the room with Amy while she had a tantrum to be sure she was safe. They should stay quiet while Amy was angry. I told them about the work of researchers Green and Potegal, who studied children's vocalizations during tantrums and have observed that the vocalizations of screaming and yelling, both angry expressions, are intertwined with whimpering, fussing, and crying, which are expressions of sadness. Green and Potegal found that sad

5

sounds tended to occur throughout tantrums, with angry spikes of yelling and screaming superimposed.

They observed that children get past the angry part most quickly if the parent is quiet, and that after the anger subsides, what is left is sadness. When the child feels sad, a parent can use that opportunity to comfort the child and strengthen their intimate connection (Green, Whitney, & Potegal, 2011).

The time to approach Amy and begin to comfort her would be when Amy was sad and whimpering. Emily could say, "I'm your mom, and I'm here for you. I won't leave you. When you're ready we can cuddle and I'll rub your back if you want, and you'll feel better." Tantrums do stop eventually, and then there is an opportunity for calming and connection. The end of the tantrum offered an opportunity for Amy to learn that she could count on her parents to comfort her when she felt sad.

Even before I met Amy, I thought about her behaviors from a trauma perspective. What were the experiences that undermined Amy's sense of safety and well-being and gave her false or distorted beliefs about herself or the world? I asked myself: What did Amy learn from her experiences in her first seven months of life? What did she learn in the orphanage? What do her current behaviors tell us about her early experiences?

I knew that Amy had been taken away from familiar caregivers at least twice. Her history made me suspect that she would have trouble trusting Emily and Peter or other caregivers, even if they were very responsive, caring people. Could she trust that she would get food when she was hungry? Given that she was small for her age and hoarding food, I assumed that she could not be certain she would have that basic need met. It made sense that she hoarded food when food was available so that she would have something when she was hungry.

Could she trust that she would have her basic need for attention and attunement met? Given that she was "charming" and indiscriminately went to strangers to be picked up told me that she probably couldn't trust that she would get attention when she needed it, so she had learned to seek it and to be charming to get someone's attention.

Amy had been abandoned by her birth parents and had multiple caregivers in an orphanage. Her early experiences had taught her that attachment leads to pain and disappointment. Trust issues are at the heart of ruptured attachment. Children who have been severely traumatized by early abandonment demonstrate self-loathing. One adopted five-year-old girl told me that she felt "like garbage" because her birth parents didn't want her, and she was "thrown away." Other adopted children have shown me their distress when they played in the dollhouse. I have seen the dollhouse baby stuffed into the oven, flushed down the toilet, and suffocated with pillows or buried under furniture. I don't interpret that play literally but see it as the child's expression of an emotional experience.

I believe that traumatized children "feel bad," and they think that means they *are* bad. Later, they attack animals or babies who remind them of their vulnerable, helpless little selves.

I guessed that if Amy could express her negative beliefs about herself, they might have been: "I can't trust anyone to meet my needs over time, so it's dangerous to connect deeply with anyone. I'm bad because bad things happen to me. I can't tolerate it when things don't go the way I expect or want." My goal was to help Amy and her parents develop a strong positive emotional bond that would feel good to all of them.

Emily began to recognize that her daughter's challenging behaviors indicated an attachment disorder. Emily went online and found the website for attach-china.org and several other sites with information about attachment. She began taking naps with Amy and stopped scolding her so often. Even with those few changes, she noticed a decrease in the frequency of Amy's tantrums.

When Amy and her mom came back to see me the following week, I used a modified version of the Marschak Interaction Method (MIM) assessment to learn more about interactions between Amy and Emily. I wanted to observe the quality of Emily's interactions with Amy: how she structured her interactions with Amy, how Emily nurtured her, taught her, challenged her and how Amy responded to her mother (DiPasquale, 2000). Emily and Amy followed the instructions to put lotion on one another's hands, and then they played with dolls, plastic dinosaurs, and stuffed animals. Emily showed her daughter how to help the baby doll be "safe and cozy."

I observed that Emily was good at paying careful attention to Amy, speaking to her in an age-appropriate way, giving her new vocabulary and expanding on Amy's words. She was gentle as she showed Amy how to pet the stuffed dog. When it was time to clean up, Emily asked, "Do you want to clean up? Do you want to put the dinosaurs in the basket?" And when it was time to leave my office, she asked Amy, "Do you want to say goodbye?" Amy's mom repeated these questions many times. Amy ignored her.

When I met with Emily the following week, I complimented Emily on the many ways she was attuned to Amy, and I shared a list of parenting suggestions with her. My plan was to start by encouraging lots of babying activities like rocking, cuddling, feeding, and comforting. I encouraged Emily to cuddle and soothe Amy every day. By starting off the day attuning to Amy and snuggling with her, Emily could help develop her daughter's capacity for connection and help fill Amy's "emotional bank." I encouraged her to notice Amy's interests, follow her lead while engaging her in play, initiate back-and-forth communication, and invite Amy to do activities with her, like singing songs or picking up toys together. Amy had such a chaotic beginning in life, as well as culture shock, that she needed to begin to see that there are patterns in life that make sense and that she could trust her mom to help her understand the world.

I also thought that teaching Emily to help Amy cooperate would bring some rewards for both Amy and her mother. By asking Amy, "Do you want to clean up? Do you want to put the dinosaurs in the basket?" Emily implied that it was really Amy's choice about whether or not to help and that she would be happy with whatever decision Amy made. Parents may think that they are being friendly by asking "Do you want to . . .?" In fact, they are giving their child a false choice. Given a real choice, most children choose not to do something like clean up a mess or stop watching TV. I instructed Emily to "only ask Amy to do what you want once. If she doesn't comply, gently bring Amy to your side or lap, and tell and show her how 'we clean up like this,' then say 'thank you for following directions' when she does comply."

Young children need explicit instructions and clear directions that accurately tell what the parent wants and expects. Children become confused by requests that are presented as choices. For example, "Do you want to hold my hand when we cross the street?" sounds like a choice, but it's tricky. The parent knows what he or she wants but presents it in a way that sounds like cooperation is optional. "Do you want to hold my right hand or my left hand while we cross the street?" is a more appropriate choice to give a young child.

I also suggested that Emily observe Amy closely and notice when she was beginning to act frustrated or upset. Then Emily could move close to Amy or hug her while she identified what Amy was feeling. She could teach Amy to use words to say how she felt. Then Emily could soothe Amy and tell her exactly what to do. For example, if Amy was becoming upset because she was having trouble trying to take off her shoes, Emily could say, "Oh, I see it's hard getting those shoes off. It looks like you're starting to feel frustrated. Let's see what's making it hard. The laces are tied. You can pull here to open them, like this, or you can say, 'Mom, will you help?' and I will help you." Amy still needed to learn how her parents could be useful to her.

I showed Emily how to set Amy up for success by giving her tasks she was capable of doing, helping her do them if she had trouble, and then acknowledging when she did something the way her mother liked. I wanted her to praise Amy's efforts to follow directions and specific behaviors that she liked rather than generalize "good girl," which implies that she is a bad girl when she doesn't do exactly what her mom wants.

When Amy and her mom came back the next week, Emily said things were going a little better. "It really helped for me to know that Amy's tantrums aren't my fault and that I can help her learn to calm herself. Now that I understand that Amy isn't just trying to defeat me, I can be calmer. I want to help her learn to regulate her emotions." Being close to Amy, talking with her calmly, empathizing with her feelings, and soothing her all began to calm Amy. Emily discovered that Amy liked back rubs. Emily started telling Amy that she loved her, because she thought it was beginning to be true. There had not been any biting, hitting, or scratching, but Amy was still obstinate and not paying attention.

I noticed that Amy was very sensitive to scary or angry facial expressions on action figures. Amy pointed to a five-inch-high, brutish-looking action figure with a small yellow head and big blue muscles. "It's scary, him scary!" she said. There has been research indicating that children who were maltreated show heightened ability to identify angry faces (Pollack & Sinha, 2002).

Emily corrected Amy by saying, "It's not scary." I modeled a response that validated Amy's feelings and also let Amy know that she's safe: "It looks a little scary, but it's just a toy, and you're safe for real." Later I would encourage Emily to teach Amy more about how to interpret facial expressions and to continue to reassure Amy that she was safe and could count on help when she needed it.

Initially, Amy's "play" consisted of pulling things off shelves. There were no themes. Nothing happened except that piles of toys and random items accumulated. She didn't exhibit any imagination—no pretending to eat or feed stuffed animals, no taking care of a doll. I determined that she needed lots of structure, and she needed to be shown what to do and even how to play.

At my suggestion, Emily began to play that a little stuffed bear was a baby. She pretended that the bear was crying and asked Amy what he needed. "Milk," Amy responded. Emily engaged Amy in giving the bear a bottle, giving him a bath, getting him dressed, and singing to him before his nap. Emily told Amy how the bear was feeling and together they figured out what the bear needed. They took turns holding him and singing to him together.

Then Emily pretended to read a book to the bear and invited Amy to sit on her lap. She was disturbed that Amy had such a short attention span and asked whether we could teach her to learn to pay attention. She showed me how she tried to read to Amy and how difficult it was to get Amy to pay attention. Amy wiggled and tried to pull or tear pages. I suggested that Emily snuggle with Amy and interact with her as she read, pointing to pictures and talking about what she saw. She could hold Amy's hand and identify objects in the illustrations and ask Amy to point to objects she named. She could guide Amy in gently turning pages. I advised her to read to Amy every day like this, extending Amy's listening time by a few minutes a day as tolerated.

By the next time I saw Amy, she was enjoying listening to short books with her mom or dad. She came into my office, pulled out the stuffed bear, sat it beside her, and pretended to read a book to her "baby." Her mom and I were thrilled to see Amy demonstrate some caregiving activity on her own for the first time. Her gentleness with the little bear told me that she was beginning to feel tenderness and connection.

When it was time to clean up, I noticed that Emily was still asking, "Amy, do you want to help clean up?" Most change of habit does not come quickly or easily. Without being told and shown what to do, Amy didn't want to help, and she didn't know what to do. I encouraged Emily to partner with Amy—show her what to do and then do it with her, making the activities fun.

Each week, there were subtle but definite changes. Emily reported that she and Amy were "happier together." Emily described Amy as "smart, busy, curious, and a good athlete."

Amy did continue to have tantrums whenever she didn't get her way. It began first thing in the morning when she woke up. Nothing seemed right. Amy cried and cried if Emily didn't give her a piggyback ride as soon as she wanted. Amy continued to be "oppositional." When Emily asked Amy not to touch some eggs, Amy picked them up and crushed them in her hands. She continued to be impulsive—and had hit their dog in the face.

Emily asked whether she should give Amy "time out" when she misbehaved. For a child who has experienced attachment trauma, being sent away for time out can trigger the hurt and the enraged feelings of a life-changing rejection. Instead, I recommended that after Amy misbehaved, Emily could help Amy calm down and feel safe, acknowledge how Amy was feeling, and then tell and show Amy what to do instead of the inappropriate behavior.

In order to understand the roots of Amy's behavior, I continued thinking in terms of her early experiences that probably never "felt right" because no one was reliably attuned to her needs. I formulated a list of beliefs that seemed to be triggered when she didn't get her way:

> I can't tolerate it if I don't get what I want.
> I'm bad.
> I'm not lovable.
> It's my fault.
> I'm going to be alone and terrified.

Whenever I make a list of negative beliefs a child may have, I generate a list of beliefs that will benefit the child's social interactions and foster the child's positive self-image. Here are some of the positive beliefs that would serve Amy well: "I can trust my parents to take care of me and give me what I need (e.g., food). I am safe and can be calm if I don't get what I want right away. I'm good. I'm still good at heart even if I make a mistake or do something wrong. I'm lovable (even if my parent says 'no'). I belong with my family and can trust my parents to make good decisions for me."

I think of ways that her parents and I can work toward those goals, so that the child can learn to be patient, feel lovable and good, and trust that she will be taken care of and will belong to her family forever. The next step was to help Emily and Peter parent in a way that would strengthen their bonding to Amy and strengthen Amy's attachment to them. No more punishments. No more taking toys away. No more time out. Now it was time for intensive-care parenting focusing on under-standing Amy, comforting her, and teaching her.

Children like Amy who have experienced ruptured attachment miss the normal development of "object constancy," which is the ability to believe that someone or something exists even though they can't see it. To help Amy build trust, I suggested that Emily and Peter play games such as peek-a-boo that would give Amy the opportunity to see her parents reappear repeatedly. Just as it is for a baby, Amy found this game to be endlessly exciting. She squealed each time her parent's face reappeared.

I encouraged Emily and Peter to play peek-a-boo with Amy often, to show her pictures of herself with her family, to tell her that they would love her and take care of her forever and ever. Amy needed to know that she belonged to her family and they belonged to her. She needed to trust that nothing could change that.

Emily was concerned that she was not getting Amy to cooperate when she asked her to do something. I introduced Amy and her mom to the bubble game, a game that helps develop and reinforce cooperation. Almost without exception, young children love to see and play with bub-bles. The bubble game is a useful way to teach children to cooperate because it's fun.

I instructed Emily to play the game like this: "Hold the bubble bear and make eye contact with Amy. Look in her eyes, and when you have her attention, say, 'I'd like you to pop the bubbles by poking them with your pointer finger' or 'Please pop the bubbles by clapping your hands together.' If she doesn't understand what you say, show her how to do it. Then you can blow the bubbles and watch her pop the bubbles. After Amy has finished, look her in the eyes and say, 'Thank you for doing what I asked' or 'Thank you for following directions.'" Then I taught Amy to look at her mom and say, "You're welcome."

Even children who hardly acknowledge what their parents do for them under ordinary circumstances seem to enjoy saying "You're welcome." And their parents are often astonished and pleased. (It's a parent's dream that their child appreciates their care!) See Chapter 12 for more details on how to play the bubble game.

I observed that as Amy and Emily played the bubble game, Amy calmed down. She waited for her mother to tell her and show her how to pop the bubbles and then did what her mother told her to do. Amy stood quietly with Emily when Emily said, "Let's watch the bubbles and listen to them pop together." Each time Amy followed her mom's directions, I tapped her shoulders and said, "It feels good to do what your mom tells you to do" or "It's fun to play with your mom."

Since Amy responded so well to that game, I decided to show her another activity to help calm her. I taught Emily and Amy the "butterfly hug," a calming technique originated and developed by Lucina Artigas and Ignacio Jarero, members of the EMDR International Association Humanitarian Assistance Program (HAP), when they worked with survivors of Hurricane Pauline in Mexico in 1998 (Boel, 1999; Jarero, Artigas, & Hartung, 2006).

Amy was too young to give herself a butterfly hug, so I taught Amy's mother how to pretend to be mama butterfly giving Amy a butterfly hug. I instructed, "Hold Amy on your lap, so that both of you are facing forward. Now wrap your arms around Amy so that your arms cross on Amy's chest. Now rest your right hand on Amy's left shoulder and your left hand on Amy's right shoulder."

I mirrored how Emily's folded arms resembled the wings of a butterfly, giving this special embrace its name. I asked Emily to cuddle Amy and give her a lot of love. Emily embraced Amy firmly and gently and told her to get "nice and cozy." Next, I directed Emily to alternately tap Amy's shoulders. "Can you feel your mommy holding you?" I asked Amy. She nodded. "Good. Notice that nice safe feeling of your mommy holding you." Amy relaxed a little as her mom hugged her and tapped her shoulders.

I said, "Amy, your mommy is holding you and loving you." I looked to Emily for confirmation. "Right, Mom?" Emily responded, "Yes, I am loving Amy." After a child with an attachment disorder has run her parents ragged with prolonged tantrums, lack of any cooperation, and frequently unsafe behaviors, some parents can't honestly say that they love the child. They feel that nothing they have done has helped the child. A parent who feels like a failure feels despair, not love. Love comes with cooperation and responsiveness and vice versa. Amy was beginning to respond to her mom, and her mom was able to begin opening her heart to Amy.

I asked Amy, "Can you feel your mommy loving you?" "Uh-huh," she nodded.

I suggested to Amy that she close her eyes, and she squinched her eyes shut. "Can you still feel your mom holding you?" I asked. "Uh-huh," Amy nodded. "Can you still feel her loving you?" Amy nodded again. I wanted to help her develop the sense of object constancy that could serve to calm her throughout her life.

Then I saw Amy peek out. "Amy, you can open your eyes if you want." She shut them quickly. I continued, "Or you can keep your eyes closed—whichever you want." Amy kept her eyes closed. I observed, "Emily, you're enjoying holding Amy and loving her, aren't you?" "Yes, I am enjoying holding her and loving her," she affirmed. I observed to Amy, "You're enjoying feeling your mommy loving you, aren't you?" Amy nodded, and I could see her relax into her mother.

When Emily and Amy returned the following week, Emily said that Amy had requested the butterfly hug several times during the week. Emily told me that she had even been giving herself a butterfly hug as a way to relax at the end of the day, before going to bed. I was pleased to hear that—self-care is one of the most important things a parent can do!

Emily reported that Amy was very sensitive to little physical hurts and some nearly invisible splinters she had in her feet. This is another symptom I commonly see in children who have been neglected. I think of the little hurts as symbols of all the little hurts of not getting attention and attunement. I asked Emily to examine these little (sometimes invisible) hurts, rather than disregard them, and kiss them to help them feel better. Sometimes parents worry that the child will keep having "hurts" to get attention, but I find that the hurts diminish as the child gets more attention and attunement.

I recommended that Emily make all contact with Amy a connecting activity, that she touch Amy and be near her as much as possible, that she use expressions like "stick with me" and "I think about you all the time, even when you can't see me." I encouraged her to play preschool with Amy and her stuffed animals. I also recommended the book *The Connected Child*, by Karyn Purvis.

Despite the continuing challenges of raising Amy, it was evident that she was developing rapidly. I periodically like to reevaluate the efficacy of treatment and review plans for further treatment. Her parents and I catalogued Amy's progress in the past two months:

1. She could now play with babies gently, without poking their eyes.
2. She could play with toys without trying to destroy them.
3. She enjoyed helping her mom.
4. She demonstrated nurturing behavior to a stuffed animal.
5. She read to stuffed animals for the first time.
6. She could sit and listen to a whole book.
7. She showed compassion and kissed "boo-boos."

Two and a half months after we started working together, Emily told me that she had learned what she needed to learn to have a positive relationship with Amy. She felt it was time to stop our weekly sessions, and she assured me that she would call if they needed help.

The family went away for a two-week vacation together. When they returned, Emily and I had a phone appointment. She reported that Amy spontaneously said, "I love you, Mommy. I want a butterfly hug." Her mom enthused, "She's becoming a real joy! She's really sweet. She's really funny. She is smart and gets it when something is funny. She has a good imagination and loves pretending. She's very generous and helpful—she cleans up with me! She's gentle with animals now."

Amy still dreamed and now talked in her sleep instead of crying in her sleep. Amy still held food in her mouth. Emily often reminded her, "There's always yummy food." She still thought toys' expressions were scary. Rebuilding trust and developing intimacy and establishing emotional regularity are processes that always take time when there has been severe early trauma.

Amy's mom ended our conversation with the best news: "I feel like we are a unit now."

Perspective

According to the American Academy of Child and Adolescent Psychiatry, approximately 120,000 children are adopted each year in the United States (American Academy of Child and Adolescent Psychiatry, 2011). U.S. Department of State statistics indicate that 249,694 children were adopted from foreign countries between 1999 and 2013 (Bureau of Consular Affairs, 2013). It is widely reported in magazine articles that a significant number of international adoptions are not successful and that the adoptive parents of these children sometimes resort to relinquishing their adopted child by making them available via the Internet. According to Nicolas Kristof, "24,000 foreign-born children are no longer with the families that adopted them" (2013, p. A35).

There were many indications that Amy was affected by attachment trauma. Amy's history of relinquishment by her birth parents at age seven months and institutionalization with multiple caregivers in an orphanage for over a year during a period of critical development indicates that her caregiving system itself was a fear-provoking threat rather than a secure base for providing protection and comfort. Initially, all of Amy's behaviors were fear-based; she was afraid of intimacy and afraid of abandonment. Her emotional dysregulation, prolonged tantrums; violent behaviors toward people and small animals, extremely oppositional, distrustful behavior with her parents, food hoarding, indiscriminant affection for strangers, and developmental delays all pointed to a history of neglect.

Clinicians use many terms to talk about trauma and its aftermath. In *Trauma-Attachment Tangle*, I define *trauma* as any experiences that undermine a person's sense of safety and well-being, and give him/her distorted or negative beliefs about him- or herself or the world. "Large-T Trauma" refers to the kind of experiences in the Diagnostic and Statistical

Manual of Mental Disorders, Fifth Edition (DSM-5) that cause posttraumatic stress disorder: catastrophic experiences like abuse or natural disaster. The term "small-t trauma" refers to events such as faulty attunement, criticism, or teasing that cause feelings of helplessness, anxiety, shame, or humiliation (Shapiro, 2001). When I talk about *treating trauma*, I am referring to addressing the memories, thoughts, and feelings that have arisen from traumatic events. These memories, thoughts, and feelings inform a child's behaviors.

Amy experienced abandonment and ruptured attachment, both of which are large-T Traumas. Although Amy may not have been physically abused, she had suffered innumerable small-t traumas during periods of neglect and lack of attunement by caregivers. Children who have been debilitated by both large-T and small-t traumatic events require "intensive-care parenting." Both are amenable to EMDR therapy.

One of the foremost authorities on psychological trauma, Bessel A. van der Kolk, MD, asserts that severely traumatized infants and children demonstrate complex disturbances of cognitive, language, motor, and socialization skills with a variety of different, often fluctuating presentations that do not meet criteria for a diagnosis of PTSD. Dr. van der Kolk proposed that the complex of symptoms presented by children who were severely traumatized over a period of time be named "developmental trauma disorder" (van der Kolk, 2005), a term that is applicable to Amy.

All parents want their child to cooperate. The precursors to cooperation are connection and attunement and clear instruction. Concurrently, parents must provide predictability, clear expectations, and positive reinforcement. Showing parents how to nurture their young children and provide developmentally appropriate structure establishes patterns of relationship that will benefit both the child and family, as well as provide a foundation for trauma resolution.

The ability to be soothed and to self-soothe is a prerequisite for trauma processing. Trauma processing stimulates distress that is stored in the nervous system. A goal of trauma processing is to bring the child's emotional response to a traumatic memory to a tolerable level. If the child's distress is too high, he/she will not be able to tolerate the intensity of the emotion and will not process the stored distressing emotion.

Play is an essential part of a child's development. Through play, children communicate their emotions, express their creativity, develop their imaginations, and solve problems. Through play, children learn to cope with their feelings as they act out being angry, sad, or worried in a situation they control (Erikson, 1963). Play allows children to work through their responses to both pleasant and unpleasant experiences.

The bubble game can be used as part of the preparation phase of EMDR therapy. The butterfly hug strengthened Amy's connection to her mother and introduced her to the relaxing effect of alternating bilateral stimulation. Amy's newly developed ability to take care of her baby doll, cooperate with her mother, and enjoy alternating bilateral stimulation was important preparation for beginning the desensitization and reprocessing phases of EMDR. If Amy returns for therapy, her ability to trust adults and cooperate, as well as her ability to show nurturing behavior toward her baby doll, will make it possible to begin the trauma work related to her own experiences as a baby.

If Amy's parents had not sought therapy, Amy, who had such severe problems with mood regulation and inattention, may have eventually been diagnosed as having ADHD and bipolar illness. Increasingly, children in the United States are being given psychoactive pharmaceuticals to treat their anxiety, depression, disturbing behaviors, and emotional outbursts, even though the drugs can have serious side effects ranging from suicidal thoughts to seizures and diabetes. These medications may simply dull children's emotions and responses, without addressing the underlying cause of their behaviors. While medication can be a valuable partial solution for helping parents cope with their children's difficult behaviors, it is essential to treat the underlying trauma that caused or contributed to these maladaptive behaviors in the first place.

2

MONICA
EMDR and Early Childhood Trauma

Lance and Jayne came to see me about their adopted daughter, Monica, now age four. Jayne launched into her concerns: "Monica is terrified of the sound of toilets flushing, so terrified that she screams and covers her ears. She refuses to be in the bathroom when the toilet is flushed." Lance added, "That makes it especially hard if we have to go in a public bathroom and there are toilets flushing. She just can't be there, and she's upset for a while afterward."

Jayne continued, "We both love Monica. She's really sweet. We just want to help her feel more relaxed and help her get over her fears. She seems sad, even though we pay close attention to her, cuddle her a lot, feed her a baby bottle when she wants it—the way attachment experts recommend—read to her, and give her whatever she needs." Jayne looked at the shelves of toys in my office and then reflected, "Her play is unusual too. A lot of the time Monica lines up her toys instead of really playing with them. When she plays with baby dolls, she plays that they're getting hurt or scared."

Lance and Jayne recalled the history of how they decided to adopt a child. "We went through years of infertility evaluations and treatments," Lance told me. "That was really stressful. After five tries at in vitro fertilization, we gave up trying." Jayne interjected, "But we didn't give up wanting a family. We both love kids, and we couldn't envision a life without children. We knew we could provide a loving home for a child, so we decided to adopt."

Lance paused and then told me more about himself: "I worked in summer camps all through high school, I have three younger siblings, and I've coached Little League for years. I figured I could handle any kid." Jayne agreed, "I love children, and I had a lot of experience babysitting as a teen," she said. "I also studied child development in college and worked as an aide in a preschool for four years, and parents often praised me. All their preschoolers loved me. I thought I could be a really good mother, and I wanted a child so much."

Lance continued, "We thought it best if we started with a foster child. If it worked out, we could adopt. It just seemed that 'foster-adopt' would give us a chance to get to know the child before we did the legal part. We found Monica through an agency when she was nine months old. She needed an emergency placement because Child Protective Service (CPS) had determined that her mother was unfit, and I think her mother wanted to relinquish her anyway. Then her mother was put in jail."

"Monica was a quiet baby," Jayne interjected, "with fair skin and hazel eyes, and she was very alert, observing everything. She even had pierced ears and wore little earrings when she was only nine months old. We had to take Monica to visit her mother in jail monthly until she was two and a half and the adoption was finalized. It was during those visits it became clear to me that Monica's birth mother was unable to take care of her or provide Monica with a stable life. We loved Monica, and we wanted to protect her and give her all the love and care she deserved."

Jayne told me that Eye Movement Desensitization and Reprocessing (EMDR) had helped her get over the grief of a miscarriage and helped her cope with the stress of the infertility treatments. Her therapist thought that EMDR might help Monica get over the trauma of neglect she had experienced during her first months of life. Jayne said, "I thought that EMDR just worked for treating isolated traumatic incidents, but my therapist pointed out that neglect is like thousands of traumas. She thought Monica showed many signs of trauma from neglect and abandonment: Monica doesn't ask for help even when she needs it, and she resists and whimpers whenever she has to transition from one activity to another. Generally she seems quiet, but sometimes she throws tantrums with an intensity that seems way out of proportion to the situation."

Lance expressed another concern. "Monica won't come out of her bedroom to look for us in the morning. Jayne and I go downstairs early to have breakfast together. We want Monica to come down when she's awake, but she doesn't come. We go upstairs, and there she is in bed with her eyes open, but she never comes out of her room unless we come in and pick her up." Jayne added, "I really want Monica to feel securely attached, and I wonder if it's a sign that Monica doesn't feel safe and comfortable in our home. I don't remember her ever coming out of her room unless we go get her."

Lance looked at his wife as he said, "Jayne is the early child development expert in our family, and she thinks that it's Monica's quiet, slow-to-warm-up temperament that makes her reluctant to do things and may be connected to why she waits in her room for us to come get her. Even if it's temperament that makes Monica so tentative, we want her to be able to overcome her fears so the world seems less scary to her."

I agreed that temperament could be contributing to Monica's shy behavior, but I also speculated that her early experiences contributed to her state of hypoarousal, low energy, and sensitivity to sound. I told Lance and Jayne that babies are distressed if they don't have an attuned caregiver and don't experience appropriate sensory stimulation. Given what we knew about Monica's birth mother, it was likely that Monica's needs often were not met and that she was understimulated.

Jayne and Lance agreed that Monica's early experiences must have affected her deeply. Lance looked quizzical and asked, "We don't think that Monica was physically abused. How do we know Monica was traumatized?"

I explained that trauma is any experience that undermines a person's sense of safety or well-being and gives her false beliefs about herself or the world. Using that definition, Monica's mother's erratic behavior and her inability to respond consistently to Monica's needs qualify as traumatic experiences for an infant. "So are you saying," Lance asked, "that those experiences may have taught Monica to believe that she couldn't trust adults to help her, and that there was no point in trying to communicate what she needed?"

"Yes, that's exactly what I am saying," I affirmed. Traumatic experiences are stored in the nervous system as if the situation is current and dangerous, instead of in the archives of experiences that are over and no longer a current threat. Whenever Monica faces a situation that reminds her of an early traumatic experience, strong emotions or physical sensations similar to those experienced at the time of the actual trauma may surface, and she feels as if she is in danger.

Jayne, who had been listening quietly, added, "It makes sense to me that Monica's brain was programmed to respond to the scary situation she was in as a baby. I've read that even a traumatized brain can integrate new information and can change. It sounds like EMDR can help Monica update her brain's computer program so she can adjust her responses to her current, safe situation."

Lance wanted to know more about EMDR. "Jayne has experienced EMDR, but I haven't," he said. "I'd like to know more about it. From what Jayne's told me, I don't understand how you would use it with a four-year-old who can't sit there and tell you about the worst part of her infancy."

I reassured him, "Yes, EMDR can be modified so that it's appropriate for a young child, though there are a lot of differences between using EMDR with an adult and with a child. Adults who come for therapy are motivated to resolve their trauma and are able to tolerate some emotional distress if they know that they will benefit. Children often can't remember or talk about painful memories, but they give us clues about their experiences and feelings through their play. The desensitization phase of EMDR can be integrated into play or artwork or stories."

The principles of EMDR are the same with children and adults. EMDR is based on the premise that everyone has an innate information processing system. Memories of traumatic experiences get stuck, undigested, in isolated neural networks. In EMDR therapy, we ask the person to remember the traumatic event and its accompanying sensory information. Then we activate the adaptive information processing (AIP) with alternating bilateral stimulation (ABS) to metabolize the memory. Alternating bilateral stimulation refers to visual, auditory, or tactile stimuli that are provided in a rhythmic left-right pattern. Visual bilateral stimulation could involve a toy or hand or lights moving from left to right and back repeatedly to guide eye movement. Auditory bilateral stimulation could involve listening to tones, clicks, music, or other sounds that are delivered through headphones, alternating between the right and left sides of the head. Tactile stimulation could be provided by small buzzers that are held in the hands and buzz alternately between the right and left hands. Adults usually have knowledge and information that helps them process the traumatic memories. We often have to give a child the information and reassurance he/she needs in order to resolve the trauma.

We want to desensitize or take the charge off of her distressed feelings and reduce her physical reactivity that goes along with the feeling. With a child, we can do ABS by tapping with a toy, by offering auditory bilateral stimulation through headphones, or by having the child hold buzzers that buzz alternately to deliver tactile stimulation.

Some posttraumatic beliefs seem to form in infancy, when the child is preverbal. For example, a child who was neglected and had unpredictable care as an infant might behave as if he/she has beliefs like "I can't trust adults to help me," "I can't be OK unless I have my way," "I can't tolerate change," or "I have to have attention or I will die." These trauma-informed beliefs may lead to feelings of anxiety, distrust, fear, and anger. The resulting trauma-informed behaviors might include lack of cooperation, tantrums, rejecting behaviors, controlling behaviors, clinginess, or extreme difficulty with transitions.

We want to eliminate the child's negative beliefs, and to do so we sometimes need to tell children what to believe instead. For example, some children believe they were bad as a baby and that's why they were neglected. If the child is playing with a baby doll and says, "bad baby," I can give the child ABS while I say, "Babies are always good. Babies and children just need to be taught what to do. It's never a baby's fault when a parent can't take care of her." While that statement alone may not necessarily make a child feel "good," it would help her begin to develop a sense of compassion for her baby self and help her attain a healthier view of herself currently.

Monica seemed to have learned that being quiet and not moving much was the best thing to do in order to please her birth mother or stay safe.

Maybe she gave up trying to get attention because her efforts were futile. Even though a baby or young child can't verbalize beliefs, we can imagine what those beliefs might be. For example, like most of the adopted children I see, Monica resists transitions. Any change signals alarm, as if *every* transition means, "I'm going to be uprooted from everything familiar, and I can expect pain and sadness." The same types of belief might explain Monica's need to line up her toys. If there is order, she knows what to expect and that helps her feel safer.

Jayne said, "It would be helpful if we could change those types of beliefs so that moving from one activity to another isn't such a big deal. We'd like her to trust that her parents can take good care of her and make decisions that are good for her, and we want her to know that she can relax even if she has to stop playing to get ready to go out with us." I assured Jayne that I wanted either her or Lance to be in the room and help with therapy for Monica so that they could help her through the process.

I wanted to meet Monica and develop a relationship with her before I could decide how and when to introduce EMDR desensitization and reprocessing to her. Jayne and Lance seemed to understand Monica's needs. They also knew about attachment and were doing their best to help Monica feel safe. I guessed that I wouldn't have to do a lot of parenting education.

During my first meeting with Monica and her parents together, Jayne and Lance talked about how they were so glad to be a family with Monica. They said that they loved snuggling with Monica and reading to her and taking her to the park. Monica sat quietly between her parents as they talked about the things they liked about her and the things they liked to do with her. After a while, Monica went over to the sand tray and began to line up Disney characters in the sand.

While Monica played, I asked Jayne and Lance what they wanted to have go better for Monica. Jayne smiled, "I'd love to have Monica come find me when she wakes up. I'll be so happy to see her in the morning." Lance answered, "I want Monica to feel safe and know she's OK when she hears a toilet flush." Monica looked unsure when her mom asked if she would like that too.

The next week, Monica came to my office with her mother. After clinging to Jayne for a few minutes, Monica went over to the dollhouse. Monica put a baby doll on the floor of the dollhouse, then toppled all the furniture in the dollhouse and piled it on top of the baby. I doubted that Monica had ever had furniture piled on top of her. I interpreted her play as a representation of her emotional experience. I had seen children with a history of neglect and abuse stuff baby dolls in the toy oven and in the toilet.

From past experience, I've learned that children don't let me protect or rescue the baby doll. The child finds a way to "hurt" the toy baby. The children usually won't let me "help the baby feel better" until they sense that their parent and I have gotten how bad it was for them. Monica seemed to want us to understand that she felt unimportant and worried she would die.

Instead of trying to help the baby, I empathized, "Oh no, the baby is hurt. It's so unfair. She's just a baby, and she didn't do anything wrong." By narrating what was happening, I gave meaning and structure to Monica's play. "She's all alone. There's no one there to help her. She's a little baby. She can't get up by herself. She needs help and she's not getting it."

We went through several sessions of a similar pattern of play. Monica organized Disney characters in the sand tray while Jayne and I talked. Monica was clearly listening as her mother told me about the things that had gone well with Monica during the previous week. Monica rearranged the order of the Disney characters in the sand while Jayne named one thing she wanted to be better for Monica. "I'd like for Monica to feel safe and relaxed at home."

After listening to our brief conversation, I asked Monica to assign roles for Jayne and me to play in the dollhouse. Monica wanted her mom to play with the "mom doll," and I got the role of the baby, as usual. I made baby crying sounds—sounds that said "I need," sounds that meant "I'm angry," sounds that meant "I give up. I can't do anything that gets me what I need." Monica loved it. She came over to pile all the furniture on top of the baby so I could cry more. I think she really wanted her mom and me to "get it" that she suffered terribly as a baby.

Within a few sessions, when the baby was buried under furniture, I asked Monica, "What is the baby feeling?" "Sad," Monica said, and she sat on her mom's lap. "Where do you feel the sad feeling in your body?" I asked Monica. Monica responded by pointing to her heart. I directed Monica, "Notice the sad feeling in your heart, and let's help your baby feel better." I tapped Monica's shoulders as I said to Jayne, "I think the baby was so scared and sad because she felt she would die, but she needs to know that she's safe now." After I tapped for about a minute, I asked Monica how she was feeling. "Better," she responded. The sadness of a prolonged period of mistreatment never disappears so quickly, so I asked, "Point to where you feel the sad feeling." Monica pointed to her chest, and said, "My heart." I tapped her feet as she snuggled closer to Jayne. I was happy to see that Monica could go to her mom for comfort and that ABS decreased her distress.

I thought about how to treat Monica for her fear of toilets. I wondered how Monica's history had some bearing on this terror. When Monica was a baby, she visited her birth mother in jail. Did that explain her extreme fear of toilets—had there been a toilet with an industrial-strength flush in or near her cell?

22

In this case, I didn't need to identify the root of Monica's fear in order to treat it. When she played with the toy toilet in the dollhouse, I asked Monica to notice the scared feeling while I tapped her shoulders. I reassured her, "You're safe around toilets, even when you hear them flush." Even though Jayne and I made a lot of flushing sounds while I worked to decrease her fear, Monica was still afraid of the toilet at home and in public places.

We decided to go into the bathroom in my office and do "in vivo" desensitizing with bilateral stimulation. Jayne held Monica while I tapped Monica's shoulders and reassured her that she was safe when she saw the toilet, as well as when she heard the sound of the toilet flushing. Soon Monica became comfortable hearing a toilet flush—but she still didn't want to flush it herself. At age four, it wasn't essential that Monica flush the toilet herself, and with her parents' encouragement, I felt sure she would eventually be able to flush the toilet.

Next, I needed to figure out how to address Monica's fear of leaving her room in the morning. When she woke up in the morning, she stayed in her own room and refused to leave the room unless one of her parents came in to get her. The door to her room was always open, but she wouldn't leave. While this was not a debilitating problem, Jayne and Lance really wanted Monica to come find them in their bedroom or the kitchen when she woke up.

One day, while Monica was playing with the Disney figures in the sand, I asked her what was scary about leaving her room. Monica looked at me with a worried expression on her face and said, "Monsters." I asked Monica to imagine seeing the open bedroom door, walking out, and going into her parents' bedroom and to imagine that her parents smiled when they saw her. While I tapped her hands I encouraged her, "It's safe to go out of your room in the morning."

The next week, Monica and her mom came into my office, and Jayne reported happily that "Monica spent the weekend at her grandmother's house, and when she woke up in the morning, she went downstairs to look for her!" I smiled, "Great. Is she doing that at home now too?" Jayne answered, "Well, now, after the work we did, she does come out of her room to our bedroom to find us in the morning, but even if she hears us downstairs, she won't come downstairs." I asked Monica why she wouldn't come downstairs. "Scared" was her answer, and she wouldn't or couldn't say why or anything else about how she felt or what might happen if she did go downstairs.

It's certainly not serious if a child doesn't come out of her room when she wakes up in the morning. But Jayne had mentioned that problem to me almost every week we had met over the past six months. She told Monica that she wanted her to come find her when she woke up in the morning. Jayne felt that if Monica really felt that she belonged in her family, she would feel free to walk around her house and find her parents.

One day Lance came to the appointment with his daughter. I asked, "Did anything happen to Monica that would have made her scared to leave her bed or scared to enter the kitchen?" A flash of memory crossed his face. I had asked the question a little differently—instead of focusing on how Monica was fearful about leaving her room, I had brought up the possibility that she was afraid to enter the kitchen. Bingo!

There was only the one time something had happened, but it didn't seem like much to Lance. Lance recalled, "One morning, when Monica was about two years old and still sleeping in a crib, I was in the kitchen in the morning and Monica came in. I was shocked and a little scared, really—it hadn't occurred to me that she could climb out of her crib. She could have gotten hurt! Then I picked her up and took her to her room. Her drawers were open and there were clothes strewn all over the room. She had emptied her drawers before coming downstairs."

I asked Lance if he had been angry. He replied, "I wasn't angry—just startled and scared. It hadn't occurred to me that she could get out of her crib."

Lance continued, "I put her back in her crib and told her never to get out of bed before I came into her room." We looked at one another. Monica was still taking that admonishment literally. A surprised, scared parent is enough to leave an impression on a child, especially a child who had been subjected to a lot of intense, scary emotions when she was a baby.

Now that we suspected the source of the problem, it would be easier to treat. As usual, Monica started the play part of our session by going to the sand tray, then moving close to the dollhouse. She asked her dad and me to play in the dollhouse. I asked her if she wanted us to act out what happened when she was a baby and got out of her crib. Monica nodded. She wanted me to play the part of the baby in the dollhouse and her dad to play his part with the dad doll.

My little girl doll climbed out of the crib, pulled the clothes out of the miniature dresser, and went to the kitchen. Monica's dad's doll turned from the stove, startled, and said, "I'm so surprised to see you. I'm scared too! I'm worried you could get hurt climbing out of the crib!" Then Lance picked up the little girl doll and took her back to her bedroom. "Look at that! You got the clothes out of the dresser too. I'm going to put you back in bed, and I want you to stay there. Don't get out of bed by yourself again. I'll come to get you when it's time to get out of bed."

Monica leaned over and peered into the dollhouse. I asked how the baby girl felt. "Scared," she whispered. I began to tap Monica's shoulders. I asked, "How did the daddy look when he told the girl to stay in her bed?" She shuddered, "Scary!" I tapped her shoulders. "How does the girl feel now?" I asked. "Angry," she said. The fact that Monica's emotion changed indicated that bilateral stimulation was working to process the range of emotions that were packaged with the disturbing memory.

I kept tapping until Monica's facial expression changed and she moved a bit. I explained, "You're a good girl. You didn't do anything wrong. Your dad was upset, but not at you. He was just worried that you might have gotten hurt climbing out of bed. Now you're older and you don't need a crib, so it's OK for you to leave your room and go to the kitchen." Then Monica went back over to the sand tray. That was the end of that window of opportunity for processing Monica's feelings surrounding the memory of leaving her bedroom and going to the kitchen in the morning, but it was apparently enough. The next week her father announced that Monica had come out of her room in the morning and come into the kitchen without prompting.

Perspective

EMDR is based on the premise that everyone has in innate adaptive information processing system (AIP), which integrates new experiences into existing memory networks. Memories of overwhelmingly distressing experiences remain stored in an isolated neural network in a dysfunctional, excitatory state. These unprocessed memories are triggered by a variety of internal and external stimuli, resulting in inappropriate emotional, cognitive, and behavioral reactions. EMDR therapy, based on the AIP model, involves accessing the dysfunctionally stored memory and connecting it with "adaptive" information that is true, useful, and empowering, information that most adults have attained as they mature into adulthood.

The eight phases of EMDR with children can look very different from those of an adult (see Appendix). When working with a child, the therapist usually meets with the parents alone first to learn about the child's issues and disturbing behaviors, experiences, or traumas that might be contributing to the current problems, losses, medical history, growth and development, family history, and goals of therapy. The therapist is always treating the parents and the whole family when working with a child, and must learn about the parents' relevant history as well as their beliefs, concerns, and fears and hopes for their child.

The second phase of EMDR involves developing a relationship with the child and teaching him/her calming techniques that will help the child tolerate emotional upset. Parents come with an agenda for their child, and the therapist must find goals that the child also wants. Parents may want their child's cooperation in doing what they say to do, or they may want their child to sleep in his/her own bed, or they may want their child to be agreeable when the parent says "no" to a request, but most children will not sign up for these goals. However, the child might agree that he or she would like to feel good and important, even when the parent says "no" to a request. Having a child agree to one goal is a good place to start!

In the third phase of EMDR, children may not be able to or choose to talk about traumatic memories for processing. In these cases, children's play and artwork, as well as the parents' descriptive story of events, offer metaphors for children's emotional experience. In play, children's rich inner life comes alive in the form of flying plastic snakes or good guys fighting bad guys. They may line up toy cars in a traffic jam and/or submerge dinosaurs in mounds of sand. Children may draw rainbows and flowers or guns and blood. They may calmly roll a ball back and forth or throw the ball wildly. It is up to the therapist to interpret the play in the context of the child's history.

Some play, like when a six-year-old boy engages "good guy" and "bad guy" action figures in repetitive fighting, or when a girl of the same age draws hearts and flowers, is typical and normal play for their age and gender. However, if the therapist has the history that the boy has witnessed domestic violence and that the girl is mourning for a deceased parent, the play and drawings may reflect the child's traumatic experiences. The child's therapist has to be able to take the family history and trauma history into consideration, to engage in the child's world of play, to see the world from the child's perspective, to understand what the child's behavior is saying, and to be alert to the child's teachable moments.

The clinician's strategies for implementing the fourth phase of EMDR, desensitization, depend on the child's willingness and ability to focus on the trauma and participate in the standard EMDR protocol. Some children as young as three or four years old can participate in the standard EMDR protocol, but many cannot. For some young children, like Monica, desensitization may consist of five minutes of bilateral stimulation with an action figure hero "helping" the child feel better about the time when her dad was surprised and upset.

In focusing on a toy's emotions (e.g., "How do you think the baby (doll) felt when her dad told her not to leave her crib?"), the child can elicit her own emotions in a way that is not overwhelming. The therapist can provide bilateral stimulation as the child helps the baby doll get over feeling scared remembering her dad's reaction when she climbed out of the crib. Or the therapist can "treat" the toy figure and enlist the child to notice how the baby doll feels in her body when she remembers what happened and to let the action figure know that "It's all over. That was a long time ago. Now you're much bigger and it's OK for you to get out of your bed and come downstairs in the morning."

While Monica couldn't talk about—and may not have remembered—climbing out of her crib when she was two years old, she showed interest in the story her dad and I told. She was able to empathize with the baby doll and feel sadness. She was also able to localize the sad feeling in her heart. When a child can feel the emotion and localize it in her body, we know that the neural network holding the traumatic memory has been

26

stimulated. In that moment, ABS can be effective in promoting desensitization and reprocessing of the memory.

It can be difficult to determine how much a child can tolerate hearing about a painful memory. The therapist does have to elicit or allow some of the child's painful feelings in order for the desensitization phase of EMDR to be effective. However, if the child is too distressed by the painful memory, he/she may become extremely disorganized, shut down, or avoidant. The child may be unwilling or unable to pay attention to the feeling and sensations of distress. If the child is overwhelmed by painful feelings, he/she may not be willing to allow bilateral stimulation in the future.

In addition to titrating the level of distress for a child, the therapist often has to provide additional information in order for the reprocessing phase of EMDR to proceed to adaptive resolution. Children do not have the "adult perspective" and need the assistance of a trusted therapist to learn a new perspective that will help resolve early trauma. Even though children have a well-functioning information processing system, they may lack the information or life experience necessary to reach an adaptive resolution. For example, Monica was not able to process the memory of her father's upset until she understood that he was upset because he was scared that she would be hurt rather than angry because she was bad.

"Cognitive interweaves," or questions about safety, responsibility, and choices, elicit the "adult perspective" in adults or older children. For example, if an adult is stuck in his belief that as a child he "drove his father to drink" so that he became violent, the clinician can challenge this belief by asking whether the adult or the child is responsible for what the adult drinks and how he behaves. An adult knows that a child cannot make an adult drink or become violent. However, children often need cognitive interweaves that provide developmentally appropriate information necessary for resolving trauma, such as "It's never a child's fault if a parent drinks and hurts people." I think of these interweaves as "educational" interweaves.

Memory storage is different in young children and adults. Adults are usually able to form and describe a consolidated image of the worst parts of their traumatic experience, and EMDR therapy proceeds as the adult naturally links his or her "adult perspective" with events that happened in childhood. However, there is a similarity between memory storage in children under the age of (about) six and adults traumatized before the age of six: In both, the memory is stored like a recent memory—that is, frame-by-frame-by-frame—rather than as a consolidated memory that is representative of the whole experience. Therefore, EMDR processing must proceed frame-by-frame-by-frame in order to completely clear early trauma. With young experiences stored in a frame-by-frame way, laying the framework for gauging all future experience, it's no wonder that adults repeatedly traumatized in childhood don't always clear trauma simply by targeting "the worst part" of a specific memory.

It sometimes helps to view those early critical incidents as a video, starting well before the upsetting part. Often, feeling good gets connected into the neural network as a sign of foreboding (negative cognition: "It's not safe to feel good because that means something bad will happen"). If this association is not recognized and specifically addressed, the client may continue being depressed, despite considerable desensitization and reprocessing.

I like to think in terms of "umbrella cognitions": There are certain positive cognitions (the spokes of the umbrella) such as "I am lovable," "I am good," and "I can understand," all of which must be gained before the "umbrella cognition" ("I am safe, good enough as I am, and I can relax and be me, confident I can know when to trust myself and the world") can be achieved. So, for the young child who has been repeatedly traumatized by neglect, abuse, etc., or the adult traumatized as a young child, each aspect of their experiences (cascade of traumatic experiences) must be processed individually.

In adults traumatized as young children, as in normally developmentally egocentric young children, there tend to be three elements in common: (1) the negative self-referencing beliefs or cognitions, such as "It is my fault" (or "I'm responsible"); (2) "I am bad" (or "I'm not good enough"); and (3) confusion about what happened and the meaning of what happened. Confusion, or not understanding, happens because the child is not developmentally mature enough or experienced enough to make sense of the experience, or the event (like abandonment of a child) is not understandable for anybody. After the traumatic situation has passed, confusing situations, or simply not having the structure provided by a schedule, can trigger a sense of danger and anxiety.

Often, processing does not come to adaptive resolution without educational interweaves to dispel the physical sensation of confusion (i.e., telling the child or inner child what's what in a developmentally appropriate way). In addition, it helps to address the confusion, the "I can't understand this" cognition, and body sensation. After targeting "confusion" sufficiently, I find that many children start doing schoolwork, especially math, reading, and/or written expression, better: I think math, reading, and written expression require being able to tolerate not knowing what's going on long enough to be able to comprehend them.

As described in this chapter, Monica's father and I spontaneously offered a brief healing narrative through play. A more formal healing narrative, detailed in Chapter 14, is especially useful as a framework for EMDR desensitization and reprocessing for young children, for children who experienced trauma when they were preverbal, and for children with complex and confusing experiences that are beyond the developmental scope of their understanding. The therapist and parents or caregivers collaborate to write a story that describes the child's strengths and personal resources, tells about the traumatic experiences, and helps the child to differentiate between *then*, during the traumatic experience, and *now*, when the child is safe or has support to help him/her through a difficult situation.

3

DANILO
Trauma from Hospitalization

Medical trauma is not uncommon. For Danilo, even a one-night hospitalization for asthma was traumatic. Danilo's parents said that after the hospitalization, Danilo had a completely changed personality. They also felt traumatized and unable to provide their best parenting because they felt helpless, guilty, and sad about what had happened to their child.

Danilo

Amelia and Armando felt sure they knew the reason for their three-year-old son's problem. Amelia explained, "Danilo changed a lot after that hospitalization for asthma almost two years ago, when he was only 16 months old. I think he was traumatized by that experience. It was very scary for him and for us too." Armando described their son: "Danilo is a good boy. He's very smart and observant. He's imaginative and he really cares about how people feel. Those parts of his personality are constant, but aside from that he's all different."

"How did he change after he was in the hospital?" I asked.

Amelia glanced at Armando and he signaled her to begin. "Danilo was very friendly before he was hospitalized. That was almost two years ago. He smiled a lot then—he liked people and even smiled at strangers. After the hospitalization, Danilo has rarely smiled and rarely makes eye contact, and he has become much quieter than before he went in the hospital. He still shies away from his father, and he looks anxious when he asks me, 'Are you happy?' He asks me 'Are you happy?' several times a day, and I've asked the other parents in our preschool—none of the other kids ask their parents that. He doesn't like to be hugged anymore—he doesn't even like having his hands held—I think it reminds him of being held down for the intravenous needle."

Armando reflected, "There are other things we've noticed, but we don't know for sure that they're related to the asthma or the hospitalization. He's seems sad a lot, and he's so indecisive. He wants something, then doesn't want it, then wants it again. It's like he doesn't know what he wants and nothing feels right."

Until he was two years old, Danilo spoke only Tagalog. At age 16 months, he spent only one night in the hospital where lots of people examined him and spoke in English, a language he didn't understand. He had a chest X-ray and needed a nasal cannula for oxygen, an intravenous line, and a nebulizer for medication. As Amelia and Armando recounted the story of their son's hospitalization, it was apparent from the language they used that they were traumatized too. Amelia described the scene: "Danilo had to be in a metal cage. So many people looked at him and examined him. He was examined with a cold stethoscope. His father and a nurse had to hold him down while the intravenous line was put in. Danilo had to have a tube stuck in his nose for oxygen. It was scary for us too—it's frightening to have your child have so much trouble breathing."

Since then, Danilo had had to go to the emergency room two other times. Both times, nebulized medication made it easier for Danilo to breathe, and he was able to go home after a few hours. Armando said, "We're worried that he might need another hospitalization someday. That would be terrible. He was so afraid in the hospital, and he doesn't even like to hear the word hospital, so we have to avoid saying it."

I knew that my first job was to work with Danilo's parents to help them view the experience more positively. I find that writing a story for a child is useful to parents who have been traumatized by their child's trauma. Danilo's family was Filipino, and they spoke Tagalog at home, although they were all fluent in English. His parents thought that it would be a good idea to write the story in both Tagalog and English so they could read to him in both languages to make sure he understood every word.

I explained the structure of the story: "The story has three parts. The first part tells about Danilo's positive qualities—what he likes to do and what his family likes about him now; the second part describes what happened to Danilo in the hospital; and the third part explains what Danilo can understand now that he couldn't understand at the time of the hospitalization. I make it a 'once upon a time' story because that makes it easier for children to listen to. Danilo can claim it as his, or he can talk about 'the boy in the story.' I leave feelings out of the story because I want to ask Danilo how he, or the boy in the story, felt."

I met with Amelia and Armando twice without Danilo present, and we came up with this story:

> Once upon a time there was a boy who lived with his mommy and daddy. This little boy was strong. He liked to climb to high places and ride his bike. He learned fast and liked to help. His mommy and daddy appreciate that he is affectionate and cares

about people and animals. He is gentle with their old dog and even helps to feed him.

Like everybody else in the world, some things in this boy's life were wonderful and some things were scary. Some wonderful things were that the boy was born lovable and good and *friendly*. One of the scary things that happened was that the boy sometimes had trouble breathing. Usually his mommy and daddy gave him medicine at home and he got better.

A couple of times when he was a baby, his parents took him to see a doctor at the hospital. In the hospital he was in a crib with high sides to keep him safe. His mommy and daddy were beside him the whole time. The doctors and nurses helped to take care of him.

The little boy needed to get special medicine through a little tube attached to his arm. His daddy and the nurses held him still while a doctor put the little tube in his arm. He also had a tube in his nose to give him air, and he wore a mask to get both air and medicine to help him feel better. There were other times when his daddy and other helpers held him still to take special pictures of his lungs to understand his breathing problem.

Doctors came and used a stethoscope to listen to the little boy's breathing. They wanted to make sure that his breathing was getting better, and it was. The next day he was breathing fine and he went home.

Now that he's older, the boy can understand some things he couldn't understand when he was a baby.

He can understand that everyone has times when they do not feel well.

He can understand that doctors and nurses are there to help people.

He can understand that if a baby moves a lot, it is hard for the doctor to put the tube in just the right spot on his arm.

He can understand that his daddy and the helpers held him still so that the doctor could put the tube in quickly, and he would feel OK fast.

He can remember that when he was in the hospital his mommy and daddy were worried and not happy, but they weren't unhappy with him. He didn't do anything wrong. He was a good boy. Now he can understand that they were worried because their boy didn't feel well.

Then, when he was a little baby and it was hard to breathe and he was coughing a lot, he didn't know what was happening. Now he knows to stay calm and take deep breaths.

It's important for him to know that he is a healthy boy, and he can play and speak with family and friends.

When he speaks or plays, it's important for him to look at the eyes of family and friends so that they can see his brown eyes.

His mommy and daddy say, "We love you so much. We are so proud of our healthy, sweet, and smart boy."

He can trust that when he is not feeling well or needs help, his mommy, daddy, grandma, aunts, uncles, teachers, and friends can help him. We can help him feel better with hugs and smiles. Sometimes we may need to give medicine or ask a doctor for help too.

We kept the information the parents conveyed to me, and by changing the language a little, we had reframed the hospital experience. We changed "he was in a metal cage" to "In the hospital he was in a crib with high sides to keep him safe."

"His father and a nurse had to hold him down while the intravenous line was put in" became "He can understand that if a baby moves a lot, it is hard for the doctor to put the tube in just the right spot on his arm. He can understand that his daddy and the helpers held him still so that the doctor could put the tube in quickly, and he would feel OK fast."

We wanted to repair the relationship between the boy and his father, so it was really very important for Danilo to know that his father was not holding him down for punishment. It's literally true that Armando was restraining his son by holding him down, but restraining by "holding a child down" sounds aggressive. "Holding a child still" sounds more caring and gentle.

A nasal cannula might sound punitive when described as a "tube stuck in his nose for oxygen." There are other explanations for the medical equipment that are understandable by a three-year-old. His parents settled on "He also had a tube in his nose to give him air, and he wore a mask to get both air and medicine to help him feel better."

We suspected that Danilo was avoiding eye contact because he associated people looking at him with his traumatic hospitalization. It was important to present the examinations of so many doctors and nurses as friendly, helping eyes. "The doctors and nurses helped to take care of him. Doctors and nurses came to look at him and used a stethoscope to listen to the little boy's breathing. They wanted to make sure that his breathing was getting better, and it was."

We used the story as a framework for EMDR processing. Danilo sat on the sofa between his parents while I read the story aloud. Danilo cried a little as I read the story in English, the language he had acquired in pre-school. The first time I read the story, Danilo held the buzzers while he listened to the story from beginning to end without stopping. Then Armando read the story to him in Tagalog. When he heard the story in Tagalog, Danilo sobbed harder. It made sense that Danilo's early memories were stored in his primary language at age 16 months and that his emotional response was stronger when Tagalog stimulated the early memories.

On a subsequent visit, we read the story to him a second time. I read each paragraph first in English, and then Armando read the paragraph in Tagalog. I stopped frequently to ask how the little boy felt. His response to every question I asked was "sad." I asked him to notice the sad feeling to help the boy feel better. Each time he tuned in to the sad feeling, Danilo cried a little, but less than the first time I read the story.

After I read the part about the father holding him still so the doctor could put in the needle in the right spot fast, I asked Danilo, "Do you forgive your daddy for holding you still? He was doing it to help you, so the needle would go in fast and you could feel better fast." Danilo nodded shyly and then smiled. Armando smiled at Danilo and gave him a hug. Armando looked at him and asked, "Will you forgive me?" Danilo nodded. Through the rest of the story he giggled frequently.

By the third time we read the story at the next visit, Danilo was laughing a lot, putting the buzzers on his nose (did that help desensitize the feeling of the tube in his nose?), and smiling directly at me and his parents. I thought that he had done all the work he needed to do, but his parents asked to bring him one more time to use my hospital set and little dolls to act out the story of what had happened.

Danilo's mom reported that at home he was still looking at her frequently and asking, "Are you happy, Mommy?" So when we played out the hospital scene, I said, "Look, the mommy and daddy are frowning. They're worried." I asked Amelia, "Why are they worried? Are they worried because their boy is sick or because he did something wrong?" Amelia responded quickly, "Oh, they knew that the boy didn't do anything wrong. What happened was not his fault. He was a good boy. They were worried because they were sorry he felt sick." I tapped on Danilo's hands and asked him to tell me when he felt better. In less than a minute, he said, "better."

Danilo's parents brought him back one more time. He was making eye contact with his parents and preschool teachers routinely and even waved at strangers sometimes. His mom informed me, "We're getting used to the way Danilo is now. He can make decisions—in fact, he's opinionated. We're so surprised when he says 'no.'" She smiled, "It's like Danilo is a normal kid now. He even gets angry."

Meanwhile, Danilo was playing with his dad, climbing on him. I asked Armando, "Do you think he forgives you for holding him still when he was in the hospital?" Armando smiled and nodded and looked at his son. Danilo smiled back.

Perspective

According to the Healthcare Cost and Utilization Project, there were nearly 6.4 million hospital stays for children 17 years or younger in the United States in 2009. Nearly 1 in 10 children in the United States has asthma, and it is the third-ranking cause of hospitalization of children (Yu, Wier, & Elixhauser, 2011).

Working with three-year-old Danilo gave me some insights into medical trauma. Medical trauma usually involves the discomfort of illness or injury, uncertainty about prognosis, confusion (confusion about the situation and/or confusion induced by medication), physical restraint for painful or frightening procedures, an unfamiliar environment, examination by lots of strangers, and worried parents. From a toddler's egocentric point of view, Danilo may have thought he did something wrong, causing his trouble breathing and his parents' distress. He may have felt betrayed by his father who restrained him.

Danilo's story illustrates the value of writing a story reframing the medical experience for the benefit of the parents as well as the child. The story provided clarification about what happened, reframed the hospital as a place where everyone helped, and established the event as something in the past, with three-year-old Danilo able to understand what one-year-old Danilo could not understand.

Note that Danilo had the strongest emotional reaction when he heard his story in the only language he understood at age 16 months, when he was hospitalized. When using EMDR to target an early memory, it's helpful to stimulate the neural networks in which the memory was stored by using the language that the child understood and spoke at the time of the trauma.

Untreated, this medical trauma may have resulted in lifelong consequences for this child and his parents. Danilo's story offers an example of the need for "detachment therapy." By deliberately detaching the painful memory of the trauma from the parent who participated by restraining him, the parent whose face registered fright, and the health care professionals who examined him, Danilo was able to resume a trusting, friendly relationship with people. A few sessions of treatment resulted in a more confident, happier child who enjoyed meeting people, loved his dad, and was no longer hypervigilant about his mother's emotions.

4

MAX

Following Unusual Symptoms Back to
Their Traumatic Preverbal Origin

Six-year-old Max had eating issues. I have seen hundreds of young children whose parents were concerned because they weren't eating the right foods, the right amount of food, or the way their parents wanted them to eat. There was something unusual about Max's food issues. My clinical judgment told me that Max's symptoms were posttraumatic; however, when I investigated his history, neither Max nor his parents could think of anything that could have happened to him that would cause his symptoms.

This story about Max illustrates some basic principles of how to approach an unusual behavioral problem with no clear cause or explanation. First, take a thorough history. When I meet with parents alone, before I meet their child, I start our meeting by saying, "Please park your problems outside the door and tell me a little about yourselves." Then I ask about their child's concerning behaviors and what events or experiences might have contributed to what's going on currently. I ask detailed questions about the child's and family's history: pregnancy, labor, delivery, growth and development, hospitalizations, illnesses, injuries, medications, allergies, somatic symptoms, sleeping, eating habits, screen time, relationships with parents, siblings, friends, school, and extended family. I learn about what interventions they have tried in addressing the problem, and what has helped and what hasn't helped.

I ask parents to tell me about traumas and losses the child or family has experienced. I explain trauma as any experience that undermines the sense of safety and well-being and gives a person distorted or negative beliefs about himself/herself. Sometimes, events happen to a child when a parent is not present or when the child is preverbal. Often, parents are unaware that events that did not happen to their child directly can initiate maladaptive behaviors and even affect the development of their child's personality.

The following story illustrates the clinician's process of history taking, sorting through diagnostic possibilities, getting to know the child and family, struggling with deciding how to focus therapy in a confusing situation, utilizing language and imagery offered by the child, motivating the child to participate in therapy, and choosing a variety of therapeutic modalities to help the child and family. Sometimes none of the information we gather leads us to a diagnosis or treatment plan. Sometimes we need to rely on clinical judgment or consultation with someone who has had years of experience with children. What is clinical judgment? Regardless of whether a clinician is a surgeon, cardiologist, or therapist, he/she uses a combination of knowledge, experience, and intuition to guide diagnosis and treatment. Clinical judgment functions like a gut feeling that tells you someone is following you, even if you cannot see him/her. Yes, that gut feeling can be wrong, but it's worth respecting because attention to the feeling might be life saving.

Max

Max's story didn't fit together. Six-year-old Max refused to eat dinner with his family. David and Jennifer, his parents, described the situation. David began, "Max says he's disgusted by the sight and smell of food, especially meat. He hates to watch anyone eat." Jennifer chimed in, "He wants to eat alone in a separate room. Of course we don't let him do that. We insist that he stay in the dining room with his family during dinner. Max's two older brothers sit at the dining room table with us, but Max insists on sitting facing away from them, at his own table. He makes a terrible fuss and won't look up if we make him sit at the table with us."

When Max ate away from home, the complications were magnified. When the family went to a restaurant, he sat at a table by himself. He looked down at his plate the whole time, so he wouldn't have to see anyone else eating. His mother began to cry when she talked about their vacation. "It was so painful to see him at a separate table facing away from us all the time at every meal. We've tried making him eat with us, but that's even worse. He screams and won't look up. He's so sensitive to the smell of food, particularly meat. And when we go to friends' houses for dinner, it's embarrassing. He will not eat at the table with anyone, no matter what."

"What does he do for lunch at school?" I questioned. Jennifer grimaced and said, "That's a problem too—he sits at a table, alone if possible, and looks down at his food. The kids think he's weird. He's a great kid and other kids love to play with him, but I'm afraid he's losing friends because of his strange behavior around food."

In my career I had seen plenty of children who were picky eaters or who refused to eat, but I had never before encountered a child who described himself as "repulsed" by food or consistently refused to sit at the table with others for meals. I needed more history.

"When did this start?" I inquired. Jennifer and David looked at one another and then slowly turned their heads from side to side as they puzzled over how to answer. They reviewed the history of Max's eating habits. Jennifer remembered, "When Max was an infant, I breast-fed him for his first 12 months, then he sat on my lap or David's lap to eat or sat in a high chair to eat, but as soon as he could talk and run around, he refused to be at the table." They didn't remember him ever watching anyone eat, but maybe it just didn't register. Their other two children had eaten with the family, and there was no history of similar problems in the extended family.

I wondered whether Max could have sensory integration issues that made it difficult for him to tolerate the smells or textures of food. Is he sensitive to odors other than food? No. Is he bothered by any particular clothes or tags? No. Do certain textures bother him? No.

Jennifer remembered something that she thought might be pertinent. Max had stopped eating with others when he was about two years old and they switched preschools. Between the ages of two and four, he had changed preschools and childcare providers three times. While it's always a little stressful to change childcare and preschools, neither Jennifer nor David remembered it being too big a deal. Max was never reluctant to go to school or childcare and never seemed upset when he came home. No, nothing upsetting had happened to him when he was in preschool or childcare as far as they knew.

Hmm. I inquired about Max's early history. I have seen "oral sensory avoidance" in children who were intubated in their first weeks of life. But Max had had a normal perinatal period. He had never had medical procedures at all, other than immunizations. To be thorough in investigating oral sensitivity as a possibility, I asked, "Can he brush his teeth? And tolerate the dentist?" Yes. No problem.

How did he get along with his siblings? Fine. Did he have friends? Yes. How did he get along with them? Fine. David elaborated, "He's a great kid and other kids like to play with him. He's our youngest child and his siblings adore him. He's just weird about eating." How did he get along with his parents? They loved him and felt close to him, and he was very affectionate with them. This appeared to be a healthy, intact, caring family that had a lot of fun together.

The only negative quality his parents could come up with was that Max was hard on himself and a bit stubborn. He "marched to his own drummer" and just wanted to do what he wanted to do. They said he "liked to be different" and frequently said, "I want to be different." This is very unusual for a six-year-old child. Most first graders want to be like the other kids their age—that is, the boys want to be like the other boys, and the girls want to be like the other girls. "How is he different?" I inquired. David answered, "As far as I can see, the main thing that's different about him is that he says he likes to be different, and he finds food repulsive and won't eat with anyone or watch anyone eat."

I was curious about whether Max had any other quirky behaviors, other than his intolerance of food odors or being in the presence of people who are eating. No other quirky behaviors that his parents could identify. They were very likeable, socially adept, friendly people, and I trusted their judgment that their son's behavior was generally age appropriate.

My mind was going in the direction of trauma again. Had anything happened at the dinner table that made him want to avoid meals with his family? I steered the conversation back to food. Had Max ever choked on anything? No. Had he ever witnessed anyone at the dinner table have a problem—like choking on food? No.

David provided some family history: "My sister had an eating disorder when she was a teen. I think she was anorexic, but she's an adult and she's better now. Could this be related?" Could it? I wondered. But what eating disorder did Max have? He was in the 90th percentile for height and weight. He was "repulsed" (his word according to his parents) by food, but he did eat and he didn't vomit. I had never seen an eating disorder present quite this way.

Then David volunteered a bit of juicy information: "I forgot to mention that Max does eat what we call a 'dude's sandwich.'" "What's that?" I asked. David explained that he had been worried about Max not getting enough protein, so about once a week he made a patty with onions, garlic, hamburger, and spinach and put it in a bun and called it a "dude's sandwich." Max ate that smelly sandwich just fine. Max's dad had never told Max what was in a "dude's sandwich."

How could a kid be fine eating a "dude's sandwich" when he couldn't tolerate meat or the smell of food?

Jennifer began to cry. "Eating together and enjoying good food is so important to our family. Eating is so important for bonding. It's sad for him and for us. We're very social, and we love to travel. He can't enjoy some of the things we enjoy most, and we've almost stopped going out for dinner at restaurants or friends' or relatives' homes. We don't know what to do."

When Jennifer mentioned "bonding," I wondered whether Max had some kind of attachment disorder. Not eating with others sure can cause problems in relationships, but would refusing to eat with others be considered an insecure, avoidant attachment? I explored his early history— he was a full-term baby and had gone home from the hospital with his mother 24 hours after birth. He nursed successfully and was a cuddly, responsive baby. His parents felt they bonded with him as soon as he was born. They loved him and enjoyed being with him. He was responsive and joyful when he was with them, in any activity that didn't involve food. This was not an attachment disorder!

I prodded for more history and a review of systems. No particular illnesses or injuries. No allergies. Occasional stomachache—usually seemed to be related to constipation. Growth and development—fine. Slept well. No nightmares.

I probed about traumas and losses. Max's parents said he had never had any losses other than the family's goldfish, but he had never seemed that concerned. The only trauma in the family happened when Max was two years old. Jennifer's sister's child (Max's first cousin), who was three years older than Max, had a near drowning. Max's parents denied that it was upsetting to Max. They had not witnessed the tragedy. Jennifer mused, "Max loves his cousin Chiara and is very affectionate and gentle with her. She had brain damage and has to be fed through a gastric tube, but she sits in her wheelchair and comes to the table for meals. That family lives in a different city, and we only see them occasionally."

I wondered aloud whether Max's unusual habit could be related to Chiara, but I had no idea how, and his parents felt that neither her accident nor her disabilities were related to his food avoidance. I could hardly wait to meet Max.

Max turned out to be a six-year-old boy who was affectionate with his parents and played calmly with toys in the sand tray while we talked. I drew a large circle on a piece of paper and added dotted lines for the spokes of the wheel, what I call a "power wheel." I asked Max's parents to tell me some things they appreciated about Max and qualities and resources that helped him in life, and I wrote one on each spoke of the wheel. I asked Max what books and music and activities he especially liked and what strengths he saw in himself. His parents named a lot of great qualities for his power wheel (see Part Two: Cultivating Positive Emotions, Chapter 11). He "knows how to welcome people and makes them feel comfortable, he's kind and loving, he loves books and learning and he's learning to read, he has a great imagination, he knows how to make rules that are fair and safe, and he's good at figuring out how things work." David enjoyed bike riding and hiking and playing catch with him, and Jennifer liked to cuddle and read and joke with him. Max examined his power wheel and was pleased to see that he had so many powers.

I asked Max what he'd like to have go better or be easier for him. He responded "school" but couldn't say what it was about school that he'd like to be easier. I asked his parents what they would like to be easier for Max and their family. As planned, his mother asserted, "I want it to be easier for him to be around food," and his father concurred. "I want Max to eat dinner at the table with the rest of the family."

I asked Max if that's what he wanted too. He shrugged. I asked Max what got in the way of him eating with his family. He mumbled, "The Terrible." I expressed my curiosity: "What is The Terrible?" He shrugged again, so I looked to his parents. "How does The Terrible mess things up for Max?" Jennifer was quick to reply, "The Terrible makes it hard to go to friends' houses and restaurants to eat, it makes Max sit alone in the cafeteria instead of with friends, and it ruins birthday parties—he misses the fun and then he feels terrible about it."

Max himself introduced this "narrative therapy approach" described by Michael White and David Epston in their book *Narrative Means to Therapeutic Ends*. Max externalized the problem, personified it, and gave it a life of its own. This is a useful conceptualization of the problem as separate from the child. Max's naming of "The Terrible" allowed some perspective on the problem and gave us an opportunity to talk about it without spotlighting it as a flaw in the child himself.

At the end of the visit I gave Max and his parents homework: "Notice when The Terrible wins and prevents Max from enjoying eating with your family or friends, and notice when Max wins and gets to have fun doing those things." I thought I would address the problem, The Terrible, with the narrative therapy approach and maybe it would yield a target for EMDR processing.

Max returned with his dad the next week. David reported, "The Terrible was messing things up a lot this week. One night Max did eat at the table with the rest of the family when his brothers persuaded him to join them, but he shielded his eyes so he couldn't see anyone eating. I think The Terrible makes Max really unhappy. I know it makes me really unhappy."

I decided that treating the symptom as anxiety and helping Max learn to calm himself was a good place to start, regardless of what was causing the problem. I guided Max to describe a "safe or relaxing place" (see Chapter 11). He described a fun place where there were lots of swimming pools and beaches and people and friends. It was warm and breezy and he could play ball in the water. I taught Max the "butterfly hug" (see Chapter 11), but he quickly lost interest and said he wanted to do something else. Since most children love bubbles, I offered the "bubble game" (see Chapter 12). Max was cooperative and affectionate with his dad, who blew bubbles for Max to pop.

The following week, Max came with Jennifer. She reported that when they went to a restaurant one night, Max asked to sit at a separate table, but one night at home he had sat with his family at their dinner table and had dinner together with them! Jennifer beamed. I was surprised—"Max, how did it feel for you to have dinner with your family?" Max's response surprised me too: "It felt great because I got to sit with my family!"

I had no idea why Max hadn't been able to sit with his family before or why he had been able to sit with his family that one night. I handed him the buzzers to reinforce the positive experience and asked him to remember what had happened when he sat with his family and how he felt. He did what I asked. I showed him all the gadgets for delivering alternating bilateral stimulation (ABS) and asked him to think of a resource as he tried each of the four different sounds through the head-phones, held the buzzers and watched the lights, and followed a "super-hero" figure from side to side. As I showed each one, I "installed" or strengthened a positive memory as a resource—a good time with mom, a good time with dad, a good time with his siblings, a protector, a learning experience, and a "yes" experience when he accomplished something dif-ficult. And I reinforced the good feeling of eating at the table with his family.

When it was time for the family to leave, I gave another homework assignment: "I want Max to eat at the table with the family every night, even if it's hard for him. And Max, I want you to notice and tell your mom or dad what was hard about it."

I figured that if Max could eat with his family once, he could do it again. I also thought that if Max were required to sit at the table, and he felt uncomfortable doing it, he might be more motivated to work toward feeling comfortable. Max didn't balk at the assignment.

When I wrote my notes in Max's chart that day, I mused, "Why not able to sit with family? related to cousin being fed through a gastrostomy tube?" I didn't see a direct connection, but I hadn't found any other explanation for Max's strange behavior.

At the next visit, Jennifer reported that Max was eating at the table most of the time because they insisted, but he didn't want to do it, and he said he was "repulsed" and kept his eyes down, even when his siblings tried to get him to laugh or tried to make him angry. "Repulse" is such an odd word for a six-year-old child to use. Max's mom observed, "When we tell Max he has to come to the dinner table, he looks more *scared* than repulsed."

Max pulled out some stuffed animal dogs and played he was the shy dog who didn't want to eat with his friends at lunch. Jennifer participated in Max's play and did a great job of following Max's lead and also expand-ing on his themes. Playing with them was fun, but it didn't yield any new themes or insights into what was making Max behave as he did.

At the next visit, I was disappointed to hear that progress had reversed. Jennifer reported, "At school, Max is beginning to have tantrums because he refuses to have lunch at the table with his friends. At home he's having meltdowns when I insist that he come to the table." Max protested, "It's too disgusting." Then he muttered something about a secret. His mother and I looked at one another in alarm. "What kind of secret?" she probed. Max said he couldn't tell us because he didn't know.

Later, Jennifer called me to say she had drilled Max about "the secret." Had anyone said anything scary to him? No. Had anyone touched him inappropriately? No. Had anyone told him not to tell something? No. Max told her that there was a secret, but even he didn't know what it was.

Jennifer assured me that she had told him many times that it's never OK to keep a secret and that he was supposed to tell his parents any time someone told him a secret. She felt sure that he had always been safe and supervised so that there most likely couldn't have been a significant event that she didn't know about.

I had seen Max weekly for two months, and I still didn't know what was going on. Had I missed some point in the history? Why would Max be scared to sit with his family, unwilling to sit with others while they ate, repulsed by the smell of meat, but only if he knew it was meat? I reviewed all of my notes and still didn't have a new clue. If there had been an identified traumatic incident, standard EMDR therapy would have been the most effective treatment.

Max's parents and I decided to try systematic desensitization. I did think exposure was a reasonable idea, so I asked David to bring a meal with him to eat in front of Max. David came in with a Tupperware container full of food, including meat. Max kept repeating, "It's disgusting. It's repulsive."

I gave Max the buzzers to put in his jeans pockets and kept them on to facilitate desensitization of anxiety and reprocessing Max's beliefs that it wasn't safe to look at people while they ate and that it wasn't safe for him to smell or eat meat. I kept the bilateral stimulation with buzzers on the whole time we did the exposure. Max loved cheese puffs, so he got one every time he looked up to watch David eat, looked at meat, smelled meat, or fed David with a fork so that he was forced to look at David's face while he ate. And every time he got a cheese puff reward, I said, "It's safe to watch people eat. You're OK if you see someone eating." I chose the word "safe" for the positive cognition because his mother had told me that he looked scared when they tried to get him to sit at the table.

I had thought a lot about my hunch that disabled cousin Chiara might have something to do with this. I remembered one seven-year-old child I had seen years before who would eat only white food—white bread, mashed potatoes, white rice, cauliflower, crackers, cheese, and pale applesauce.

When the mystery of the preference for white food was unraveled, it turned out that the child had finished eating mashed potatoes and started eating broccoli right before his parents screamed at one another and announced they were getting divorced. Somehow, his young psyche decided that it was safe to eat only white foods, as if the divorce never would have happened if he had continued to eat his mashed potatoes. We used EMDR to desensitize and reprocess the memory, and after that he was able to eat everything.

So as David ate slowly and Max reluctantly did as he was told for the cheese puff reward, I inquired, "What were you doing when you learned that Chiara had had the accident?" Max shook his head. He didn't remember anything about it. His father didn't remember much either: "We were having lunch at a neighbor's house when we got the call telling us what had happened and that Chiara was in the hospital." "Were you at the table eating?" I asked eagerly, but David didn't remember the details of what had happened four years before, when his phone rang to deliver the shocking news.

I'm so used to telling stories to children that I just started making up a narrative about the day Chiara was injured. I turned off the buzzers and looked at Max: "Let's just imagine that you were at your friend's house. You were very little, just two years old. Everyone was sitting at the dinner table enjoying a meal and having a good time. You smelled the food and especially the meat. Imagine that." At that point, I turned the buzzers on. Max was looking down—in a minute he looked up, and I responded to his change of posture by turning the buzzers off to check in and find out what he was experiencing. Max didn't say anything but appeared to be waiting for me to continue with the story.

"The phone rang and all of a sudden everyone looked frightened and upset. Imagine that." I turned the buzzers on and waited for Max to look at me. I continued, "Sometimes when parents look scared and upset, little children can't figure out why, so they think that somehow they caused the problem. Imagine looking at the parents' faces and seeing how scared and upset they look." I turned the buzzers on again. David nodded, "We sure were scared and upset when we heard the news about Chiara. We stopped whatever we were doing and left the children with our friends so we could go to the hospital."

I made more guesses: "So the boy's parents suddenly left for the hospital, and the little boy had to stay with his friends who were scared too. Imagine that." Buzzers on again. When Max looked up again, he appeared more relaxed.

I asked Max what the little boy might have felt and thought when his parents looked scared and then hurried away. How did the little boy feel when his parents left him all day with his friends who were also scared? How might the boy have felt when his parents came home and they were even more upset? The news was not good. Chiara had severe brain damage from a freak accident. Max couldn't tell me what he thought or felt, but I could see he was following my story with interest. His father nodded affirmation—he looked distraught just remembering the shock of the day.

I looked at Max's eyes and when I felt he was connected with me, I informed him: "The little boy needs to know that what happened wasn't his fault. A child can't cause an accident like that, and a child can't prevent an accident like that. It wasn't your fault. It didn't have anything to do with you. I want you to think about this: Back then, *a long time ago* when you were just a little boy, something really scary and dangerous happened while you were at the dinner table and watching people eating and smelling food. *Now*, when you smell food, it means that you are safe and everyone is well and enjoying life. That's the way it's supposed to be." Max looked relieved.

I remembered that in addition to having trouble tolerating food, Max also insisted that he wanted to be "different." That would have been perfectly normal in a teen. It was very unusual for a six-year-old boy. So I turned on the buzzers as I added another part to the story: "After that, Chiara was different, not you. Chiara couldn't eat the way everyone else eats, but you can. You're normal just like the rest of your family and your friends. It's OK for you to eat normally at the table, even though Chiara can't."

It's not unusual for a child to identify with the key person in the memory and to confuse himself with that person or to feel guilty that he was OK but she was not. My job is to separate the identities of the two people so that the safe, healthy person could feel OK even though the person he cared about was not well. EMDR is useful for putting the past in the past and for clearing confusion and blurred interpersonal boundaries.

I haven't seen Max again. A few weeks after I last saw him, Jennifer sent me a nice note of thanks telling me how great it was to have Max normal—he could eat at the table without a problem. I haven't heard anything else since then, so I assume Max wants to be like everyone else his age and is eating with his friends at school.

Perspective

Max had experienced an event that did not affect his own safety. However, he saw that his parents were very frightened and assumed that something he did caused their distress. It's typical for developmentally egocentric young children to think they caused the problem, and they know that their parents get upset when they do something wrong. Max's young age—he was just two years old at the time of the tragic accident that caused his cousin Chiara to become disabled and changed the family forever—contributed to the huge impact that event had on his own development. Max not only felt sad, he felt terrified for himself and his family, and he felt responsible for keeping his family safe. His two-year-old mind reasoned that the frightening problem happened when he was eating with people, so eating with people must be a dangerous thing to do. Two-year-old Max thought that he was protecting people by not watching them eat and by avoiding the smell of meat.

Preverbal trauma, especially experiences that even the parents don't know or remember, is especially tricky to detect and treat. It's often helpful to explore the experiences around the time of birth, and, as was the case for Max, it's helpful to ask the parents about times when their child may have seen them frightened. The history that Max's parents were shocked and scared by the call about their niece's accident was the clue that led to the source of Max's unusual behaviors. A frightened parent always makes a child uneasy—parents provide their most reliable cues about safety and danger.

5

AIDEN

Including Parents in Their Child's
Trauma Resolution

Storytelling is a way to help children make sense of their experiences, and it provides good scaffolding for EMDR therapy. Writing a story focuses the clinician on making a sound, goal-oriented case formulation that will guide treatment. Involving parents in the story writing provides a means for assessing the parent's perspective and learning about the family's belief system. Parents who have been traumatized by their child's experience or who have been overwhelmed by their child's distress and disruptive behaviors find it difficult to help their child. Parents feel more competent when they participate in deciding what they want their child to understand, what they want their child to believe, and what they want their child to do.

Aiden

Like many of the parents who enter my office, Susi and Steve knew that their family was in crisis. Susi's eyes filled with tears: "We thought that by adopting Aiden at birth we would avoid some of the problems we've seen other parents have when they've adopted an older baby or child." Steve shook his head and said, "Aiden is seven and we're going through a really rough period. Aiden has been running around the house screaming, 'I hate you! I'm stupid. I hate myself!'" Susi added, "Yesterday he was yelling, 'I don't want to be part of this family. You're not my real parents. Why don't you run me over with a car?'"

Susi told me that she and her husband had read my first book, *Small Wonders: Healing Childhood Trauma with EMDR*. Susi was a therapist. She asked if she and Steve could write a story for their son because it seemed that the kids I wrote about benefited so much. I thought there was no harm in having them write a life story for Aiden, so I gave them guidelines to take home. The next week, Susi handed me the story that she and Steve had written.

This is the story they wrote on their own:

An Adoption Story

This is the story of a boy who lived happily in a big house with his mother, his father, and his little brother. They loved each other very much. Their favorite times were when they watched movies together.

The parents wanted their son to be happy. But sometimes the boy talked and cried about his birth mother, saying he missed her. He asked a lot of questions about her and wished he could meet her someday. He was sad knowing he never would because she died when she was hit by a car when he was two. Sometimes the boy had trouble sleeping at night, and he said things like "I only slept five minutes" when he was awakened in the morning.

Whenever he heard certain songs, he cried a lot. He didn't want anyone to sing when he was around.

The boy wanted to have many friends. But there were times when some other boys teased him or refused to play with him. That made him feel very sad. Sometimes he felt as though nobody liked him or wanted to play with him.

There were times when he didn't like his brother and wanted to hurt him. Then he would play roughly with him, threaten him, annoy him, or say mean things to him until he cried.

There also were times when his mother wanted him to do things to help around the house, but he didn't want to. He would do all sorts of things to avoid doing what she wanted. That made her very mad. When she got mad, he got mad too. They would yell at each other and sometimes they would hurt each other. Then nobody was happy, and he would feel like he was a bad boy.

At school he had a hard time staying focused and doing his seatwork. He usually knew what to do, but he would rather talk to the other children or read or find something more interesting to play with. Writing was hard for him. Another child told him his writing was sloppy. He didn't like to write because he thought he was a terrible writer.

After a while the boy began to feel happier. When he thought about his birth mother, he could remember her love for him and feel glad he had such a good family to be a part of. He had several friends whom he liked and who liked him. They played together often. He was able to listen to all songs without crying. At school, he was able to stay focused on his work, and his writing was improving. He knew he was a good boy who was loved by his family and friends.

The end.

When I read the story, I felt dismayed. The story written by Susi and Steve told me a lot about their own concerns and struggles, but if I were a child listening to it, I would probably feel terrible and tune out fast. I didn't think a child could bear to hear so many sad and discouraging facts. And to make the story worse, the very first line and the happy ending were not true.

Reading the story written by Susi and Steve brought up memories of *The Stuffed Owl: Anthology of Bad Verse*, a book I read in college. I remember class discussion about why we were assigned a book with bad verse . . . why not good verse? Wasn't reading good poetry the way to learn what makes a poem good? We talked about how judgment that a piece of writing is "good" is very subjective. The professor urged us to read the bad verse as a way to help us recognize good verse. We were skeptical, but of course we read the *Anthology of Bad Verse*. Although I haven't seen the book for many years, I recall reading the verses and sensing that they were a collection of words that didn't hold emotional truth.

I felt it wouldn't be useful to read that story to Aiden. I left his parents' story in my office that weekend. At home, I wrote a story that I hoped kept the spirit of their intention, but that I thought would be more true and useful. After that, I never asked parents to write a story by themselves. I always worked on it with them in my office, where I could listen with "my child's ears" and at the same time contribute what I knew from my years of clinical practice. Even with guidelines for writing a story, it's challenging for parents to write a story that can be used with EMDR.

So I told Susi and Steve that I used some of the ideas from their story to write one that would work as a basis for EMDR. They read my story and fortunately they liked it—I think it helped them see their son's experience in a different, more realistic and hopeful way.

Here is the story I wrote:

Once there was a boy who lived in a big house with his mother, his father, and his little brother. They loved each other very much. Their favorite times were when they watched movies together or went hiking or camping.

Like everybody else in the world, this boy had some sad things happen in his life and some wonderful things. The very first thing that happened in this boy's life was both wonderful and sad. The wonderful part is that he was born healthy and lovable and good. His birth mother knew this, and she loved him. The sad part was that his birth mother was too young to take care of a baby, and she was blind, which made her decide she could not take care of the baby she loved. This was confusing for the boy.

Another wonderful part was that his birth mother was determined to find a good family to raise the baby she loved. She chose parents who really wanted a baby and couldn't have a birth baby of their own. She thought long and hard and finally made the decision that she had found the right family for this precious little boy. She chose a mom and a dad who had so much love for the precious boy. The mom and dad were just right because they . . . (I asked Susie and Steve to fill in the blanks).

and they appreciated the boy for his . . .

And they loved to hike and go camping and do . . . other fun things with him.

The baby loved his family as much as they loved him, and he grew just fine. When the boy was two years old something else sad happened. His birth mother died in an accident. The boy was sad and he wondered . . . why she had died. "It's sad, but it's not your fault," his mom said.

"I'm sorry she died, but I'm so glad she chose us to raise you," his dad said.

Sometimes the boy's birth grandmother came to visit. She talked to him about her daughter, his birth mother, and helped keep her memory alive. Sometimes the boy didn't know what to do about the memory of his birth mother. He thought about her a lot and sometimes couldn't stop thinking about her.

Now that the boy is getting bigger, he can understand some things that he couldn't understand when he was very little. These are some things he can understand:

Everyone has some sad things and some wonderful things that happen to them.

It's sad that his birth mom had big problems and died in an accident.

It's wonderful that he got a great mom and dad who can take care of him.

And now he's learning something very important: Love keeps growing, and we can love a lot of people all at the same time. He has enough love for his birth mom and his adoptive mom and dad and his brother and his grandmother.

And when someone dies, it's OK to find a special, safe place in our heart where we can feel their love and love them back.

Once he found that special place in his heart to keep his birth mother's love, he was free to love his adoptive mom and dad and brother even more, to play, to make friends, and to do his schoolwork.

Aiden's parents allowed me to video their family's work with me and were willing to share it so others could learn from it. The content of this chapter represents much of the work shown in the videos.

Both parents came to my office to be with Aiden while we read the story. During the first part of that session, I let Aiden choose the type of alternating bilateral stimulation (ABS) he liked best. He chose to hold the buzzers and to listen to the synchronized tones through speakers on either side of the love seat where he and his parents were cuddled together.

Aiden told me he wanted to think about how he was adopted. I probed, "What do you think about when you remember that you were adopted?" Aiden replied, "Um, I think of loving people, like my mother, who gave me up." I reflected," You think of loving people, like your mother, who gave you up. OK. Do you want to think about that while you hold the buzzers? What's that feeling?" Aiden responded, "Sad and happy at the same time." I asked, "Where do you feel that in your body?" When Aiden pointed to his heart, I directed him to notice the feeling while Steve held him.

When Aiden wiggled a little, I turned off the buzzers and checked in with him, "What came up for you that time? And when I say what came up for you, I mean any pictures in your mind, any memories, any feelings or thoughts? What did you notice?" Aiden replied, "I don't know. I don't know." I focused the question "How are you feeling now that we did that?" Aiden smiled, "Happy." I smiled too. "Happy? OK, where do you feel the happy feeling?"

Aiden waved his hands around his body and said, "Everywhere." I turned on the ABS, saying, "OK. Stay with that."

Aiden stretched a little, so I turned off the ABS to check in: "How was that for you?" Aiden smiled again and said, "Happy." I asked Aiden if he felt ready to hear the story, and he nodded. I told him that I would turn on the buzzers and the sounds and that I wanted him to listen to the story all the way to the end because there was a good ending. Then we would talk about the story, and he could hear it again if he wanted. Aiden nodded a big nod. He was ready.

When I finished reading the story, I asked, "How was that for you, Aiden?" He responded thoughtfully, "Happy and sad." I paused to give Aiden time to consider his thoughts and feelings, then asked, "Would you tell me the parts that are upsetting to you?" Aiden looked sad: "My birth mother dying."

I remembered that Aiden was only two years old when his birth mother died. Susi and Steve had told him right away. I thought that the memory of finding out that his birth mother had died would be a good target for EMDR: "Do you remember finding out when she died?" Aiden nodded, "Yeah, I think I was looking out of a window and . . . Maybe that was in a dream." Dreams also make good targets for EMDR, so I reassured him,

"It's OK if it was in a dream. It doesn't have to be exact. I just want to know what you remember or what seems to be what happened. What do you remember about what you heard?" Aiden considered: "Um, my birth mother dying." I explored the details of the event: "And who told you?" Aiden looked at his parents and responded, "My mom and my dad." I probed for a negative cognition: "And what do you remember thinking?" but Aiden told more of his experience: "I think I cried."

I decided to proceed with desensitization and reprocessing since Aiden was already expressing the sad feeling: "And when you remember being told that, how upsetting does it seem now, if this is zero (with my hands together), not at all upsetting, and this is 10 (with my hands about 10 inches apart), the most upsetting you can imagine; how upsetting is it now when you remember being told?" Aiden's eyes widened: "Ten." I thought we were ready to launch into processing the memory, but when I suggested we do some work to help it not be so upsetting, Aiden hesitated: "It's not really upset . . ." Susi understood: "Just sad?" Aiden nodded his agreement.

I was eager to help Aiden start feeling better: "Can we help that sadness feel a little bit better?" Aiden shook his head: "I don't think so. The only person who can help that is my birth grandma." I was curious: "And how does she help?" Aiden explained, "She tells me stories about her." I offered Aiden the buzzers: "How about, will you think about your birth grandma and remember the stories and how she helps?" Aiden consented.

I followed up: "What came up that time?" Aiden sounded like he was recounting a confusing dream: "Um, when the, when, um, my birth mother and her mom, my grandmother watched, I mean, um, walked along the road and sang different words to a song, words that they made up. I think of the love that—the happy and the loving times they spent together."

I turned to Susi and Steve: "Are you learning some things about Aiden and his experience right now?" His parents nodded agreement. I continued, "I think your learning those things about him is one way of helping him, and having you close to him while he's processing some of his feelings is a big help to him too. So you can think about how this is one of the many ways you help Aiden."

I stopped to have that conversation with Aiden's parents because they were both listening to the sound of the alternating tones, and I didn't want them to start processing any of their own traumatic experiences. I wanted them to stay present and to focus their attention on Aiden. I also wanted to install positive cognitions that were true and useful to them. It was true that they helped Aiden in many ways.

I turned back to Aiden: "Do you want to think of the fun and loving times your mom and your grandma had together?" He nodded his assent, and I turned on the buzzers. Then Aiden smiled: "I feel good." I smiled too: "You feel good? You are good. Where do you feel the good feeling in your body?" Aiden was exuberant: "Everywhere." Susi watched Aiden and observed, "You look almost blissful!"

I directed Aiden back to the original target to check how disturbing it was: "Aiden, when you look back and remember being at the window and hearing that your birth mom had died, how sad does that feel now, if zero is not at all upsetting and 10 is the most upsetting you can imagine?" Aiden estimated, "Probably five."

So we were going in the right direction. I considered how to shape the next part of the session. I knew that a major problem for Aiden was that he always felt a need to be in control, even when his parents wanted him to do something they knew he would enjoy. That strong need for control is not uncommon in children who have experienced early trauma. In this instance, if Aiden had had control, he would have made sure his birth mother was safe. That need for control continued to surface whenever anything didn't go his way, even though it was safe for him to relax.

I decided to explore the topic of control since it was so problematic for Aiden and his family and teachers: "OK. One thing I want to mention, I want to check with you, is back then, when your birth mother died, did you have any control over that at all?" Aiden looked dejected: "No." I pursued, "If you had had control, what would you have had happen?"

Aiden knew exactly what he wanted to control: "I would rewind time and stop the car and let her cross the street." Aiden agreed to think about that. "What came up for you that time?" Aiden answered, "Sadness." I explained, "That's right. Because you didn't have control. Nobody had control, right? If your dad had been there, had been able to be in control, would you have stopped the car?" I checked with his dad, who responded, "I definitely would have stopped the car if I could have." Aiden's mom agreed, "If there's any way I could have stopped it I sure would have."

I wanted to let Aiden know that we all understood his need to be in control in order to save his mother. I made the comparison between then and now: "Back then, it was kind of dangerous not to have control, right? Because without you having control, your mom died. But you know what, Aiden? Now, in everyday life, when you don't have control—like when your teacher has control, or your mom and dad have control—it's OK to let them be in control. Because it's just day-to-day life. It's not life and death. Do you know what I mean? Will you hold on to the buzzers and just think about that?"

Aiden sat quietly until I turned off the buzzers and looked at him: "What came up for you that time?" Aiden looked puzzled: "I don't really know. It's a confused feeling." I turned on the buzzers: "OK, good. Hold on to the buzzers and just notice the confused feeling. Where in your body do you feel the confused feeling?" Aiden swirled his hands around his body to indicate he felt it everywhere.

Confusion is a typical accompaniment of childhood trauma. Posttraumatic confusion interferes with learning and functioning in new or unfamiliar situations. At the time of the trauma, not understanding what was happening was a portent of a life-changing event. Life is full of situations that are normally confusing. For example, when we learn something new, there is usually a period of time when it's impossible to understand exactly what's happening or what to do. When confusion continues to trigger anxiety in a learning environment, the confusion and resulting anxiety interfere with a critical step necessary in the learning process.

I turned to Susi: "Was some of it confusing to you? About how things happen in the world?" His mom nodded in agreement: "Life can be very confusing. Especially when people die when it doesn't seem like the right time for them to die. It's very confusing."

I turned to Steve: "Was it confusing in some ways for you?" He nodded too.

Both parents understood the confusion troubling their son, and I confirmed, "So was it normal for Aiden to be—to feel—confused?"

I had imagined that all the confusion made Aiden's mind feel cluttered and may have made him even feel crazy. I wanted to normalize his experience of confusion. Aiden picked up on the idea: "I was only a tiny itty-bitty baby."

I offered, "Can we process through the confusion? Just notice it, and it's going to change . . . Just tell me when, and notice the confused feeling. Because then, confusion meant that—meant what?" Aiden sighed, "That I was lost almost."

I suggested, "Let's see if we can make the confusion stop bothering you. Just notice how back then it was confusing. What did you need to know then? What did you need to understand that you couldn't understand when you were just two years old? What was confusing? What did you need to hear or need to know?" Aiden pondered the question: "The questions I asked myself were: Why did she have to die? Why? Why did God plan it this way? Those were my feelings."

"Just notice those feelings. They are good questions. What came up?" Aiden responded, "The answers to the questions: God didn't just plan it this way; crazy things happen. And God doesn't plan things. It happened. It was a flash."

I asked, "Do you want to know what your mom and dad would say if they were talking to a two-year-old child who was confused about what happened? What would you say? Who wants to go first? Just hold one buzzer in each hand and listen to your parents. Is there anything you want to tell him? Imagine he is a confused two-year-old who just heard that his mom died." I turned to Susi: "What would you have said to

Aiden when he was two years old if you had known that he was feeling confused and had these questions?"

She began, "I think I would say something like that the confusion is a very real experience, and that when people die, we all kind of feel confused about how God was involved in all of this, or if there's something that we could have done to make things different. And you know what we're going to miss out on, because things are the way they are even if we wanted them to be different."

I wanted Susi to comfort Aiden in language that would be easily understood by a child who was two years old: "What would you say to comfort him—to let two-year-old Aiden know that you're there for him, that you can understand his feelings, that you love him, and that you'll always care for him. What things would you say to Aiden?" I wanted to reach the young "two-year-old part" of Aiden that was stuck in confusion and distress.

Susi met Aiden's eyes: "The thing I remember telling you is—about two hours later and you were on my lap, and you were crying, and I was telling you and just sharing how sad that I felt, and that no matter what, we would always have each other and love each other, and you could still love (his birth mother). That she is in our hearts and that she'd never be separate from us because we'd always have her memory in our hearts. And your birth mom loves you just as much now as ever."

Steve shared his thoughts: "I'd say that I feel very anguished that it happened, and I want right now to express that your mother and I will be loving you for a long, long time. And you're a very precious son. It's something that happened that you had no control over."

I concurred, "It sure wasn't his fault in any way," and turned to Aiden: "Aiden, how are you doing?" Aiden indicated that he felt good. His parents voiced their pride in Aiden. Steve said, "I just feel like you've done a lot of beautiful and hard work. This is not easy stuff to think about. You've been really brave."

One of my goals was to keep separating the past from the present and to show how behaviors like being controlling might have made sense at the time, but now it's safe for him to do what adults ask him to do. Another goal was to help Aiden's parents empathize with him. Empathy strengthens connection, and connection is a prerequisite for cooperation.

Since grieving was such a big part of Aiden's feelings at the time, I proposed that he do a candle-lighting ceremony to honor the people he loved. Aiden was very eager to light candles! I let Aiden choose a different colored candle to represent each person he loved. Then we set them on an aluminum foil-covered tray to keep our ceremony safe. He lit each candle with a large taper and told something about each person represented by the candles: "This is my birth mom. I know she loves me and would care for me if she had me. This is my birth grandma. I know she loves me. This is my dad. I love him; he loves me too. He plays an important part of my life." (This was especially interesting because we didn't know much about Aiden's birth father, and he had not been mentioned.) "This is my mom. She's special. I love her. This is me. I love myself and my family and friends."

Aiden's ceremony was beautiful. I directed him, "Look at those candles, and think about all that love you have and the love that you're receiving from all those people who are special to you, and all the love that you have to give. Where in your body are you feeling that love right now?"

Aiden beamed, "My whole self."

I concluded, "Just notice that . . . Aiden, can you imagine that love being just as strong and feeling that just as strongly in a little while after you blow the candles out? Yes? Because the candles are symbols of that love, but the real love you have is inside you and all around you, right? Yes? And it's up to you, Aiden, you can decide whether you want to say anything more about how you are feeling or whether you feel ready to blow each of the candles out, knowing that the feeling of love is inside you and it will always stay there." Aiden said eagerly, "I feel ready." He blew the candles out and grinned.

When Aiden and his parents returned the following week, I asked about his experience the previous week when we worked on the story the first time.

I rechecked the original memory: "So Aiden, when you look back at that memory of being two years old, and hearing that your birth mother had died, what would you like to believe about yourself now? Would you like to believe—it's over, I'm safe, I have my family and can still love my birth mother. What other beliefs do you think would help?"

Aiden came up with his own positive belief: "That I know even though she's dead she can still watch over me. Actually a better one is 'not alive.' Even though she's not alive . . . I know she will watch over me." Susi interjected, "And how about, I think too that she would want me to be happy." Aiden liked that idea. "And peaceful," he added. He thought a little more: "Not 'would want,' but my mom *wants* me to be happy and peaceful."

I repeated Aiden's positive cognition: "Even though she is not alive, I know that my birth mom will watch over me. My birth mom and my mom want me to be happy and peaceful." Aiden refined his comment: "I want to say my moms want me to be happy and peaceful."

I summed it up: "That sounds just right. Even though my birth mom is not alive, I know that she will watch over me. My moms both want me to be happy and peaceful. So what is the picture or the memory of that moment? When you were two and you were looking out the window and you heard the news that your birth mom was not alive anymore, that she had been in an accident. Is there a picture or a moment that you remember?"

Aiden considered: "I don't know. Yes." I checked in to make sure I understood: "So the picture is the window? Looking out the window and then hearing the sound—you hear the words?" (Yes, he nodded.) "And when you remember that, what feeling comes up? Aiden said, "Sadness." I followed his lead: "And where do you feel that in your body?" Aiden indicated that he felt sadness everywhere, and he noticed the sadness as he held the buzzers.

I waited until Aiden shifted his position and then, "What came up for you?" Aiden replied thoughtfully, "Sadness and joy because even though my birth mother died I know I still have my adopted family." Aiden had processed the sadness sufficiently to begin to allow joy to present itself.

Aiden continued, "In one of the stories that my birth mother told me when—I mean that my birth grandmother told me about my birth mother—she was very into science, and this buzzer moving across my leg reminded me of that, and I just went to science camp last week and I made a hovercraft, and it actually vibrates when it moves across the floor . . ." I was impressed, "Oh, cool."

I wanted to know if we were on track to clear the original memory or if this was an important diversion: "OK, good. Aiden, when you look back at what we started with, how upsetting does it look now if zero is calm and relaxed and 10 is the most upsetting you can imagine?" Aiden said, in a matter-of-fact, tone, "None."

It's important to clear the body sensations as well as the visual memory: "Just check your body from head to toe and notice if there is any place in your body still holding any tension when you remember being two years old and hearing that news that your birth mom was no longer alive . . ." Again Aiden replied, "None." Now it was time to install the positive cognition: "And think this thought: Even though my birth mom is not alive, I know that she will watch over me."

Then I checked the Validity of Cognition (VoC): "And how about this time—when you hear that statement: 'Even though my birth mom is not alive, I know that she will watch over me'—how true does that feel in your body, if zero is not at all true and seven is completely true, that she will watch over you?" Aiden didn't hesitate: "Seven."

I turned on the buzzers to reinforce the positive cognition: "How about when you hear this one—when you remember looking out the window, hearing the news, how true does it feel in your body now when you hear, 'My moms both want me to be happy and peaceful. I can be happy and peaceful. How true does that feel?" Aiden responded decisively, "Seven."

I did one more round of installing positive cognitions: "So remember that memory that we're working on and think those thoughts: 'My moms both want me to be happy and peaceful.' Where do you feel that peaceful feeling in your body?" Aiden looked very peaceful as he said, "Everywhere."

Second Story and Candle-Lighting Ceremony

When Aiden and his parents returned the following week, I offered Aiden the story again. Some children like to hear their story 10 or 12 times. Each time, they seem to find a slightly different focus and they seem to "own" the story more and more.

I offered, "Aiden, are you ready to hear your story?" He nodded, and this time Susi read the story. I gave Aiden a choice: "Shall I turn on the buzzers while you are listening to the story?" He nodded and looked pensive while his mother read the story.

Then Aiden wanted to light the candles again. Aiden pointed to each of the candles and used a long candle to light them: "This is my dad, my adopted dad, my adopted mom and my brother, my birth grandmother, my birth mom, oh that's me."

I encouraged him to tell more: "Is there anything more you want to say about each of the candles or about lighting the candles?" Aiden smiled, "I love all of them, but there is one special thing about my birth dad. He's very spirited and did lots of bad things. He went to jail. And I'm not sure if he's still alive or not. But alive or not, I still love him."

I was surprised that Aiden mentioned his birth father, and his parents were surprised that Aiden knew his birth father had been in jail. It felt important to say something positive about Aiden's father: "And we know he did one good thing in his life: He helped to give you life."

Susi added, "And he helped pick out your dad and I to be your adopted parents too. He was very concerned that he was finding a very wonderful family for you to be in." I reiterated, "Those are two good things he did in his life that we know about." "That's right," his mom agreed. We wanted Aiden to hold on to his birth father's positive characteristics.

At Aiden's next visit, I wanted to see how he had absorbed the work we had done to help him understand and accept his family. I wondered aloud whether Aiden would like to pretend that he was a sculptor and that he got to model himself, his mom, and his dad into a sculpture (a modification of Virginia Satir's "family sculpture"). What would it look like?

Aiden grabbed Susi and Steve's hands and pulled them into a standing hug. Then he stretched out his arms for them to lift him into the middle of an "Aiden sandwich." He peered at me, grinning. I smiled and asked, "Will you tell us some about the family hug?"

Aiden grinned even more and began, "I love my dad and mom. I love my family." Susi responded, "We love you too, sweetie pie." And then added, "Oh, you want to do our family song?" Aiden nodded. I asked, "What's your family song?" Steve replied, "The Barney song." I pointed to Aiden, "Will you lead them?" And the hugging family sang, "I love you. You love me. We're a happy family. With a great big hug and a kiss from me to you, won't you say you love me too?" And they all exchanged kisses.

Perspective

Aiden's parents were initially so distraught by their adopted son's sadness, anger, and wild threats that they couldn't hold on to the possibility that he could be better. They couldn't say anything positive about him, and they couldn't say what positive beliefs they wanted him to have about himself. The first story they wrote for Aiden told the story of their despair rather than offering a healing story. After working with Aiden's family, I decided not to encourage parents to write their child's story at home, even if they had my guidelines. I realized that writing the story with the parents was healing for them and gave them an opportunity to help their child.

While Aiden's parents were in no way responsible for causing Aiden's distress, their supportive participation and compassion made it possible for Aiden to face his painful memories, voice his fears, and resolve his trauma. Treating trauma made it possible for Aiden and his parents to feel they were on the same team—their family—together in mutual respect and love.

6

CHARLES AND TOMAS
Angry Boys, Out-of-Sync Parents

I have seen a number of young children who are furious, and they direct their anger toward their parents, especially toward their mothers. One five-year-old boy attacked his mother daily by biting, hitting, scratching, and kicking her and never expressed remorse. Another boy who was four years old repeatedly yelled at his mother and told her that he hated her, and another child of five frequently hit his mother, telling her that she wasn't his real mother, that he hated her, and that he wanted to go to another family so he could have a new mother. All of these angry children were living with both of their biological parents. All behaved well in pre-school. All of these children had experienced early childhood trauma that their parents had not identified as related to their disturbing behavior.

Angry children are usually scared children—scared that they don't measure up, scared that they are all alone, or scared that they are unlovable. Once a child's distress is so severe that his/her parents are afraid, worried, and frustrated beyond their tolerance, it's time for professional help. Even though Ella and Lane were smart and caring and described themselves as close to their son, they couldn't understand him. What made Charles scared? What made Charles so angry? And what could they do about his behaviors that were making family life almost unbearable?

Tomas's parents were also smart and caring. Although Charles and Tomas presented with very similar behavioral patterns—appearing angry and aggressive and sad—their troubling behaviors arose from different circumstances.

Charles

Charles posed major challenges for his parents every day. His parents, Ella and Lane, were bewildered by his behavior and dismayed that Charles yelled so much. Ella was on the verge of tears when she described his outbursts: "He makes a terrible face and he screams at me, 'I hate you. I'll shoot you. Go away! Shut your mouth!'"

60

Charles spent many hours away from his parents. Ella was a lawyer in a prestigious firm. She worked long hours and often had meetings at night so that she was rarely home for bath time, story time, or bedtime. Her job required her to travel frequently, staying away from home three to five days at a time. Charles's father was a graphic designer who had a flexible schedule, so he picked Charles up every day at 5 p.m. Charles was in preschool and afterschool care from 8 a.m. till 5 p.m. five days a week. His preschool teachers described him as smart and emotionally fragile—often angry and sad.

Ella said, "I feel like Charles is a lot like me, and I feel close to him. I spend a lot more time with him than my parents ever spent with me. I pay attention to Charles. My parents weren't attentive to my feelings at all. They drilled me on spelling words and math equations at the dinner table because they were most interested in my achievements, and they never showed interest in how I felt."

Ella had been raised by a nanny whom she dearly loved. Her nanny had died suddenly the day after Charles was born two weeks prematurely. And the same day, Charles had to be admitted to the neonatal intensive care unit because he was having difficulty breathing. It was frightening for his parents to see their tiny baby in an incubator with monitors attached to him, an intravenous line in his scalp, and a nasal cannula for oxygen.

Ella became teary when she talked about the mixed feelings she had had around the time when Charles was born: "I was happy that I had my baby, then worried that he had to be in the neonatal intensive care unit for 10 days. At the same time, I was grief-stricken about my nanny's sudden unexpected death. It was such a stressful time." Ella sometimes told Charles the story that shortly after he was born she called her nanny to let her know about his birth. Her nanny heard him crying in the background and exclaimed, "Oh, wonder of wonders!"

Charles's mother suffered from postpartum depression as well as grieving the death of her nanny for the first year of Charles's life. She started back to work full-time six weeks after Charles was born, and she coped with the stress of depression and grief by working long hours at her law firm. Lane and a nanny took care of Charles most of the time. Charles began preschool at age two. He had three different nannies before he was three years old, and he was increasingly violent toward them.

When Charles was a little over a year old, he developed asthma. Although he didn't have to be hospitalized, he frequently had to go to the emergency room for treatment. Whenever he got a cold, he had to take steroids and albuterol to keep the asthma under control.

On the positive side, Ella and Lane described Charles as extremely smart and articulate. The first time I met Charles, I was struck by what a handsome child he was and how he had an impressive command of language for a four-year-old. Charles looked depressed and angry. His face was cloudy, and his eyes became glazed and unfocused when something wasn't right for him. He played in the sand tray with tiny ceramic pandas. He told me a long, involved story about the pandas. "The mommy panda could not find her babies, and this baby felt not happy. A scarlet macaw picked up the baby panda and began to fly away with him. The panda karate-chopped the scarlet macaw, and the bird fell and hit a rock and broke his wing and could never fly again." Even without analyzing Charles's play further, it was obvious that the themes were separation, loss, and injury.

When it was time to leave, Charles told me that he would be rude to me when he came back. Then he said, "I want to stay here forever."

When Charles returned with his dad the following week, he wasn't rude. He cuddled with Lane, who was very attentive and affectionate with him. I showed Charles and Lane how to do imaginary face painting. Charles would say what color he wanted parts of his face "painted," and his dad would dip his finger into an imaginary pot of paint. Lane pretended to give Charles the magenta ears, peach lips, pink eyebrows, white nose, and purple and blue eyelids he requested.

Then I began to talk about the magic cord that connects children with their parents. "It's invisible, but it's incredibly strong—it can stretch anywhere in the world and nothing can ever cut it." I talked about the cord going between Charles and his dad and the cord going between him and his mom. Charles said sadly, "Mommy's always at work."

Charles also played in the sand tray, with his dad and I beside him. Charles put a white kitty and a gray kitty in the sand tray. The white one kicked the gray one away. I asked, "How does the gray kitty feel?" Charles was quick to respond, "Not good. I feel like that sometimes."

"What does she need?" I asked, pointing to the gray kitty. "Hugs and kisses" was his ready response. Lane picked up on his cue and gave Charles hugs and kisses. "How does kitty feel now?" I inquired. Charles said, "Good. Her heart is filled with love." I asked Charles's dad to take care of the kitties and give them love while Charles continued to play.

Charles was a very loving, caring child whose play was transparent. He made it perfectly clear that he felt rejected, that he needed physical affection, and that he could respond positively when he got what he needed. He wasn't despondent yet, but I feared that he would be if he didn't receive the attention and care he needed. Charles was able to express his feelings through play, and he was able to receive comfort personally, as well as through the metaphor of play. He was very pleased that his father and I were cradling both kitties. We understood that the kitty that was doing the kicking needed affection as much as the one who was kicked.

Charles came back with his mother for his next visit. He wanted her to watch him play and to hold the kitties. At one point, she absentmindedly put the kitties back on the shelf. In Charles's play, animals were scratching each other, eating other animals, and poking one another in the eyes. Ella watched. Occasionally she made a factual comment about what she observed, but she never mentioned feelings.

I asked Charles to tell us the things his mother did that helped him feel loved. He said he liked when his mom watched him play, he liked cuddles, and he liked when his mom said nice things to him. I asked if he felt full of love after she did those things. Charles sighed, "No." I knew I needed to work on increasing positive interactions between Charles and his mother.

The following week, I met with Ella alone. I told her that Charles needed "intensive care" to help him out of his depression. I asked her if she could cut back on work time so she could be with him more for the next few months. She told me that she felt guilty and at fault because he was having problems. She was going to weekly therapy herself to talk about her parents and to stop feeling so bad and guilty. Nevertheless, we would have to find a way to help Charles accept that his mother was a busy professional. She felt she could not cut back on her work schedule. In fact, she was leaving town that night for a conference and would be gone for a week.

I felt sad that Ella wouldn't spend more time with her son, but I know that when I want something for a child more than the parent wants it, what I want never happens. Just like Charles, I had to accept the sad fact that although his mother loved him and wanted him to be well, he was not her top priority, even for the next few months. I talked to Ella about how we could work on developing Charles's "object constancy," the sense that she was there for him and connected to him even when she was at work or out of town.

Ella liked the idea of strengthening Charles's sense that she was close to him and cared about him even when she was away. She agreed to write a note for Charles for each day that she was gone so that his dad could read him a note from her every day. I told her she could tell him that she was thinking about him, that she was looking forward to seeing him, and that she hoped he had a good night's sleep and a good day at school.

Ella agreed to give Charles a picture of himself with her, another with her and his dad, and a third of the whole family. She said she would tell him to look at the picture and know she cared about him. She would give Charles a calendar and show him the day she would return.

Ella was eager to know what to do about his terrible daily outbursts. She recognized that traditional discipline like "time out" did not work. When told to go to time out, Charles would either refuse and scream uncontrollably for an hour, or he would go in his room, empty his drawers, knock toys off shelves, and then break them. She also recognized that routine and predictability were important for Charles. She told me that she was working on not taking his anger and insults personally, but it was hard to be calm with him when he was so angry with her.

I appreciated Ella's honesty and her willingness to learn. She was able to listen while I talked with her about "time in" instead of "time out." I suggested that she "front-load" their interactions with plenty of physical contact and interest in watching him play. When he began to be upset, I suggested she ask him how he felt and wonder aloud if he really needed a hug. She took notes and agreed to try it.

I talked a little about partnering so that Charles wouldn't feel so alone. She could talk with him while they did things together, and she could use the expression "let's do this . . ." instead of just telling him what to do. I suggested that she read about "floor time," and I gave her an article on "one-to-one time." While many generations of children have never had a parent—or any adult—play with them, I find that participating in a child's play is as meaningful and as soothing as sharing a cup of tea with a friend and telling one's life story.

I expected Ella's parenting to look like "paint by numbers"—a little stilted but eventually recognizable as attuned parenting. We would work more on attunement at the next opportunity. I was happy that Ella had made the commitment to come to see me with Charles every week or two.

Next time Charles came to my office, he was dancing and singing. He looked a little happier. The calendar and letters helped him feel calmer while his mom was away.

Then Charles played in the sand tray and gave his mom and me the kitties to hold "for safe keeping." As Charles was playing, his mom missed some cues. She put the kitty back on the shelf. (I handed her the kitty and told her to keep it safe and help it know it was loved.) She missed a chance to hug Charles when he talked about how much the kitties needed a hug. I told her, "I think Charles needs a hug," and "Hug Charles." Charles talked about how the kitties loved to be swooped up and hugged. I prompted Charles's mom to "swoop him up" and hug him. She grabbed Charles so quickly that he was frightened and cried.

It was obvious that Ella had not had attuned parenting. She simply didn't know how to do it consistently yet, but she was capable of learning. I thought that once she became more attuned to Charles, he would be such a pleasure to her that she would continue to provide connecting parenting. At least, I hoped so.

That session, Charles's mom paid for her mis-attunement. When it was almost time to leave, Charles announced that he wanted to read a book. Ella told him there wasn't time. Charles threw a world-class tantrum, screaming and kicking. It took a while for him to calm down. I asked Ella if she would read the book to him in the waiting room. She agreed. I was looking forward to the day when Charles wouldn't have to throw fits to get the kind of attention he needed.

In the next sessions, Charles played in the dollhouse. The play was about babies getting taken away from their mommies. At one point he said, "I'm happy and angry. I'm so angry I want to eat my head."

Then the theme changed, and Charles chose to play with the hospital set. I took my cue from Charles's choice of toys, and I started talking about when Charles was a baby in the hospital. I asked Charles how the baby in the incubator (he knew that word!) felt. He said, "The baby was sad because he couldn't talk." I asked, "If the baby could talk, what would he say?" Charles smiled and said "Goo-goo ga-ga." I was pleased that he was able to start paying attention to his "inner baby."

On the next visit, I introduced Charles and his mom to one of the lollypop games. I asked Charles to cuddle up on his mom's lap and snuggle with her. He was eager to take his shoes off and start snuggling and having a lollypop. I always ask parents ahead of time without the child present if the lollypop offer is OK. Some children have allergies. Some parents don't want their children to have sugar. Some are worried about the child's teeth. Some ask about the kind of lollypop I use. When I tell them it's organic, with natural flavors, they usually relax.

I instructed Charles to look at his mom's eyes when he wanted her to put the lollypop in his mouth and to open his mouth when he wanted her to take it out. I instructed Ella to pay careful attention to his cues. Charles looked like a nursing baby while he sucked on the lollypop. Ella did fine responding to his nonverbal cues, so I asked Charles how his mom was doing getting his cues. He turned to me and smiled, then cuddled closer to his mom and looked at her. I alternately tapped on his toes, saying, "Feel your mom holding you and notice how she is learning to get your cues."

Charles and his mom began to have synchronized breathing and looked at ease. I started talking about how there was a magic cord connecting him and his mom and that she was always loving him and sending love to him through the cord. Charles reacted quickly, as if he had had an anaphylactic reaction—he began angrily chomping on the lollypop. I had spoken about his mother's love before Charles could reliably feel it.

In the next session, Charles became mad within five minutes in my office. Ella sat on the love seat, and Charles commanded angrily, "Get off that couch so I can sit there." Ella started to get up. I urged her to continue sitting on the couch and to tell Charles that she would like for him to sit beside her. I knew that Ella had developed the habit of "walking on eggshells" around Charles. She did what he wanted because she was afraid he would launch another tantrum.

Charles yelled, "I'm so angry I could eat you! You stress me out. I've had enough of you. I'm not going to talk to you." He moved to throw over my standing lamp. I caught the lamp and said, "Charles, you can have strong feelings and still control your behavior. It's not OK to hurt anyone or anything in my room."

Charles yelled at his mother again, "Get off the sofa!" She stayed seated. Then she said, "Charles, I love being with you even if you are mad." It was a nice sentiment, but it wasn't true. Charles went wild. He threw himself on the floor and screamed, "I've had enough of you!" Charles's mom meant well and truly wanted to give Charles unconditional love. Children almost always know when a parent isn't telling the truth, and it insults them. While I do not believe parents have to tell their children everything, I feel strongly that they should be honest in what they do say—in a developmentally appropriate way.

Charles screamed at his mother, "I hate you!" Ella said, "Will you sing me a lullaby?" Charles's face became cloudy and his eyes drifted to the side. In her attempt to distract Charles, his mom had totally missed the content and intensity of his feelings. Charles appeared to dissociate—his facial expression was flat and his eyes were unfocused. His mother's lack of attunement made him feel helpless and want to disappear.

Charles rallied enough to lash out at me too. He tried to knock over the lamp again and shouted, "You do not need that lamp, you mean old wizard!" (I was secretly flattered and amused that Charles called me a mean old wizard!) He flung his insult at me, "When I go to school, I'll ask the big kids to tell me all the bad words they know, and I'll say all of them when I come back to your office!"

Then he turned to his mom and said, "You are a poopoo head." For the next 40 minutes, Charles yelled at his mother and tried to hit her. I thought that Charles needed for Ella to set limits rather than always bow to Charles's wishes, so I thought it was good I could keep her company and show her how to stop Charles without yelling at him. I felt that Charles was testing to see whether we thought he was still good and lovable even when he was behaving badly, and maybe he was asking for "time in." I asked if Charles could play the lollypop game for a few minutes before we ended our time together. His mom agreed, and Charles took the lollypop as if nothing had happened.

It had been a painful, tiring hour together. When it was time to go, Charles got up, put on his shoes without being asked, and waved goodbye. "Have a nice day," he smiled.

Ella reported by phone that Charles had had a good week until the night before, when his father had to go out for a meeting. Charles's good week told me we were on the right track. Charles needed to be assured that we cared about him even if his behavior was impossible. It occurred to me that Charles was giving Ella and me a homeopathic dose of what it felt like to have someone unwilling to do what you want.

When Charles and Ella came back, we had to go through a session similar to the one before. His mom sat on the sofa again, and Charles told her to get off. This time she stayed put without prompting and invited him to sit beside her. He became enraged, hit her repeatedly, and knocked off her glasses. Charles's mom told him she loved him no matter what. Ella's timing was off. Charles screamed, "I'll kill you when I grow up!" Ella looked shocked. I think she was deeply worried that she was raising a murderer.

I told Charles, "I'm sure you will never kill anybody when you grow up. Even when you have strong feelings, you can learn to control your behavior. You'll learn to calm yourself when you have strong upset feelings." I felt Charles was worried about himself. Children really don't like controlling adults by raging. He seemed relieved to have reassurance and hope that he would not always be so angry.

Despite my reassurance to Charles, I was concerned about his obvious depression and mood instability. I had worked with Charles and his parents for six months. It was very possible that he had endogenous depression that had nothing to do with parenting that was slightly out of sync with his needs. I made a note to discuss him with his pediatrician and a child psychiatrist. I also wanted to check for possible celiac disease and to consider omega-3s.

I never medicate a four-year-old child with psychoactive medication. I also resist labeling four-year-old children as "bipolar," even when there is a history of depression and bipolar illness in the family. I focus on improving the environment, working with parents, and treating trauma, usually integrating EMDR into play and sand tray work and artwork.

After I have done everything I can, I consider medication. I personally don't have enough experience with psychoactive medication for children under five to feel comfortable prescribing it. At that point, I want another opinion from a child psychiatrist. When I've called child psychiatrists around the United States to inquire about their approach to young children with excessive rage, I've gotten a wide range of opinions, from "do play therapy" to "prescribe mood stabilizers." There is little research or consensus on how to treat disturbed preschool children.

Then Charles and his family went away for a two-week vacation. Ella e-mailed me to say, "Charles controlled his temper better."

When he came back, Charles came in singing and dancing. He looked happier, and he and his mom were connecting better. When Charles talked about something, his mom picked up the thread of the conversation instead of asking him a random question. He and his mother were able to look at one another and respond appropriately.

Charles wanted to play the bubble game. I could see that cooperation felt good to both of them. Charles was following directions so easily that I decided to change the game to help him learn to ask for what he wanted.

Children need to learn three steps on the way to being able to get their needs met: (1) recognize the feeling, (2) express the feeling, and (3) make a request. First, a child has to notice that she/he has a feeling or a need. Then the child must learn to express her/his feelings, wants, and needs. Young babies cry to express feelings and needs. As she/he grows older, a child learns to say, "I'm hungry" or "I want to play in the sand tray." Then parents can teach their child to make a request. So instead of, or in addition to, saying, "I'm hungry," the child can ask, "May I have something to eat?" Instead of saying, "I want to play in the sand tray," the child may make a request: "May I play in the sand tray?" or "Will you help me take the lid off the sand tray?"

While statements of needs or wants versus making requests are subtle differences in language, I find that children who make requests feel more confident. Parents notice the difference very quickly—usually within a week or two. I tell children that they can always ask for what they want. It's a parent's job to decide whether the answer to the request is a "yes" or a "no." For most children, the most challenging part is to learn to be calm and OK even if the parent says "no" to their request.

I taught Charles and Ella a bubble game I developed for children who have a hard time when they don't get their way. In the game, the parent and child face each other while the child asks the parent if he may pop the bubbles with his fingers or elbows or whatever he wants. In front of the child, I instruct the parent to say "yes" to the first request and "no" to the second, and to continue alternating the response to the child's requests. Charles was happy with his mom's "yes" response. When she said "no" to his next request, Charles fell down screaming and yelled, "I don't like you, Dr. Lovett! I like Mommy." That was the best news I had heard from him, but he had a way to go before he could be OK with a "no" response. No wonder his parents felt they were "walking on eggshells" around him.

Which children can't tolerate a "no" response and why? Most children want what they want and try hard to get it. However, "no" is especially hard for children (i.e., traumatized children) who already believe that they are not good enough and that whatever happens is their fault. These children want to be in control, as if nothing would go wrong if they had their way. "No" also becomes difficult to accept for children who are accustomed to having adults do whatever they want, often before they even ask. The traumatized child who throws fits whenever he doesn't get what he wants can train his parents to anticipate his needs and wants. When parents "walk on eggshells," it's a sign that they are parenting out of fear or guilt. The traumatized child has his distorted beliefs reinforced (i.e., beliefs that he can't tolerate not getting his way and that he is in control of what adults do).

A "no" response simply means that the parent doesn't want to do something, or doesn't think a "yes" would be in the best interest of the child or the family, or perhaps the parent just doesn't feel like doing whatever the child wants. The traumatized child is much more likely to interpret "no" as "I don't like you," "You don't deserve good things," or "You're bad." That child is likely to throw a tantrum, withdraw feeling hurt, or lash out in anger, "You're mean!" The parent also has to decide when to allow the child to negotiate.

One day, Charles drew a picture of a heart with "cords" attached. He explained about all the cords connected to the heart. As he drew the first line from the heart, he said, "This is the sorry cord." Second, "This is the mad cord." Third, "This is the happy cord." Next, he drew another "mad cord." He pointed to the heart: "This is the heart and all the cords connect to the heart. All the cords give it some power. Sometimes they don't give it power but sometimes they do." He named all the feelings again and said, "And that's how everybody feels." He pointed again, "This is the really happy one that feels good. And those are the mad feelings—that mad is the big mad feeling that booms across the world, and the other mad one is the quiet mad feeling. And that is the sorry feeling." He drew a little picture of a face with a tear. He pointed and said, "and that's the tear." He sat back looking satisfied: "And those are all the feelings in the big heart."

Charles's explanation of how feelings work was amazingly perceptive and articulately explained! His sensitivity, intelligence, and big-hearted feelings had both contributed to his distress and provided a way of working through the distress.

I could see that through her own therapy, Ella was becoming more perceptive and appreciative of Charles's feelings—feelings that resonated with the experiences she remembered having as a child when her parents didn't "get" her. She became determined to understand Charles's feelings instead of ignoring his feelings the way her parents had ignored hers. She began to see parenting Charles as an opportunity for personal growth and as a way to heal her own past.

She even left work early one day a week so she could pick Charles up at school, and she set up a weekly "date" with him. She taught him "sweet talk" for helping him calm himself in school. Together they worked out a signal for Charles to give her when he felt she didn't understand his needs, and when he really needed for her to "get his feelings." She agreed to pay close attention when he rubbed his cheek—their special signal.

Charles clearly enjoyed the lollypop game now and agreed that his mother was doing a good job of getting his cues. We started talking more about the magic cord connecting him and his mother. He began to believe that there was a strong, invisible cord connecting him with his mother—a cord so strong it could never break and so magical that it could stretch anywhere in the world. He began to agree that he could feel her loving him.

A few months earlier, when I had talked about the cord of love connecting him and his mother, Charles had chomped on the lollypop. He simply could not believe that his mother loved him. He couldn't feel it. Having her care about him (she always did) was not enough. Ella had to be attuned to him, and he had to feel that love. Now he could even believe that his mother was loving him when he was asleep or when she was away for a business trip. She said that she missed him when she was away, and that was the truth. He began to say, "I love you, Mommy."

Charles wanted to play with my hospital set. When he brought out the small incubator with a tiny baby, I talked about when he was a baby. "He was born a little early, and he had some trouble breathing. His parents and the doctors and nurses all took care of the lovable little baby. The mom was upset, but not about the baby. She was upset because she felt sad that her baby was sick." For the next few sessions, Charles played with the hospital set and wanted to hear more about the baby. Then he cuddled with his mom on the love seat and she gave him a lollypop. With some guidance, she pretended she was seeing him and feeding him for the very first time. Charles looked so content, wrapped in a blanket, cuddled by his mom. I asked him to feel her holding him and feel her loving him, and I tapped his toes to strengthen the feeling of being held and loved by his mother.

Charles's school was reporting "amazing changes." His teachers had always known that he was smart and creative—now they were seeing that he was becoming resilient. His parents reported that he had "more good moods than bad moods." When he got upset, his mom told him to breathe, and he was able to calm down.

Meanwhile, Ella and Lane spent about six sessions writing a life story for Charles. Here's the story they wrote, changed to remove identifying information:

> Once upon a time there was a boy who lived with his mom and dad. They lived in a house surrounded by a big sunny yard where the boy had a climbing structure and lots of room to play. The boy loved to dance and sing and play "catch." His parents appreciated that he was so interested in the world around him, and he had even learned to read. They knew that he liked to tell stories, and they liked to listen to him.
>
> Like everybody else in the world, some things in this boy's life were wonderful and some things were confusing. One wonderful thing was that he was born good and lovable and strong.
>
> Some things that were confusing happened when the boy was born. He was born a few weeks early. A lot of babies are born early, and nobody knows exactly why.
>
> Like many babies who are born early, the boy had trouble breathing at first. The doctors and nurses had all the right tools

for giving him oxygen and helping him get better quickly. His mommy and daddy stayed by his side and touched him and talked to him and rubbed his back every day that he was in the hospital. His mommy and daddy were happy about and proud of their new baby boy and couldn't wait for him to go home with them. Soon after the baby was born, his mommy spoke with her nanny on the phone. Her nanny was eagerly awaiting Charles's birth. When she heard he was born, she said, "Oh, wonder of wonders!" She was so happy that she had lived until he was born and even got to hear him on the phone.

The next day the mommy's nanny passed away.

The boy's mommy was so, so very sad about her nanny. Even though it was sad that the nanny had died, everybody was glad that she had known that the baby boy was born and that she had gotten to hear him on the phone.

After 10 days, the baby boy was all better and was breathing fine. He was able to come home to his mommy and daddy. After six weeks, his mommy went back work. Even when the baby boy's mommy was at home playing with him and when she was at work, she was feeling sad and missing her nanny.

What did the baby think when he saw that his mommy was so sad?

What did he feel?

What did he wonder?

What did he need?

If he could have talked, what do you think he would have said?

Sometimes, when a parent is sad and grieving, a baby may feel that his parent is sad about him. A small baby can't understand how his mommy can feel happy about him and sad about her nanny at the same time.

Even though his mommy had to be away from him to work, she made sure he had her breast milk to help him grow healthy and strong. His babysitter helped his mommy and daddy take care of him all summer. The baby boy had lots of fun with his babysitter and friends during the day, and mommy and daddy were with him most nights and most weekends.

Soon the boy had a nanny who loved him very much and he loved her.

The boy grew bigger and stronger. He learned to crawl and walk and talk and play.

When the little boy was two he started preschool, and his special nanny needed to go to school too, so she couldn't be his nanny anymore. She still cares about him and thinks about him and visits sometimes.

It was also hard for the boy that his mommy stayed at work when he wanted to have time with her. The mommy missed the boy too.

His mommy and daddy realized that when the boy was screaming and throwing things, he was having strong feelings that were hard to talk about.

His mommy and daddy went with him to someone who helps children and parents understand one another better.

They did special games like the lollypop game so the boy's mommy could get his signals better. The mommy began to realize that she needed to make changes so she and the boy could have more time together.

The mommy and the boy started having special play dates that were just for the two of them, and they started enjoying being together more.

His daddy and mommy did their best to understand how he felt. The boy learned more about how to say how he felt, he learned more about how to help calm himself down and feel better, and he is learning to control his words and his body.

His mommy says, "No matter how close or how far away we are, our love cord is strong, and no one and nothing can ever break it. I promise to do my best to listen to what you have to say, to understand how you feel, and to help you feel full of love."

His daddy says, "Doing things with you is fun. The part that is most important to me is being with you. I'll always do my best to take care of you. I love you for who you are with all of your feelings—whether you feel happy or sad or frustrated or silly."

Now that he is older, the boy can understand some things that he couldn't understand when he was a baby.

He can understand that when he was a baby and his mommy and daddy were sad and upset, they were sad about the mommy's nanny, not about their precious baby. They were so very happy about him.

Now that he's older, he can understand that everybody has strong feelings sometimes. He can trust that his mommy and daddy will do their best to understand how he feels and help him learn how to express his feelings.

Now that he's older, he can understand that his parents always love him—no matter what. Even when his parents are at work or away on a trip or asleep, they're always loving him.

Charles held the buzzers while he listened to the story. When the story was over, I asked which part of the story he liked best. "I liked all of it," he replied. Then he was ready to play.

The next session, when I read the story to Charles, I stopped and asked, "What was the baby thinking when his mom was upset and crying?" Charles responded, "He was thinking that the mom's nanny died because she heard him cry on the phone." Of course. Young children are developmentally egocentric, so they think that they are the cause of everything that happens.

The story reframed the event for Charles. His mom's beloved nanny did not die because she heard him cry. It was fortunate she heard the sound of his voice before she passed away.

The next big concepts Charles had to deal with were how his mom could be happy and sad at the same time and how she could have loved him even when she was sad and distant. We talked about it a lot while he played with the hospital set and the baby in the incubator. Finally, Charles found his own way of understanding the duality: "Being happy and sad at the same time is like having chicken and noodles in the same soup." Brilliant!

Charles wanted to hear the story several times. He liked talking about the baby and what he felt and what he needed. With help from his mom and me, he imagined what it would have been like if the baby had gotten everything he wanted and needed.

When Charles was five, about a year after we started working together, he was ready to graduate. He and his parents were getting along well. He still had some difficulty when he didn't get his way, but both of his parents knew that meant he needed some extra attention. Overall, he was thriving—fun to be around and socially competent.

Perspective

Many factors contributed to Charles's difficulties. He had experienced a premature birth, early separation from his parents, and medical treatment in the NICU (neonatal intensive care unit). His mother's beloved nanny had died the day after Charles was born. Charles's mother had suffered from grief and postpartum depression, and she had spent long hours away from him. Ella had been raised by parents who were not attuned to her emotional needs, and she didn't understand her son's feelings or needs. Initially she was unable to pick up on his cues.

Children are excellent observers and poor interpreters. Charles saw that his parents were upset and assumed that he was the cause. That was further complicated by the fact that they *were* upset by his tantrums, hitting, and name calling.

As a result of his early trauma and mis-attuned connection, Charles believed that he was responsible for the death of his mother's nanny, that he was bad, and that he couldn't trust others, especially his mother, to meet his needs.

Charles's therapy included attunement training for his mother, helping Charles and his parents identify and respond to his feelings and needs, teaching Charles how to make requests, and developing a coherent narrative that helped his parents and him make sense of his life. Talk, play, and artwork gave him ways to express his strong feelings in appropriate ways. Repair of early trauma involved "inner baby" work through the lollypop game, play, and Charles's life story.

EMDR and a trauma perspective offered a framework for understanding Charles's symptomatic behaviors, a way to strengthen his positive connections with his mother, and a way to desensitize and reprocess his traumatic experiences. Therapy with EMDR helped him to become more resilient.

Tomas

Four-year-old Tomas's parents, Camila and Mateo, described him as "impossible." Mateo said, "Tomas doesn't do anything we ask him to do. He won't agree to do activities with us, even ones that he enjoys, like going to the park. On top of that, he hits us and kicks us whenever he's frustrated or unhappy, which is a lot of the time." Camila added, "He seems to take pleasure in chasing our small dog. When Tomas catches Blueberry, he pulls his tail and squeezes him until Blueberry squeals." Tomas's parents were worried that their generally friendly dog would finally lose patience and bite Tomas.

Other behaviors also made Camila and Mateo concerned about their son's safety. When they reached for his hand to cross the street, he repeatedly tried to escape and managed to run into the street several times. He climbed up on high walls, even though they told him to stop.

While Tomas was very challenging for both parents, he reduced his mother to tears by screaming, "I don't have a mother!" When she sobbed, Tomas came to her and gently said, "I'm sorry, Mom."

Camila and Mateo were very sociable, friendly people. They both came from loving families and did their best to be good parents. They described Tomas as a "smart, articulate child." His parents knew what he liked and tried to provide what he needed. They listened to him, talked with him, and played with him. They were proud that he had toilet trained early, he knew the names of all the dinosaurs, and he knew about the dinosaur's feeding habits. They were happy that he slept all night in his own bed.

So what was going on? Tomas's parents, grandparents, aunts, and uncles all thought Tomas had ADHD and possibly oppositional defiant disorder. He was far more difficult than any of the other four-year-old children they had known. He had always been active and had become

74

progressively more impulsive, oppositional, and aggressive over time. Tomas's pediatrician agreed that Tomas was a "handful" but was unwilling to diagnose ADHD at the age of four. It did cause Tomas's pediatrician to raise his eyebrows when he asked Tomas what he liked to eat and Tomas replied, "Garbage." Lots of four-year-old children are wild and out of bounds, as well as wonderful.

Tomas's parents could not identify any specific experiences that could have contributed to his current behavior. There were no traumas, hospitalizations, or losses. No one in the family was ill or had drug or alcohol problems or rage. They had a stable home and promised that there was no pushing, shoving, or yelling going on. Tomas was a healthy, full-term baby who had had the same daycare situation since he was three months old. He had been cared for in a home childcare from 8 a.m. to 6 p.m. five days a week for four years, and Camila and Mateo trusted the caregivers. Tomas's parents were puzzled by his behavior and expected me to prescribe medication for Tomas to help calm him and treat possible ADHD.

A diagnosis of ADHD is as nonspecific as a diagnosis of fever. Both can have a number of root causes. ADHD and PTSD or a stress reaction can present with inattention, lack of cooperation, hyperactivity, defiance, and impulsivity. Most attachment disorders are caused by traumatic experiences that have affected the child or the parents, and lack of cooperation is largely about relationship. Especially because Tomas was only four years old, I wanted to understand and address the root of his difficult behaviors and not use medication to suppress them.

I asked what Tomas's childcare provider observed and how she managed him. Camila responded, "She never tells us she has a problem with him. She and her cousin take care of eight children, and now Tomas is one of the oldest. She is a sweet woman and she loves Tomas. She is very warm and caring. She never spanks the children."

"When children misbehave she has them stand with their nose touching the wall for a few minutes, but she doesn't do that often. We tried that to punish him, but we couldn't get him to put his nose anywhere near the wall. My mom told me that wasn't a good idea—she said I should just reprimand Tomas and then distract him. I also read books on positive discipline, but he rejects me even if I say nice things to him or ask him nicely to do things. I tried '1–2–3 Magic,' but when I start to count he yells, 'Don't count me!' and he continues to yell. I think it makes the situation worse."

Mateo said, "Maybe I have contributed to the problem. I tried to get him to try things he's not particularly good at—like I encourage him to color in the coloring book, and he doesn't like it. Sometimes I turn on classical music, which he doesn't like. I just want him to be exposed to art and music. But I also play with him and play what he wants." His parents agreed that they "walked on eggshells" and did their best not to "set him off." Tomas's tantrums were relentless—no matter how careful his parents were, Tomas was "set off" by anything and almost everything they did.

Tomas's parents had done a lot of soul searching and investigated different child-rearing methods. They were warm, caring, and generally well attuned, but Tomas was spending more of his waking life with his childcare worker than with his parents. I needed to learn about Tomas's experience in childcare, and I asked for permission to speak with Tomas's childcare provider, Ming. I wondered whether Tomas behaved the way he did because he was afraid of Ming's punishments.

I called Ming. When Ming answered the phone I had trouble understanding her heavy accent. English was obviously her second language. Her message was brief: "Tomas is normal. He does what I tell him. I give children special food when they do the right thing. He sometimes gives my cousin trouble. She has to take care of him more now because I have four children under two years old, and one is a new baby."

Ming had given me very helpful information. It was especially interesting that Ming said that Tomas was "normal." If he could behave fine with her, why couldn't he behave with his parents? Also, Tomas started going to Ming's home when he was a baby, and now that he was one of the oldest of eight children, he must have been getting much less attention. Tomas was a smart, articulate kid, and I wondered how well Ming understood him and responded to him. Camila and Mateo told me that a few months before, they had tried having Tomas go to a private preschool for part of the day because they wanted him to be with kids his own age and learn more, but Tomas wouldn't cooperate with his new teacher, and the school director advised that they wait a year and try again when he was more mature.

Tomas was away from his parents for 10 hours a day. Even though Tomas's parents had pictures of him at work and thought about him all day, did four-year-old Tomas have a strong enough sense of object constancy? I decided to start by focusing on attachment.

My decision to focus on attachment was substantiated by Tomas's play in the sand tray and the dollhouse. He played family—sometimes with toy people and other times with families of dinosaurs or cars. Every time he played, the mother was missing. "Where is the mommy?" I asked. His response was startling, "She hasn't been born yet."

Tomas was oppositional about almost everything. He didn't want to be in my office when he arrived and tried to run out. When it was time to leave, he refused. He wanted to stay. When I asked if he wanted to play the bubble game, he refused. When I offered a chocolate chip animal cracker for the animal cracker game, he played the game cooperatively with his mother, a relief after he had screamed at his mother during most of our hour together.

I met with Camila and Mateo the following week. They agreed that Tomas needed "intensive care," and they were willing to do anything to help him. I explained that children who are stressed tend to start doing better quickly, regardless of the source of their distress, when they have time with attuned parents who can stay calm while acknowledging the child's feelings of anger, frustration, disappointment, and that "nothing feels right." Mateo and Camila didn't hesitate when I suggested that they cut back on work temporarily and spend more time with Tomas, even though it was sometimes an ordeal to spend time with him. Camila agreed to pick Tomas up at school mid-afternoon every day and give him a snack, play with him, and nap with him if he needed a nap. Mateo would spend extra time and cuddle with Tomas in the morning before taking him to daycare and would have "special time" with him on the weekends.

We talked about the need for object constancy—the sense that they were connected to Tomas, thinking about him and caring for him, even when they were away from him. I suggested that they give Tomas a picture of him with each of his parents and a picture of him with both parents. He could keep the pictures in his backpack and look at them whenever he wanted. I recommended that they read him books like *The Kissing Hand* by Audrey Penn and *The Invisible String* by Patrice Karst.

I also instructed Camila and Mateo to have expectations for Tomas's behavior—not just "walk on eggshells" around him. They could teach him to make requests politely and to model what they did want to hear when he was inappropriate. The "atmosphere of eggshells" had included asking Tomas's approval or agreement with each of their requests. So, they were asking, "Hold my hand when we cross the street, OK?" and "Do you want to get dressed now?" even when staying in pajamas was not an option. Tomas needed to know that he could count on his parents to have rules and that they were in control, even if he acted unhappy.

Within two weeks, Tomas was happier and cooperating a little more at home. His mom started our visit by telling how he helped her at the grocery store and that they were having happy times doing their bedtime ritual, which now included brushing teeth, feeding the fish, talking about Tomas's day, and reading two books. Despite some improvement at home, Tomas's play in my office still spoke of his distress. In the dollhouse, the toy dad wouldn't let his son have his birthday, and his mom had not been born. When it was time to leave my office, Tomas hit his mom—he didn't want to leave. I advised Tomas and his mom that it's never OK for him to hit and that it's his parents' job to stop him right away. I modeled for Camila how to teach Tomas words for feelings: "It's OK to say I don't want to go or I feel angry. Feelings are OK. Hitting is not. You can have feelings and still control your behavior."

Within the next week, Tomas became less rude and disrespectful and more affectionate with his parents. There was still about an hour a day of

Tomas screaming. In my office, Tomas's play became more informative. He loved playing Baby Bird whose parents were away and the babysitter put his nose to the wall. Baby Bird needed love. Baby Bird got abandoned by his parents and then rejected by the babysitter. I began to wonder whether Ming was paying so much attention to the seven younger children, including the infant, that Tomas was feeling rejected. His English was quite advanced for a four-year-old child, and from my phone conversation with Ming, I speculated that his command of English had surpassed hers. I wondered whether he felt lonely and misunderstood because she couldn't communicate with him at his level anymore.

In the following weeks, Tomas's play shifted from the sand tray to the floor of my room. He pretended he was Baby Bird, or a baby frog or koala or skunk or lion cub that was crying because his mom was not there. He said he felt lost and admitted that he thought that his mom died when she didn't come home. This play gave Camila the opportunity to find her "baby" and have a happy reunion, letting him know that she was thinking about him the whole time and that she had missed him too. It also gave me an opportunity to help Baby Bird and all the other babies get over feeling sad as I tapped on Tomas's knees: "Notice that sad feeling, Baby Bird, and let me know when you start to feel better." In a few minutes Tomas nodded, I stopped tapping, and Tomas turned around to hug his mom. Then I tapped his shoulders and told him, "Your mom loves you all the time." I looked at Camila and she took her cue, saying, "I love you all the time, and you're lovable and important to me all the time, even when I'm not with you."

Over the next weeks, as Tomas pretended to be various baby animals and Camila played the role of the baby animal's mother, they played the lollypop game, did pretend face painting, and played the bubble game and the animal cracker game to strengthen attachment and cooperation. Through each of these activities, I used bilateral stimulation to desensitize the anger, fear, frustration, and sadness that the baby animal felt, and I reinforced the feelings of trust, safety, and pleasure as they arose.

Over the course of about five months, Tomas became calm, cooperative, and affectionate. He returned to the preschool he had visited unsuccessfully in the past, and it accepted him. He loved his new school and thrived there, and his language, friendships, and self-esteem blossomed.

Perspective

Tomas and Charles both exhibited similar behaviors initially. They both had extremely tense relationships with their parents, were quick to anger, demonstrated extreme anger, were very controlling, and were seldom satisfied, causing their parents to "walk on eggshells" around them. Both knew how to behave when they were away from their parents. Both were bright and sensitive and imaginative, and both cared deeply about their parents, even though their rage was directed at their parents.

Despite the similarities in Charles's and Tomas's presenting behaviors, there were different root causes for their behavior. Charles got off to a rocky start when he was born—he was sick, in the NICU, and his mother's nanny died, launching grief and postpartum depression that affected Charles as well as his mother. Tomas did not have any identifiable critical incident trauma, and his parents were not going through difficult times of their own.

Although Tomas had well-attuned parents, he was spending most of his day with a caregiver who was busy and could not speak English fluently. While some children would have loved being the oldest of seven children and could have thrived in that environment, Tomas needed concentrated one-to-one time with someone who could understand and attune to his sensitive feelings and had time to soothe him and help him learn to comfort himself.

I have seen many children who are "horrible" with their parents but can behave and even excel in settings outside their home. Often the parents have been told that their child behaves badly with them because they feel safe at home. This advice is meant to help the parents feel that they are good parents, but it doesn't help them know what is causing their child's out-of-control behavior or what to do about it. When the "horrible" behavior makes the parents afraid or excessively angry and when it is much more intense, frequent, and longer lasting than that of other children of the same age, it's time for professional help.

7

ZACHARY

Dealing with the Loss of a Parent

The death of a parent is a child's worst nightmare. And when the parent has died, the child experiences the grief of ongoing loss. No one can completely replace that parent.

Angela Nickerson, of the Massachusetts Veterans Epidemiology Research and Information Center and the University of New South Wales in Sydney, Australia, and her colleagues analyzed data from 2,823 adults who had all experienced the death of a parent during childhood. They used the World Health Organization Composite International Diagnostic Interview to assess psychological impairment, parental care, and other factors that could contribute to difficulties later in life. They found that the younger a child was at the time of the loss, the more likely the child was to develop mental health problems, including anxiety, mood, or substance abuse issues (Nickerson, Bryant, Aderka, Hinton, & Hofmann, 2013).

Zachary

The main source of eight-year-old Zachary's distress was obvious. When he was four years old, Zach's father had died after a three-month battle with cancer. The school counselor referred Zach and his mom to me because Zach was having such a hard time in school. Elizabeth, Zach's mother, enumerated the problems that concerned her: "Zach stole a book at the book fair and takes things like erasers from other children in his second-grade class. I find them in his backpack and make him return them and apologize. He knows it's not OK to take other people's things! One day he wrote his friends' names on the walls of the bathroom, and he had to go to the principal's office. He 'blows up' whenever he loses a game or perceives that someone played unfairly. When someone bumps him, he feels that they're trying to hurt him." She paused and reflected, "I feel bad for him—he's so smart but he still says, 'I don't know anything.'"

Elizabeth had been devastated by her husband's death and spent about two years mourning heavily. Then she decided she had to move on: "I was determined that I had to do my best to carry on with my life and to live joyfully again." She continued to work in the same job with flexible hours so she could be home in time to pick Zach up from school most days. She had done everything possible to keep Zach's life stable after the death of her husband. She kept a routine for Zach, stayed in the same house, and sent him to the same school. She had friends who always included her and Zach in their family activities. They attended church regularly, and the church community was very supportive. During holidays they visited relatives on both sides of Zach's family.

Elizabeth was concerned about her relationship with Zach too. "He gets angry with me a lot, and I yell at him more than I like," she confessed. "Zach has a very low frustration tolerance, and when he's frustrated he even hits the dog." Elizabeth continued, "I'm worried about Zach's obsession with weapons. He talks about weapons, he draws guns, and he plays that his action figures are attacking and killing each other." She perceptively wondered, "Maybe he's so obsessed with weapons because I used to have conversations with friends and relatives about how the doctors were using 'the big guns' to fight his dad's cancer."

Elizabeth described one of her frustrations: "When Zach steals something, he lies and says he didn't take it, even though I know he did. When I call him on it, he screams, 'You don't believe me!' And he's right, I don't believe him, but then he turns away and doesn't want to talk about it." While Zach was inquisitive, curious, and smart, he used angry actions rather than words to express his feelings. He was also having nightmares but didn't want to talk about them.

Zach never cried, and he became very upset if anyone else cried. Zach's mom remembered, "The first year or two after my husband's death, I cried a lot." She recalled, "One evening, near the end of my husband's life, I returned home from the hospital, and Zach found me curled up on the floor of my bedroom, sobbing." Could those be the reasons he never cried and couldn't stand to see anybody else cry? It brought up too many painful memories.

Zach's recent behavior was worse than it had been immediately after his father's death. This year had been particularly hard because Zach played baseball, and all the other boys had dads who were involved. Several were umpires, several were coaches, several drove car pools, and all of them came to at least some of the games. Although Elizabeth came to most of the games, Zach acutely felt the absence of his father and repeatedly said that it wasn't fair that his friends had dads, and he didn't.

When I met with Zach and Elizabeth together for the first time, Elizabeth listed Zach's good attributes. She said that Zach was loving, witty, inquisitive, sensitive, and athletic. He loved to cuddle and he cared about how others felt. He enjoyed reading and playing baseball.

I decided to make a "power wheel" (see Chapter 11, Figure 11.1) for Zach. I drew a circle with dotted lines for the spokes of the wheel and put a positive attribute or resource on each spoke of the wheel. Zach looked with interest as his power wheel filled. Children who come in with a problem like stealing or lying seem grateful that they are seen as a whole person—not just as a thief or a liar.

When I asked Zach what he would like to have go easier for him or for him and his mom together, he shrugged and said, "Everything is fine." That's a typical response for a child, even when there is a lot of distress at home and at school. That's why I meet with parents alone to discuss the question "What would you like to have go easier or better for him/her and your family?" Many parents tell me, "I'd like to have my son/daughter happier."

Then I probe further: "What would be happening differently if he/she were happier?" The typical responses from parents include "He wouldn't get so angry over little things, like if he thinks it's unfair if he plays a game of chance and loses," or "He wouldn't be stealing or lying or bullying the dog." All that is true. I might ask, "If he were happy, he wouldn't do any of those things. *What would he be doing instead?*"

Parents also get trapped in negative thinking about their children. It's a worthwhile exercise to encourage them to describe what they would like—in positive terms. We might come up with statements such as these: "He'd be able to use his words to express his feelings." "He would learn to calm himself when he feels frustrated." "He would go to an adult for help if he doesn't know what to do to help himself."

Finally, I ask parents, "What would you like him to think about himself if something is disappointing/unfair or he doesn't get his way?" My goals in asking all these questions are to move from blame and anger to understanding and compassion and to help parents discipline their child effectively with a goal in mind and teach their child coping skills.

Elizabeth said, "I'd like for both Zach and me to learn to use words instead of exploding, and I'd like for Zach to not get so frustrated over little things." She gave an example of the kind of interaction she wanted to change: "He asked me 'Can I go to Jason's house to play?' and I said 'no' because it was almost time for dinner. He got really angry and yelled, 'I hate you!' That happens a lot. For example, we drove to a store to get him some new baseball gear, but the store was closed, and he blamed me. I think that when I say 'no,' Zach feels not heard or not important. Of course he's important to me—and when a store is closed, it's closed. I didn't do it."

I asked her what she would like Zach to think about himself when something didn't go his way. She knew exactly what to say: "I want him to think he can be OK with little disappointments and little things that aren't fair."

From a trauma perspective, I guessed that Zach reacted to little disappointments so strongly because he had experienced the big, life-changing disappointment of his father's death. After so much trauma, big unfair and little unfair felt the same to him. Anything that was unfair triggered a huge reaction. And I thought it was interesting that Zach blamed his mother when things went wrong. Young children always believe that when something happens, it's someone's fault. They don't understand that some events are no one's fault. It's not uncommon for a child to say something like, "That stupid table tripped me." I wondered whom Zach blamed for his father's death. His mother? Himself?

I also guessed that Zach was confused about what had happened to his father. What would a four-year-old think when he hears (or overhears) that "the doctors are using the big guns" to fight the cancer. I imagined that Zach was also confused and upset about his own urges to steal. I find that children who steal have often had something or someone important taken from them.

Parents ask if their child is stealing on purpose and whether they can control themselves. Parents also want to know how to handle it. The answer is "it depends on the situation." Children who have had a big loss tend to steal unconsciously, just the way their play might show action figures losing their home, losing their way, or losing life. Sometimes children do steal deliberately, but that is more likely to happen when a child is angry and wants to get revenge. Sometimes children steal for necessity. And sometimes they are testing boundaries and want to see what will happen.

So how can the parent handle it when a child steals? There are probably lots of right ways to handle it. When a child steals in response to a loss, I usually say something like this: "Sometimes children steal things after they have lost something really important to them (like a parent). After something as little as an eraser is stolen, all the adults get very upset and sometimes angry. Imagine how upset those adults would be if they had lost something as important as a parent."

When children know they have done something wrong, most feel embarrassed and ashamed. As a consequence of stealing, I think it's important for the child to return the object, write a letter of apology, and make amends. It's also worthwhile for the child to be asked to "replay it" the way he/she wishes it had happened. Most children recognize the urge to take something, and they wish they hadn't taken it. The message the child needs is that even if you feel like taking something that isn't yours, you know that you have to control your behavior. It's not OK to steal. When you have strong feelings or urges like that that you know are not right, you can always talk to an adult.

I might tell parents, "I think he's giving us a homeopathic dose of how it feels to have something taken. If people are so upset about a little eraser being stolen, imagine how he must have felt having his father taken away." I think it's a good idea to handle the situation as calmly as possible—to help the child to return the stolen item and to apologize. We need to teach the child to do the right thing even if it's embarrassing. We should also teach him how to calm himself, how to express his feelings appropriately, and how to help himself resist urges. EMDR can help to reduce the urge to steal, but helping the child recognize and express his emotions is essential in preventing recurrences.

I introduced Zach to bilateral stimulation to cultivate his positive feelings. He chose buzzers combined with the sound of an arcade on the headphones. For a learning experience, he chose to think about a computer game he had learned to play. For a "yes" experience, he remembered finally winning the computer game. He felt a proud feeling (see Chapter 11).

I began to formulate my plan for taking care of Zach. Of course, I would follow Zach's lead, but I intended to learn about his relationship with his father and Zach's experiences around his death. Since Zach didn't like to talk about it, I would ask Elizabeth if we could talk about his experiences of loss or what she imagined the experiences were like for him. Each week, while Zach played and listened, I would encourage her to tell me something that went well in Zach's week and something that was difficult. Zach was clearly listening, even though he was playing actively on the other side of the room. Whenever we made an error, he corrected us.

I wanted Zach to hear how his mother and I modeled the conversation about his father's illness and death. I wanted to give words to Zach's experience and teach him the words and the way to express his strong feelings. Now that Zach's mother was no longer flooded with her own grief, she was able to help Zach with his. Talking about what happened helped her feel that she was helping Zach.

I thought that writing a story would be helpful to both Zach and Elizabeth in clearing up some of the confusion about Zach's father's death and about his mom's response to her losses. Elizabeth enjoyed sharing happy memories of her husband. She brought in pictures of her and Zach with Zach's dad to show me. When she talked about the sad circumstances of his death, she was able to see how she had been resilient enough to pull herself together to make a good life for Zach and herself. Since she was getting so triggered by Zach's belligerence, I thought we would have to address the helplessness underlying her angry responses.

When Zach and his mom came back the next week, Elizabeth reported that Zach had stolen a pen from his teacher. Since Zach started stealing, she had been checking his backpack every day, and she had found it there. Zach knew that his mother was checking his backpack, so he must have wanted her to find the pen.

Zach's mom asked him to talk about what happened with the pen. Zach shook his head and said he wanted to go play. He nodded toward his mom and said, "You talk about it." So Zach played with robots on the floor, about six feet from us, and Elizabeth began to talk about angry feelings. "Sometimes, if I have angry feelings, it's that I feel sad. When I feel no one is paying attention to me I feel sad and then I get angry and then I feel more sad." (I felt Zach's mom was describing his feelings as well as hers.)

She continued, "I've noticed that Zach wants me to feel bad when he feels bad. Maybe he feels he won't feel so lonely if two of us feel the sad together." Zach was clearly listening while he played. He interrupted, "But Mom is mean when she says 'no.'" His mom looked to me: "He always says I'm mean when he doesn't get his way."

I thought that the memory of feeling extremely upset every time his mom said "no" would be a good target for EMDR. However, children don't say, "Sure I'd love to feel fine whenever I don't get my way." I had to find a way to motivate Zach so that he would want to feel better about something.

I asked Zach's mom, "What would you like for Zach to think about himself when you say 'no'?" She replied, "I'd like him to think, 'I am lovable even if my mom says "no." I can trust my mom to make good decisions for me. I can stay calm around something little.'" Now we had positive cognitions that Zach might want. Most children agree that they want to feel lovable and important, and that they'd like to trust their parent and trust that they can get over little things.

Next time they came, Elizabeth presented an example of Zach blowing up over a "no." "Last night Zach wanted ice cream at bedtime and I said 'no.'" I asked Zach if he'd like for me to show him some things that have helped other kids feel lovable and good even if their mom says "no." Zach agreed, and we were ready for the desensitizing and reprocessing phases of EMDR.

When Zach remembered his mom saying "no" about the ice cream, he felt angry, and the Subjective Units of Distress Scale (SUDS) rating was 5. His processing went like this: angry >>> she was trying to help me but I acted out >>> sad/mad >>> happy >>> she was trying to tell me I already had dessert. If I drink too much soda or eat ice cream I stay up too late. His SUD rating had dropped to zero. His body felt clear of distress when he remembered it. I asked Zach to think about what happened and hold the thought: "She made a good decision." We continued with reinforcing the positive belief, and he said, "It's a little thing; I can let it go; she's trying to help me."

Zach left feeling calmer, but the next week he returned feeling upset again. He had stolen a friend's pencil, scratched the car seat with it, and written the name of his friend on the bathroom wall at school. Zach's mother had been out of town on a business trip over the weekend. Had her absence prompted his urge to take something? Regardless of what caused him to misbehave, it was time to target his urges to steal and do things he knew were wrong.

Zach agreed to work on the memory of writing his friend's name on the bathroom wall and scratching the seat of the car and then getting in trouble. The most disturbing part was getting in trouble and the principal talking to him. His processing went like this:

Worst feeling >>> confused feeling in my brain >>> all feelings are confused >>> mad—because I did something wrong >>> sad >>> happy/ confused >>> the feeling is like bored >>> inside of the bored I don't think there is any feeling >>> white nothing inside the feeling >>> I was sad after I got caught >>> a little happier that I got over it >>> I recognize that there isn't any other feeling >>> I'm over it and I won't do it again.

I recognized that though Zach may not do those same things again, he could very well do something else because we hadn't addressed the root cause, and we hadn't cleared the urge to do things he knew were wrong. I asked him what he could do if he got strong feelings. He told me that he could go to the school counselor or one of the women who worked in the office—or that he could do the "butterfly hug." We added in a set of eye movements while he imagined getting help for strong feelings.

In the following weeks, Zach came up with a system for talking about his feelings. He started color-coding his feelings. He decided that "red feelings" were big feelings and included all feelings—"good, bad, mad, and sad." He said he remembered a "red day" when he came home from preschool and got on the couch where his dad was dying. He explained more: "Green feelings are mad and sad feelings because Daddy isn't here. Yellow is the happiest you can get. Orange is kind of happy. I feel orange on the weekend. Blue is no feeling at all. Dark blue is calm and I never feel that way."

He described his emotions-color-coding system further: "Bright red is strong. Green is calm. Black is a smidge of energy. Yellow is second happiest. White is all the happy feelings mixed together—like a good calm. Black is all the bad feelings. Orange is the happiest happy—like on my birthday and Christmas."

Wow! I could see why Zach had a hard time expressing his feelings! There were so many feelings and they were swirling in color and changing quickly and were confusing. Young children find it difficult to understand how they can feel sad and happy or calm at the same time.

Zach continued with his color-coding: "Red is hyper. Orange is happy. Blue is nothing—dead. Green is calm. Violet is mad. Black is all the feelings mixed together. Brown is going somewhere fun, but you don't think it will be fun. Purple is the angriest you can get. Blue—all the feelings are dead like in the graveyard."

I gave Zach the "strong feelings rod" (see Chapter 13) so he could use his feet to push the strong feelings out the rod while he pulled the cords and held the buzzers. He focused on being in the principal's office while she talked to him about taking pencils and doing damage with them. As he pushed on the rod with his feet and pulled the ropes with both hands and felt the alternating taps from the buzzers, he imagined all the colors shooting out from the ends of the tubes. At the end of desensitizing and processing the memory of the principal talking with him about taking erasers, he no longer felt upset about that incident.

I was concerned that we were clearing distress around little incidents, but we hadn't yet worked on memories of his father's illness and death. Why didn't I start there, desensitizing those awful memories at the beginning of our work together? There are several reasons: Initially, Zach didn't have a vocabulary for feelings but wanted to hear his mother and me talk about feelings. By listening to us, he began to develop an interest in emotions and even devised his own system for classifying his own huge confusion of emotions. There were so many traumatic experiences around his father's illness and death and his mother's response to the illness and death and ongoing loss of her husband. Zach's sense of loss had not diminished over time.

I had decided to follow Zach's lead and work on whichever piece he was willing to talk about. I also had needed time to work with Zach's mother on parenting issues—how to handle his sassing, stealing, and outbursts. Furthermore, if I started on the most traumatic memories, there was a high probability that Zach would become overwhelmed by so many feelings and refuse to do EMDR. With children who have had complex trauma, it often works best to "work around the edges" of less upsetting or current experiences that will have immediate benefit for the child.

Next I met with Elizabeth alone to review our progress and to determine which problems were still significant. Zach's mom told me that overall he was doing better and that the teacher had given him his best report card ever. She had outlined three areas that were still problematic for Zach: (1) He was easily disappointed and quick to anger over little things—like when plans changed or when he didn't get his way; (2) he was overly critical of himself—if he made a little mistake in math he labeled himself "stupid," or if he missed a ball someone threw to him he said he was "terrible"; and (3) he couldn't tolerate correction and always interpreted comments from his teacher as criticism and reacted with "You hate me."

From that list of behaviors I surmised that Zach's negative cognitions might be (1) I can't stand it when anything unexpected happens—disappointment means that terrible things happen; (2) I'm bad; and (3)

It's my fault bad things happen. Those are common beliefs after childhood trauma. I also knew that there was enormous confusion about why his father got sick and why he died.

At this point I decided to set up several sessions alone with Elizabeth so we could write a story for Zach to help clear up some of his confusion and so I could clarify my understanding of the family's belief system regarding health, illness, death, and loss.

Elizabeth and I wrote the story together during several appointments. We struggled to explain Zach's father's illness. We wanted Zach to know that his father had had cancer, but we didn't want him to think that everyone with cancer dies. We decided to tell him that his father had a severe, incurable kind of cancer and that it was no one's fault. It was important for him to know that everyone did their best to help and that he had helped by keeping his dad company and that playing with his dad made him happy.

We wanted to dispel any notion that Zach had caused the cancer or failed to prevent his dad's death. We also needed to help him understand that his mother's distress and irritability at him was because she was so upset about her husband's death—it wasn't because he was bad and caused the main problem. We agreed that we couldn't fit everything into the story, but we could answer questions as they came up. We wanted to normalize a sense of confusion after a parent's death and introduce the concept that it's possible to have something very sad in your life and still engage in life and feel happy at the same time.

We wanted to distinguish between "big unfair" things and "little unfair things." Zach had been acting as if any disappointment or unfair thing merited the same high level of distress. We talked about giving him a scale of 1 to 5, with 1 being little unfair and 5 being big unfair. He and his mom could use the 1–5 scale at home to determine how big a reaction Zach demonstrated and how big he thought it actually deserved. While we could talk about "unfair," it was useful to have a way for Zach to decide what was a big unfair (and means this is dangerous—get an adult involved!) and a little unfair (like not getting dessert) that meant everyone is still safe and it's OK to let it go.

Elizabeth also wanted to find a way for Zach to understand that his dad still lived inside him, but he wasn't just like his father who died from cancer. Zach's mom wanted to convey that love is stronger than death, but she didn't want to use the word death. She wanted Zach to believe that he currently still had a father, though his father was not alive. This was hard to accomplish, and we talked about it for a long time before we decided on a way to express that concept. It was true that he had a father, but how could we say that he *has* a father currently in a way that felt true. Zach's mom also wanted to state her love for Zach.

And we wanted to accomplish all that in a page or two!
Here is the story we wrote:

Once upon a time there was a boy who lived with his mom and his dog "Spoof." The boy loved to play piano, to challenge his mom in chess, and to go biking and play baseball with his friends. He liked to have his mom read adventure stories to him. His mom appreciated his perseverance when he wanted to do something, like learn to play a new piano piece. His mom, his grandparents, his cousins, and his aunts and uncles all loved being with him.

Like everybody else in the world, some things in this boy's life were wonderful and some were sad and disappointing.

One wonderful thing was that the boy was born good and lovable and very much loved by his family. When he was born, his parents were so very happy.

One sad thing was that when the boy was four years old, his dad was diagnosed with a severe kind of cancer that couldn't be cured.

The boy stayed close by his dad and helped him feel better by keeping him company and playing cars on the sofa with him. His dad, the doctors, and the boy's mom and family and friends did everything they could to fight the cancer, but the cancer was a kind that couldn't be cured.

Sometimes when a parent dies, a child thinks it has something to do with him. When a parent dies, it's confusing. Nobody knows why his dad got cancer, but we do know that it was nobody's fault he got it and it was nobody's fault he died.

After his dad died, lots of things changed for the boy and his mom. His mom had to work more, and she cried a lot for a while.

She was sad a lot of the time. The boy and his mom and family and friends all missed his dad.

Some things stayed the same.

He lived in the same house. He went to the same school.

And his mom always made sure he was loved and cared for.

Now that four years have passed since his dad died, the boy is older and he can understand some things he couldn't understand when he was only four years old and in nursery school.

He already knows that big unfair and disappointing things happen sometimes, like when his dad died.

There are some things that feel unfair and are disappointing, like when he loses a game or something doesn't go the way he wants.

When it's a little unfair thing, he can feel disappointed and then let it go.

A family friend said, "You get what you get and you don't pitch a fit." And before long you'll feel better. No matter what, you are always lovable.

His mom says, "You are the light of my life, and I love you when you are happy or sad, angry or funny—with all of your feelings. You are lovable because you are you."

Now the boy is growing up.

The boy is handsome and has a mischievous smile, a curious mind, and a gentle heart, just like his dad.

Even though his dad can't be with him, his love and his spirit always will be.

Zach's mom had prepared him to hear the story by telling him that she and I had written a story about his life and she wanted him to listen to it. When they came in, they snuggled up on the love seat together. I got Zach set up with the buzzers, turned on the alternating bilateral stimulation (ABS), and began to read this story. When we came to the part of the story that explained why Zach's father had died, Zach stopped me. "I thought he died from heart cancer." His mother looked surprised: "No, he didn't have heart cancer." She explained his illness.

Zach began to smile shyly when I read, "The boy is handsome and has a mischievous smile, a curious mind, and a gentle heart, just like his dad." His mom had found exactly the right way to say that his dad still lived.

Zach and his mom had come to see me almost weekly for a year and a half. During the course of the year, Elizabeth learned a lot about how Zach was feeling, learned to model for him how to express feelings of sadness, anger, and frustration, and improved her parenting skills.

As Zach settled into more appropriate behavior, blamed his mom less for any little thing that didn't go his way, cooperated more, and became increasingly articulate and cheerful, he became easier to parent. Their relationship improved, and they trusted and enjoyed one another more.

Perspective

The death of a parent affects every aspect of a child's life. There is no therapy that can help a child recover fast. The goals of grief therapy with Zachary were to help him learn a vocabulary for expressing his feelings, to resolve his feelings of guilt about his father's death, and to understand himself as helpful and as a source of comfort during his father's illness.

Initially, Zach played as he listened to his mother and me talk about what had happened around the time of his dad's death. We helped him sift through the confusion of loss, grief, and change. We modeled ways to express feelings and strategies for self-soothing. Zach willingly did EMDR to help himself get past some upsetting memories and to discharge feelings that were too intense to articulate.

Zach's improvement was slow but continuous. The preparation phase for EMDR was attenuated as Zach had to learn the language of emotions by listening to his mother and me talking about their traumatic experience. Zach was initially avoiding or unable to talk about his father's death, and it was important that we address current problem behaviors before focusing on the traumatic events so that he didn't become overwhelmed.

The process of writing the healing narrative was helpful to Elizabeth, and both she and Zach benefited from having a cohesive account of what had happened during the time surrounding his father's death. The narrative made sense of Zach's behavior, relieving him of guilt and giving him a positive way to keep his father's memory alive. The modified EMDR therapy succeeded in taking the most distressing charge off the upsetting memories and facilitated the transformation of Zach's negative self-referencing beliefs to positive, useful, and self-enhancing beliefs.

8

JOEY

Developmental Disabilities Complicating
Trauma Resolution

Some children have histories that are so full of trauma that it's hard to begin to formulate a treatment plan. This story about Joey offers a variety of ways of integrating EMDR into the treatment of chronic, complex trauma resulting from severe abuse and neglect early in life, multiple foster placements, and multiple psychiatric hospitalizations, complicated by developmental disabilities and prenatal drug exposure. Joey's history was heartbreaking.

Joey

Ken got right to the point about why he and his wife were consulting me: "We're here to try EMDR. We heard that EMDR is really effective for treating trauma. Our son Joey is 10 now and he has severe behavioral problems. His main problems are that he's violent and very fearful, despite lots of medication."

Ken paused and began again, "We adopted Joey when he was three. In his first three years of life, Joey was neglected and abused by his birth mother, who was a drug addict, and he was placed in seven foster homes. He was sexually abused in at least one emergency shelter. I think he was traumatized by all the times he's been restrained and all his psychiatric hospitalizations. Joey has probably had hundreds or thousands of traumatic events in his life. Do you think EMDR can help us?"

I must have looked dismayed because Alison quickly interjected, "Joey can be really sweet too. He's developmentally delayed, but he still loves cuddling his stuffed animals, and he gets excited over little things like playing 'Duck-Duck-Goose' or singing songs like 'The Wheels on the Bus.' That's the side of him that gives us hope. He feels things deeply, and he has a kind heart. Despite his problems he's really very lovable. But his rage gets set off by so many things, so quickly—he goes from zero to a hundred in a split second. Medicine helps tone down the rage, but it's made him gain a lot of weight, and he's sluggish and tired all the time when he takes enough medicine so that he's not violent."

Alison sighed, "Last year, it became apparent that we couldn't keep Joey at home—we had to keep calling the police to restrain him because he was so out of control, breaking things and trying to hurt us or himself. Everybody in the emergency room knew us because we were there almost every day, and in the past few years Joey has had nine psychiatric hospitalizations because he was violent and needed to have his medications adjusted."

Ken interjected, "Joey's been on all kinds of medications: high doses of anti-psychotics, mood stabilizers, antidepressants, anti-anxiety meds, ADHD drugs, sleeping pills, vitamins—he's even been on seizure medications and medicines to lower blood pressure, even though he's never had seizures or high blood pressure."

Alison added, "We've gone to dozens of therapists and psychiatrists. We thought we had tried everything to help Joey, but then one of the psychiatrists told us about EMDR and recommended that we see you."

Ken said pensively, "We were discouraged for a while. We called 40 residential settings for emotionally disturbed children, but nobody would take him because he is so violent, and the facilities that take someone who is violent just aren't appropriate for a 10-year-old child." Then Ken's face brightened: "We finally got him into a small group home for severely disturbed schizophrenic and autistic children. Joey is not autistic or schizophrenic, but he requires intensive one-on-one care in a well-structured, protective environment, and he has an aide around the clock. The group home is only about half an hour from where we live, and we can bring him home on weekends. The problem is that even though he's heavily medicated, he's extremely anxious and just about anything sets him off."

Joey had a daunting history, starting in his prenatal life when he was infused with his mother's cocaine and an assortment of other drugs. His birth was precipitated by physical violence when his mother's boyfriend kicked her in the abdomen, initiating early labor. Joey's mother abandoned him in the hospital. His father was unknown.

Joey was hospitalized in the neonatal intensive care unit for 10 days after his birth. Joey told me his version of his birth story: "A mean man kicked my mother in the stomach, and that's why I was born." He lifted his shirt to show me a scar where he had had a chest tube to treat a collapsed lung and told me, "This is where I was kicked." Joey had heard stories of his inauspicious beginnings in life, but he drew his own, incorrect explanation for the scar on his chest.

When Joey was about two weeks old, he was discharged from the hospital to live with his birth mother. She was drug addicted and homeless. She left Joey with a variety of strangers. According to Child Protective Services reports, she had locked him in a closet, either to get him out of her way, to protect him from out-of-control drug addicts, or to punish him. He was often hungry and didn't get the care and attention a baby needs.

Finally, Joey's birth mother decided she couldn't handle a baby and left him with her parents. They had their own problems. Their screaming, verbal abuse, and neglect drew attention to the family, and they were reported to Child Protective Services several times. They often left Joey in the care of his seven-year-old brother or dropped him off at relatives' homes.

Ken added to the history: "By the time he was one year old, Joey was very difficult to handle—he was hyperactive, aggressive, inconsolable when upset, and uncooperative. When he was 17 months old, Joey's grandfather died suddenly." From a toddler's point of view, his grandfather disappeared and everyone around Joey was upset.

Alison continued, "When Joey was 18 months old, he was home alone with his grandmother when she fell out of her wheelchair, hit her head, and died. The police had to break down the door to enter the house. They found Joey in a pool of blood beside his grandmother's body, trying to open her eyes. No one knew exactly how long he was home alone with her body."

Joey's grandmother's death led to a series of foster placements for Joey. Within two years, Joey was placed in seven different foster families, sometimes waiting for months in emergency shelters until a new foster family could be found for him. He was sexually molested in at least one of the emergency shelters. He was hyperactive, aggressive, and often out of control. He became infuriated whenever he saw babies, and he attacked one of the babies in a foster placement. The child needed to be hospitalized, and Joey had to be moved to a new foster placement. There were attempts to reunite Joey with his birth mother, but she took him from one drug house to another, often leaving him unfed and uncared for.

When Joey was three years old, his current parents, Alison and Ken, adopted him as their only child. Alison had been a pediatric oncology nurse and Kevin was the manager of a recreation center, where he had years of experience working with children. They decided to adopt Joey because they had the time, experience, money, and resources for a child with special needs. The judge presiding over the adoption advised them that all Joey needed was their love and consistent care to turn things around for him.

Despite the judge's good intentions, and Alison and Ken's love, attention, experience, and patience, Joey did not thrive. Joey had significant developmental disabilities. He wouldn't use a toilet until he was over seven years old. At age 10, he had not yet learned to read or write. Joey became more and more aggressive and out of control. His temper tantrums were epic, sometimes lasting hours, and it was impossible to predict or prevent them. Joey would scream, bite himself or his parents, break toys, punch holes in walls, throw furniture, and run into the street.

Ken listed more of Joey's difficult behaviors: "He sometimes poops on the floor or on someone's bed. He often won't do what people ask him to do. He especially has a hard time cooperating with Alison. I guess he's especially reactive with women because it was his birth mom who neglected and abused him most." Alison added, "He wants whatever he doesn't have, and nothing satisfies him. He continues to have tantrums that can last two hours, and he's so big now that I cannot physically restrain him or keep him safe. Joey talks in different voices too. Sometimes he talks like a baby, sometimes like an officer in the Gestapo, sometimes like another kid, and sometimes like 10-year-old Joey when he's calm."

Ken enumerated a formidable list of Joey's fears: "He's afraid of closets, showers, monsters, wearing shorts, people getting old, death of parents, pain, taking his shoes off, my jacket, and loss of control. He also has a fear of eating solid food." Alison described what happened when Joey felt scared: "He cries or screams or laughs wildly when he's afraid or sad. When he's upset, he tries to hurt himself or someone else. He has a big bite mark on his arm right now. He did that when we told him it was time to turn off the TV." Joey also had an extreme fear of having his blood drawn that made it very difficult to monitor his medications.

Joey had an equally daunting list of "triggers," or things that set off prolonged temper tantrums, which sometimes lasted several hours.

Even when the triggers were obvious, the treatments were not. If someone already had a parking space that Joey wanted for his parents' car, Joey's tantrum could last an hour or more. When his mom felt sad, Joey became mean. When anyone was injured or in trouble, Joey laughed uncontrollably. Loud noises or someone knocking on the door terrified him. He became fearful and angry when his parents were away, when another child got attention, when he was hungry, when he felt left out, and when he thought of death or loss. He was too frustrated to wait in line. He raged when meals weren't exactly what he wanted. When Joey had to return to the group home after a visit with his parents, he defecated on his bed. The list of Joey's problems seemed endless.

Joey's history was chilling, and the intensity and scope of his symptoms were overwhelming. I felt sad that any child had to suffer the way Joey had suffered. I also felt despair. What could I possibly do to help this child? I told Alison and Ken that I didn't know whether EMDR would be helpful to Joey. I wanted to meet Joey and evaluate his readiness for trauma processing and his receptiveness to EMDR.

Approaches to Complex Developmental Trauma

I decided to start by learning and understanding as much as possible about the child and his family and work toward good rapport. What next?

It is usually possible to collaborate with an adult to prioritize issues to address if the adult comes for therapy because he/she wants help. Joey was a significantly developmentally delayed child who was so traumatized that he was dissociated much of the time. I could easily say that Joey had severe posttraumatic symptoms from chronic trauma and displayed disorganized, disoriented attachment behaviors. He had a severe dissociative disorder with multiple personalities.

And what was the endpoint? No matter how much therapy Joey had or how many medications he took, Joey would never be close to normal. In fact, he would probably need a one-to-one aide for the rest of his life. It would be wonderful if he could get to the point where he didn't require hospitalization, if he were not a danger to himself and to others, and if he could be relieved of some of his debilitating fears.

I decided that I would take my cues from Joey and follow his lead. I would address current issues and be careful not to rush to open up too many of the memories of past horrors in his life. Joey was a fragile child. If I couldn't help him feel better, I certainly didn't want to make him feel worse. While focusing on his current problems, I would be alert to early experiences that had contributed to his current thoughts, distress, and behavior patterns. I would also be sure to reinforce any positive experiences, feelings, and thoughts Joey had.

I tried to figure out what distorted, false, and negative beliefs ("negative cognitions") seemed to correspond with Joey's behaviors. I started with several that are often apparent in people with so much early trauma: "I'm bad" and "It's my fault," "I can't trust" and "I can't stand it when things don't go my way," and "I can't stand it when I don't know what's happening or when I'm confused." Joey also seemed to have a lot of beliefs about safety. "I'm only safe if I get what I want. I'm not safe if someone is sad. I'll be alone and terrified if anyone is upset. I'm not safe if someone knocks on the door. I'm not safe if I don't know exactly what's happening." The positive belief "I am safe now" would help to decrease Joey's anxiety. So I wanted to reinforce Joey's sense of present safety and help him feel that he was essentially lovable and good and would be cared for.

Another approach I use when working on understanding behaviors is to look at them developmentally. For example, Joey's willingness to poop on a bed or the floor or anywhere pointed to trauma as a baby. Babies poop without regard to where they are. His "potty talk" was typical of a four-year-old child. I wanted to address the needs of his scared "inner baby" and his scared young child part. Joey might be receptive to having one of his parents in the room to comfort him and to tell stories about how they would have taken care of him as a baby. In children with multiple personalities, working with the "inner baby" and young child part is crucial.

Another strategy is to look at behaviors that seem to go with specific traumas. For example, Joey's extreme fear of sudden, loud noises or his fear when someone knocked on the door might have been related to his memory of the police knocking down the door when his grandmother died. Or perhaps when he was an infant and his birth mother moved from place to place, she may have literally knocked on a lot of doors. Joey went wild when he was restrained. That certainly made sense given that Joey had been restrained with duct tape as a toddler and later restrained multiple times by police and staff in the emergency room and psychiatric wards.

It is important to identify the confusion that always resides with early childhood trauma. I wanted to notice everything that was confusing for Joey, so I could be ready to offer an "adult perspective" and to address the confusion through play or stories. Sometimes I ask myself, "If the baby could have talked, what would he have said or asked?" If the baby could have talked, he might have asked questions: "Why is this happening to me? Why didn't my grandfather ever come home again? What is death? Why did I have to go to foster care? Why did they keep taking people away from me? Who can I trust? What can I do? Is this my fault?" I suspected that Joey felt really bad about biting a child so badly that he had to be hospitalized.

With children with complex posttraumatic issues, I think of five broad categories of approach: (1) EMDR to resolve trauma and promote attachment in a developmentally meaningful way; (2) reinforcing positive behaviors with alternating bilateral stimulation (ABS); (3) physiologic quieting and helping the child develop the capacity for self-calming—this may be achieved through nurturing by an attuned parent, neuro-feedback, mindfulness, breathing exercises, relaxation exercises, EMDR protocols, and medication; (4) a cohesive life narrative to make sense of a confusing early childhood; and (5) strengthening positive nurturing relationships with the parents or caregivers. This approach may also involve therapy for the parents or caregivers themselves. In the course of Joey's treatment, I used each of the categories multiple times, sometimes all five in the same session—at other times, one approach per session.

First Impressions of Joey

When I first met him, Joey was 10 years old. He had curly blond hair and big brown eyes and a round, pale face that reflected dramatic mood shifts. Initially, Joey wandered around my office in a disorganized way.

I felt discombobulated and helpless just being in the room with him. It was hard to know what precipitated Joey's abrupt changes in mood, and it wasn't clear what response would calm Joey when he was upset. Sometimes Joey's face looked like it belonged to a baby, particularly when he cried and his lips curled into a wailing open rectangle. If I had just heard that intensely distressed cry and not seen him, I would have thought that it belonged to an infant instead of a 10-year-old boy.

When he was delighted, Joey beamed with excitement, and his enthusiasm filled the room. As soon as something sad came up, Joey shifted his eyes and began to laugh or to sing selections from his favorite musicals. When he was angry, he roared his aggression and pounded the furniture, the floor, and whatever was nearby. And when Joey disapproved of himself, he bit his own hand, banged his head against the wall, or hit himself on the head.

The second time I met with Joey and his parents, I was surprised and pleased to see that Joey was very affectionate with his parents. He sat on Ken's lap and clearly enjoyed having Alison rub his back. Joey had brought some of his own toys, and he played on the floor with his action figures while his parents and I talked. While we were talking about Joey's good qualities, I noticed that all of Joey's play was about destruction.

I invited Joey to play some imagination games with me, and with his parents' encouragement, he agreed. I asked him if he could imagine a safe place, and he could—it was his own room at home with his parents. I asked Joey to show me where he felt the safe feeling in his body, and he pointed to his heart. I asked if he could imagine a fun time, and he remembered having fun playing in the park. I asked if he could think of something that he learned that used to be hard for him, but now was easy. With some prompting from his parents, Joey remembered learning how to dress himself.

I was encouraged that Joey was able to recall positive memories and do these imagination exercises with me, and especially glad that he was able to point to feelings in his body. For example, he could feel a safe feeling in his heart when he imagined being in his safe place—in his bedroom at home.

I also noted that Joey needed almost constant directions, reminders about rules, and instructions on how to behave. Often, Joey's train of thought was hard to follow, and he would begin to quote books like *A Nightmare in the Closet* or sing the soundtrack from a favorite musical. It wasn't until later that I understood the significance of this behavior.

Joey's Initial EMDR Sessions

Every time Joey came to see me, one of his parents accompanied him and participated in his therapy. Usually, I started each session by asking Joey and his parent what had gone well in the previous week. Joey and his mom or dad proudly told me about a time when Joey had cooperated or stayed calm in a previously stressful situation or had successfully tried a new behavior. Reinforcing current positive experiences, having his parents present and hearing that he was lovable and loved were some of the anchors that helped to prevent Joey from dissociating and helped him become more present even after he had dissociated. After reviewing the successes of the past week, I asked if they had identified one thing that they would like to have go better for Joey so he and his family or people at the group home could have more fun. Once they were used to that routine, they usually came to their appointments prepared to focus on one fear or troublesome behavior. I recognized that all of Joey's difficult behaviors were fear-based, making them potentially responsive to desensitization and reprocessing. The following section of text names the target fear, the negative cognition (dysfunctional, distorted belief) and the positive cognition (desired, true, useful belief) that Joey, his parent and I determined would be helpful to Joey.

Fear of the Closet

Negative cognition: I'm not safe near my closet.
Positive cognition: I am safe and can relax when I see a closet or think about a closet.

Joey came to the next session with his dad. I wanted to find out whether Joey could process memories with the assistance of ABS. I had to find something that Joey was willing to work on. Ken led the way by saying, "Joey wants to come home with us for Halloween, but he is afraid of his closet." I asked Joey if he wanted to get over his fear of the closet. He nodded.

I had my target: Joey's fear of the closet. And I had Joey's motivation: He really wanted to go home for Halloween. Children will put up with emotional pain or discomfort only if it promises to give them something they want. Joey had a goal, motivation, and he agreed to work toward his goal.

Fear of closets was just one of the many fears that triggered upset and prolonged crying for Joey. It wasn't until later that I learned that Joey really had been locked in a closet as a baby.

When I don't know the source of a fear, I assume that I am treating a symptom of irrational fear, rather than treating a specific trauma. When working with young children who have been neglected and abused before their adoption, we are often working with incomplete information and have to follow the child's lead and our hunches.

I decided that I wanted Joey to believe simply, "I am safe when I see a closet or think about a closet." Joey's parents had told him many times that there was nothing hiding in his closet and that he was safe. They had repeatedly opened the closet and shown them that there was nothing inside, but Joey continued to be fearful. I hoped that EMDR could erase the irrational, fearful feelings that cognitive reasoning could not touch.

I had learned that when I work with people with developmental delays and cognitive disabilities, I cannot expect them to choose their own positive cognitions. I also knew that I had to choose a specific cognition, like "I am safe when I see a closet or think about a closet," rather than the more general belief, "I am safe." Furthermore, especially if the child has intellectual disabilities and his/her learning doesn't generalize to similar situations, I might have to divide the positive cognitions into two separate cognitions: "I am safe when I see a closet" and "I am safe when I think about a closet." Then reprocessing can be achieved with each of these positive cognitions as a goal.

I decided to offer Joey the chance to draw some pictures of whatever was scary about a closet. I folded a piece of white paper into four sections for Joey and numbered each section. (This "folded paper" technique was developed by the Humanitarian Assistance Program therapists in Mexico to assist them in screening a group of children who had been traumatized, and I've found that it is also useful for addressing irrational fears, those not necessarily based on any real-life event.)

I didn't ask Joey to draw his memory of being locked in the closet as a baby because he didn't remember it (it had been noted in a Child Protective Services report) and because I didn't want him to be overwhelmed by fear. Instead, I asked Joey to draw a picture of the "fear of closets" in the first section (see Figure 8.1). Joey scribbled in the square in the upper left corner of the page, and then he looked at me. I asked, "How upsetting does the fear of closets look if this is zero (I put my hands together) and this is the most you can imagine (I put my hands about eight inches apart). Is it a little, like this, or a whole lot, like this?" Joey showed me by putting his hands wide apart.

I asked Joey to look at his drawing while I tapped his shoulders and to let me know when there was a change in the size of the fear or a change in what he was thinking or feeling. After I tapped for about a minute, I asked Joey to draw his fear of closets again. This time the picture turned into a circle with scribbling inside. We repeated the dual attention stimulation. The third picture was a circle with two eyes, and some scribbling. We repeated the process. The fourth and final picture was a circle with a smiley face, and Joey said "not scary at all." He appeared to have a happy resolution to his fear: When Joey thought about the closet, he visualized a smiley face instead of a fear.

Joey's Drawings

When Joey returned the following week, he reported that he had gone home for Halloween and that he was no longer afraid of his closet. Hurray!

Figure 8.1 Targeting the fear of someone hiding in the closet

Joey's Experience: Nothing Feels Right

Negative cognition: Nothing will help me feel better. I can't be satisfied.
Positive cognitions: I'm safe. I can say what I want. I will get what I need.

Joey had done well at home over the weekend except that he had had two meltdowns. The first meltdown occurred when he couldn't find one of his shoes. The second meltdown occurred when he had to take his medication. "I don't want it with pudding. I want it with applesauce." His parents offered pudding. Then they offered applesauce. Joey whined for an hour about what he wanted and what he didn't want. Nothing had felt right for Joey. That experience of "nothing feels right" is common in children who have a history of chronic trauma early in life and often goes along with "disorganized, disoriented" attachment, in which the primary caregiver who is supposed to be a source of protection is also a source of terror.

In my office, Joey stretched out on the floor and chose to have his dad alternately tickle his right foot and his left foot. While Ken provided ABS, I offered the positive cognitions "I can say what I need or want. Dad can give me what I need. I am getting attention." While we talked, Joey put toys in his mouth and bit on them. I wondered whether he was going back to being about six months old when he was teething. I wanted to help Joey differentiate between infancy and his current age of 10 years. When he was an infant, he could not successfully make his needs known, and he often could not get what he wanted or needed. In the present, his attentive parents were willing to do almost anything for him. However, I knew that it would take a lot of work before Joey would be able to trust that anyone could meet his needs, even though his parents had been appropriately attentive to his needs for seven years.

Fear of Having Blood Drawn

Negative cognition: I can't stand the sight of blood.
Positive cognition: I'm safe and can be calm when I imagine blood
being drawn.

This time, Ken wanted me to help prepare Joey for a blood test. In the past, it took several people to restrain Joey while a nurse drew his blood. I asked Joey how scary it looked when he remembered having his blood drawn. Joey threw his arms wide apart and said, "One hundred." Because Joey's level of distress was so high, we titrated his exposure to the memory of a blood draw.

Instead of talking about Joey's experience with blood draws or asking him to remember an upsetting memory about having his blood drawn, Ken and I pretended to draw blood from one another with a syringe without a needle. At first, Joey couldn't bear to watch, and he moaned

"Nooo . . ." and swatted at us. He refused to focus on that fear. He was overwhelmed by it.

We would have to revisit that fear another time. If the child's arousal level is too high, he/she can't process the experience. For Joey, blood drawing involved being restrained (a trauma with a long history), pain (another trauma with a long history), and loss of control (a third trauma with a long history). I would start by working toward the transitional positive cognition "I'm safe and can be calm when I imagine blood being drawn."

For Joey, as for other people with significant developmental disabilities, I would work on each of the individual components of the frightening experience rather than a single image of having blood drawn. I would help Joey feel comfortable with an empty syringe, and he could play with it and pretend to use it on a stuffed animal. I would desensitize him to the feeling of the tourniquet on his arm, the feeling of the alcohol wipe, and the feeling of sitting in the chair waiting. I anticipated that the most difficult part for Joey was the thought of being restrained so he didn't move his arm.

Demand for a Particular Parking Space

Negative cognition: I can't be calm unless I get exactly what I want.
Positive cognition: I'm safe and can relax, even if I don't get the parking space I want.

Then Joey shifted his attention to another source of distress: parking spaces. Even though he was settled in my office, he fixated on the fact that his father hadn't parked in the space Joey wanted. "I wanted that parking space—why don't you just ram them out of that parking space?" he bellowed. Ken explained calmly, "When we go into a parking lot, Joey has huge temper tantrums if we don't get the parking space he wants—even though another car is already in that spot. I tell Joey that I would park there if it was available, but it isn't. It's occupied. Joey has tantrums for one to two hours if he doesn't get the parking space he wants." Joey started to chant: "Ram them out. Ram them out. I want it!"

I gestured to Joey's dad to begin to give him ABS. Ken began to tickle Joey's feet alternately, just the way Joey liked. Then he recounted three incidents when Joey had stormed about parking spaces recently—at the mall, at a restaurant, and in my parking lot. I asked Ken what he wanted Joey to believe about himself, even if he didn't get the parking space he wanted. Ken said, "I want Joey to think, 'I'm safe and OK even if I don't get the space I want.' I also want him to know that he can make me happy by being good."

As Ken continued to tickle Joey's feet, alternating between the right and the left, I repeated to Joey, "Just think this, Joey: 'I am safe even when I don't get exactly what I want. I can make Dad happy by being good when I don't get exactly what I want.'" I didn't expect one session to clear Joey's distress when he didn't get what he wanted. I just imagined that we were whittling away at the grime covering Joey's sweet nature.

When Joey returned with both of his parents the following week, they reported that Joey had been doing really well. They gave me the report on Joey's response to not getting the parking space he wanted. Joey's tantrums over parking spaces had diminished—now he fussed for about two minutes when he didn't get the space he wanted. I was astounded by Joey's response to EMDR therapy.

In patients with complex histories and complex problems like Joey's, I've learned to appreciate every time I hear that they're doing really well. That report usually means that we've made one more step in the right direction. I've also come to expect that other issues, which have been just below the surface, will begin to emerge. The process of complex trauma resolution involves peeling back layer after layer of memories.

Leaving Parents and Returning to the Group Home

Negative cognition: I'll be abandoned and alone if my parents leave me. I'm in danger.
Positive cognition: I can count on my parents to take care of me. I'm safe.

Joey had been home for a brief vacation. Now the vacation was almost over, and Joey would have to return to his group home. In the past day, Joey had been mean to Alison, his mom. He laughed at her, made fun of her, wouldn't cooperate with her, and stayed angry with her. Whenever Joey was mean to his mom, it meant that he was sad. When Joey felt sad, he quickly felt bad, then he got mad at his mom for almost anything she did or didn't do. He refused to cooperate when she asked him to do something, he screamed or hit, and he often threatened to kill someone. The sequence: Scared of being abandoned led to feeling sad, to feeling bad, to acting mean. When Joey was mean, Joey's dad became angry. Then his mom became very sad because she seemed to be the only person Joey treated that way.

I asked Joey's parents to hold him and take turns stroking his arms, alternating from one side of his body to the other. I began to connect the experience of leaving his parents after vacation with the experience of having to leave foster families when he was a baby. I talked with Joey about how when he was a baby, he felt very scared sometimes when people left him. And then it was scary because he didn't know what was coming next or who would take care of him. Now, when he left his parents after a vacation, he could count on them coming back. Now he knew what to expect and that people would take care of him. He was still safe.

I asked Alison to tell Joey how it would have been if she had had him even from before he was born. Alison's face softened: "Joey, it would have been so wonderful to have you inside me before you were born. I would have loved carrying you inside me and feeling you growing inside me. You would have been warm and safe and happy." As she talked about carrying him inside her before he was born, Joey curled up in the fetal position.

Alison continued to talk to Joey: "When you were born, I would have held you and rocked you in my arms, and fed you when you were hungry, and changed your diapers when you needed clean diapers. I would have paid attention to you all the time, and I would have given you what you needed."

Joey responded by looking like a contented baby. At the end of the session, I wanted to make sure that his content "baby Joey" ego state got integrated into Joey's sense of himself, but I didn't want him to leave my office with a baby ego state predominating. To ensure that Joey left my office behaving like a 10-year-old boy, I said, "Then you were a little baby, and after that you kept growing up: You were one year old, and then two, and then three, four, five, six, and you kept growing bigger and bigger; and then you were seven and then you were eight, nine, and now you are 10. Stand up and show me how big you are, now that you are 10 years old." Joey stood up and looked more like a 10-year-old.

The Next Visit: The Solid Food Challenge

Negative cognition: I can't chew. It's not safe to eat solid food.
Positive cognitions: It's safe for me to chew and eat solid food. I can enjoy eating solid food. I can enjoy eating pizza (hamburger, salad, and noodles).

Our visits followed a pattern: First I asked Joey's parents to tell me something that had gone well during the previous week and then something that they wanted to work on so that everybody would feel happier. "Joey has been doing better with his mom," Ken reported. "Today I'd like Joey to work on being able to eat solid food." At that time, Joey had a very limited list of foods he was willing to eat. In addition, Joey would repeatedly ask for foods and then reject them, saying, "I want pizza—no, I don't want it." Ken didn't remember any particular incident of Joey choking on solid food. Joey just hadn't liked eating solid food ever since they adopted him at age three.

I searched my mind for possible ways that solid food might have been traumatic for Joey as a baby. I remembered times from my pediatric internship and residency when I had observed parents who were not in tune with their infants. Often they would absentmindedly push fries or hamburger into their baby's mouth. Babies are not ready to chew solid food until they are about nine months old. By that age, they have several teeth and have developed a pincer grasp. That is, they can oppose their thumb and forefinger to pick up small bits of food and steer it to their mouth. Babies who are fed solid food before that age have difficulty coordinating chewing and swallowing, and they tend to choke.

The negative cognition "I can't chew. It's not safe to eat solid food" may have been true for Joey if he was fed solids before he was ready. Now that Joey was 10 years old, it was developmentally appropriate and safe for him to eat solids. I wanted him to have the positive cognitions "It's safe for me to eat solid food" and "I can enjoy eating solid food."

I asked, "Joey, how upsetting does it seem when you imagine eating a slice of pizza? On a scale of zero to 10, if zero is feeling completely relaxed and 10 is the most upsetting you can imagine, how upsetting does it feel when you imagine eating a slice of pizza?"

Joey's voice quavered: "10." I asked him to imagine eating pizza and to notice the upset feeling in his body. Then, while his dad alternately touched his left and right arms, I said, "It's safe to eat pizza." The upset quickly went down to zero. We went through this same procedure as Joey imagined eating hamburger, salad, and noodles. Soon Joey was enjoying imagining eating foods that most 10-year-olds love.

That week Joey tried some new foods. He tried the foods he had imagined eating, as well as clam chowder and meatballs. His parents noticed that he was chewing more.

Morning Tantrums

Negative cognition: I can't tolerate it if I don't know exactly what to expect.

Positive cognitions: I can trust that adults will take care of me every day. I'm safe even if I don't know what's going to happen next.

Ken wanted Joey to work on the tantrums he was having first thing in the morning. Joey explained, "I get frustrated." I thought about what it must have been like for Joey when he was a baby and woke up in the morning not knowing what was going to happen. So much uncertainty must have been frightening for him as a baby—he didn't know who would take care of him and whether he would be fed or where he would be taken that day.

As Ken stroked Joey's arms alternately, I talked about how Joey's current life was very different from when he was a baby: "I imagine that when you were a baby, you would wake up in the morning and not know what to expect. Now that you're 10 years old, you can understand what is happening, and you know exactly what to expect every day. You know who will take care of you, you can count on having breakfast, and you know or you can ask where you will be going that day. Joey relaxed and smiled eagerly: "Now I'm in Dr. Lovett's office, then I get a treat, and then I go home." Another experience from the past went to take its proper place in the past.

Joey had been home for a school vacation all week and had had only three temper tantrums. When Joey had wanted to be in his parents' bed, they insisted that he stay in his own bed. Joey banged his head on the floor for 15 minutes. The day that Joey's parents took him back to his residential home, he pooped on the floor and on his bed. He laughed wildly. He was upset about having to leave his parents to return to his group home. We would have to do extensive work to help Joey believe that he would be safe when he left his parents and that he could trust that they still loved him and would return.

Fear of Someone Knocking on the Door

Negative cognition: If someone knocks on the door, something terrible will happen.
Positive cognition: I'm safe when someone knocks on the door.

At Joey's group home, the TV was often blaring. Loud noises stimulated rage for Joey. Joey's parents wanted to reduce Joey's sensitivity to noise. If someone knocked on his door, Joey assumed something terrible was happening and that there were mean people at the door. We wondered whether we could trace Joey's sensitivity to noise to his early experiences of violence and yelling when he was a baby. We thought that his fear of a knock on the door may have stemmed from the time when his grandmother died and the police had to forcefully break open the door.

We approached the problem by having Joey watch while I knocked on the door of a cabinet. As soon as Joey heard the sound, he pointed to the cabinet: "Scared, it might be mean people." I asked Joey to point to the place in his body where he felt the scared feeling. Joey pointed to his heart. Joey's father began to stroke Joey's arms alternately. After a minute or two, Joey said, "It might be nice people." Then "People will protect me." Then "I'm safe." Ken and I reviewed what Joey should think and do if someone knocked on the door. Joey was never left alone, so we knew it was safe for him to relax and just ask the adult to go to the door.

Death

Negative cognitions: It's my fault. If I don't understand what's happening, something terrible is happening. I'm bad.
Cognitive (educational) interweave: A baby cannot kill an adult.
Positive cognitions: It's not my fault. I'm good.

One day, Joey came into my office, sat on the floor, and muttered, "She died."

"Who died?" I asked and looked at Joey's dad. He shrugged and looked a little puzzled. "Nobody we know died recently."

I remembered Joey's early history—he was a year and a half old when his grandmother died and he was alone with her body. "Are you talking about your grandmother?" I asked. Joey whispered, "Yes."

"Would you like to know what happened?" I asked. Again, Joey whispered, "Yes." I wanted to make sure: "Do you want us to tell the story of what happened when your grandmother died?" He nodded. I asked, "Do you want me to bring out the toy grandma and the toy wheelchair?"

"No!" Joey burst out. He continued to look at the floor and quietly mumbled, "I killed her." "No, you didn't kill her," I said firmly. "A baby cannot kill an adult. Right, Ken?" I wanted his father to reinforce the truth. Ken responded, "Joey has often said he killed her, but he couldn't have killed her—he was just a baby, only a year and a half old. Babies can't kill anyone."

I explained to Ken, "Sometimes babies think they did things they couldn't have done because babies are developmentally egocentric and think they make everything happen just by being there." To Joey, I said, "You didn't kill your grandmother. Nobody killed her; she died. She died because she was old and sick. She had a stroke or a heart attack and she died. You were there when it happened, but it had nothing to do with you."

That kind of distinction—"You were there when it happened, but it had nothing to do with you"—is very hard for children to understand and accept. It's especially difficult for a child if the adult is angry with the child at the time or if there is an argument between adults about the child. So, for Joey, I had to explain over and over in different ways that he didn't kill his grandmother even though he was there when she died.

Ken and I shared the job of telling the story to Joey. The story went something like this: "Once upon a time, when you were very little, you were home alone with your grandmother when all of a sudden she fell out of her wheelchair onto the floor. Did you hear anything?"

"Bang!" Joey added as he slapped the floor.

"You heard her fall on the floor. And you saw blood." Joey pointed to his head and face. He added, "I leaded it all the way to the kitchen." (Here's more evidence of the difficulty of explaining to Joey what happened—he doesn't know the difference between leading and following.) Joey said, "I hitted her." I quickly corrected him with an educational interweave: "A baby can't really hurt an adult by hitting them. You may have hit her to try to wake her up, but she couldn't wake up because she was dead." Ken added, "I think he tried to open her eyelids, because he's always trying to open people's eyelids."

I continued, "Oh Joey, you really wanted her to wake up, and you wanted her to be OK. You were a baby, and you needed an adult to take care of you. It must have been scary to be there." We emphasized that then, no one was there to listen to Joey, but now someone is always there to listen to Joey. It was scary and sad then. Now Joey was safe.

Then Joey seemed to change topics abruptly. He said the name of an aide in his group home who was sick. Joey's expression became blank and he chanted, "Coo, coo" and laughed wildly. The wild laughter was a sign that Joey was dissociating—he was so overwhelmed by the topic of illness that he couldn't "be present." Illness, sadness, death, and danger all seemed to be clumped together in his mind. Trauma work can stir up deep feeling connected to a variety of experiences, especially when there is a history of chronic, complex trauma.

The best thing to do when a child dissociates is to re-establish a feeling of safety. Ken looked at Joey and said, "You didn't hurt your grandmother—you were only a baby. Little babies sit in strollers and get pushed around in the stroller. They eat and sleep and play. Babies are too little to hurt anybody."

I added, "If your mom and dad had known about you then, they would have been right there to take care of you, right Ken?" Ken's voice got soft, "If we had known, your mom and I would have been there to take care of you. We would have picked you up and taken care of you. We would have made sure you had attention and food and clean diapers. Who loves you, Joey?"

Until that point, Joey had not allowed any ABS. After Ken asked "Who loves you?" Joey's body visibly relaxed, and Joey said to his dad, "You do." "That's right," Ken confirmed. "Your mom and I love you so much." Then Joey allowed Ken to alternately stroke both sides of his back while we told the story again. After we were finished, Joey looked relieved, and I asked him, "How does it feel to know you didn't kill your grandmother?"

"Good," he sighed.

Biting the Baby

Negative cognitions: I'm bad. It's my fault I bit the baby. I deserve to be punished.

Positive cognitions: I'm good. An angry baby doesn't know how to behave. It wasn't my fault. Now I have parents and aides who keep me and other children safe. I deserve to feel good.

The next week was rough. Joey was in a terrible mood, and he pushed limits and swore a lot. When he came to see me, he wanted to hear the story of when he bit the baby and got moved to another foster home. Whenever Joey talked about hurting someone, he laughed as if he were a different person. The pain of the memory was so great that Joey opted not to be conscious and aware. Whenever Joey was scared, he became angry and aggressive. Whenever he started to feel good, he punished himself, as if he did not deserve good feelings.

I knew it was important to desensitize and reprocess Joey's memory of biting the baby. Joey thought he had killed the baby. Since Joey had a language-processing problem and didn't understand the difference between "kill" and "die," he didn't know whether he hurt the baby or not. Although Joey injured the baby and the baby had to go to the hospital, the baby certainly didn't die.

In fact, given Joey's history, an adult should have been supervising Joey closely and should have protected the baby. However, I didn't want to ask Joey, "Whose responsibility was it to protect the baby?" and I didn't want to say that the adult should have made sure that Joey and the baby were safe. Joey needed to trust adults, and pointing out that the adult was responsible for the baby's injury would not have been helpful to Joey. An adult remembering biting a child years before, on the other hand, might feel relieved to know that it wasn't his fault. The adult might feel anger toward the adult who should have been supervising more closely, but that anger could also be processed to adaptive resolution.

So far, I had learned some things about Joey that remained constant throughout our work together. I learned that Joey would not allow desensitization and reprocessing of a memory until he had some understanding of what had happened (i.e., until the confusion was reduced). His language-processing problems compounded the confusion. Nevertheless, he was able to point to the place in his body where he experienced his feelings, and his EMDR processing proceeded normally.

His recurrent themes were that he was bad, that he was at fault, that confusion was dangerous, and that he needed reassurance that he was lovable. He needed repeated reassurance that someone would always take care of him.

It was apparent that Joey was dissociative. He sometimes assumed the voices and personas of various people: a baby, a member of the Gestapo, or some of his autistic friends at his residential home, and sometimes he had his own voice. I thought that he had dissociative identity disorder (DID), also known as multiple personalities. The "real" Joey made it very clear that he was present when he had a calm voice and could do EMDR work. He demonstrated dissociation by singing, laughing wildly, or talking in an alternate voice. When he was dissociated, I focused on establishing safety by reminding him that his parents loved him and always took care of him. When he was fully present, we addressed a traumatic memory and focused on improving his attachment with his parents. I started each session by talking about and strengthening whatever had gone well for Joey that week.

Little by little, clearing up confusion helped make Joey available for learning. If confusion triggers anxiety, it is impossible to learn. Being able to tolerate not knowing, not understanding, and confusion are essential parts of the learning process. One day Joey came to me bouncing up and down, fidgeting with his hands, and smiling: "Dr. Lovett, I have a surprise for you!" Joey handed me a letter written in his uneven printing. He said, "My mom told me how to spell words, and I wrote a letter for you." The letter said, "Dear Dr. Lovett, My dream is reading a book. Love, Joey." At 10 years old, Joey was beginning to learn to read and write the alphabet. I was thrilled by his accomplishment.

Joey frequently wanted to hear a story of when he was a baby. He was very concerned about the mean man and woman, his version of his birth story. He liked that the doctors and nurses helped. Over several years, we addressed many issues: his memory of biting the baby in a foster home, the illness of a friend, the death of a friend and his grandparents, sexual abuse when he was in an emergency shelter, his distress when he didn't get attention, his distress when he didn't get food, his many fears, his out-of-control behavior, his urges to run away, his memories of being restrained in the emergency room multiple times, and his memories of his nine psychiatric hospitalizations. I always explained to him what happened and reminded him that the past was the past and that what's different now is that he has parents and helpers who would take care of him.

Joey at 19, Triggered by Crowds of People

Negative cognition: I am in danger if I see a crowd of people.
Positive cognitions: I am an adult now. I'm safe even when I see a crowd of people.

Recently, Joey asked his dad if he could come see me after a year-long hiatus in our visits. Joey felt bad that he had made such a big scene at church. He had been triggered by the crowd of people at church. All of a sudden, he became like a member of the Gestapo (perhaps something he saw on TV), yelling, "Kill everyone!" (naming various minority groups). "Stab them," he yelled as he laughed wildly. The police were called and eventually Joey calmed down. I asked Joey if it was OK if we talked about when he was a baby, and crowds and chaos were scary and even dangerous to him.

Nineteen-year-old, two-hundred-fifty-pound Joey nodded and curled up close to his dad. His dad explained, "I think when Joey was a little baby, there were probably crowds of strangers around when his birth mom was doing drugs, and he got neglected or locked in the closet."

"I bet he was scared," I empathized. "Joey, where do you feel the scared feeling in your body when you think about the scared little baby with a crowd of strangers around?" Joey pointed to his heart and motioned for his father to alternately stroke his eyelids.

Joey's dad added, "I bet he was angry too." Joey exclaimed, "I was so angry I thought I would explode!" I asked Joey where he felt that "so angry I thought I would explode" feeling. He pointed to his heart, and his dad resumed gently stroking his eyes. Then Joey began laughing wildly. His giddy laughter was an indication that he was dissociating and that a terrified fragment of his personality was letting us know that the pain was intolerable. I asked Joey to open his eyes and notice where he was. I wanted to help him orient to the safety of the present moment. "Your office," he responded as he settled down and resumed processing baby Joey's anger. By addressing Joey's experiences as an infant and giving voice to his distraught "baby parts" as well as the furious adult introjects that inhabited him, Joey's "parts" began to be integrated and Joey could tolerate old, painful memories.

When asking Joey to orient to place (my office) and time ("How old are you now?"), I asked him to look at his dad: "Who loves Joey?" "Joey's mom and I love Joey," his dad responded, smiling.

I questioned Joey, "And how old are you now?" "Nineteen," Joey answered in his adult voice. I wanted Joey to maintain dual attention—to be present in my office as a 19-year-old man while remembering, or imagining, baby Joey who was so distraught. We imagined comforting baby Joey and empathizing: "Of course he was scared and angry—any baby would have felt scared and angry."

Ken offered a story about how he would have taken care of baby Joey, and we reassured "baby Joey" that everything would be OK. Ken's voice was soft and comforting as he imagined soothing "baby Joey": "You will grow up to have parents who love you and take care of you, and friends and family and teachers who love you. You will have amazing experiences, like riding a horse and piloting a plane (with a licensed pilot in control). You will go to camp and ride a three-wheeled bike. You will even wear a tux and go to a prom." After hearing that, Joey said his "baby self" felt much more relaxed and safe. I reassured Joey that we would continue to help "baby Joey" grow up, and he nodded solemnly.

Ken and Alison had been amazing, dedicated parents during their 16 years raising Joey. I asked Joey's dad how he had learned to be such an effective parent. Ken said, "I noticed that when I got frustrated or angry, Joey became scared and frustrated and angry, and his bad behaviors escalated. All those times when Joey was in the hospital on the psychiatric ward, I observed the nurses. The most effective nurses were calm and clear about their expectations and talked in a very matter-of-fact way. They used rewards rather than punishments, and Joey responded really well to their calm manner."

In addition to having parents who were masters of calm parenting, Joey was fortunate to have great aides in his most recent group home. One aide frequently reminded Joey that he is a "good man." He taught him to talk respectfully and to calm himself through meditation. Good, dedicated parents, skilled aides, effective therapy, and medication all helped Joey.

Originally, I saw Joey weekly for several years, and now, 10 years later, I see him occasionally. He has never had a psychiatric hospitalization since we started our work together. His tantrums have decreased, and his relationship with his parents and friends has improved a lot. Nevertheless, Joey will need a one-to-one aide for the rest of his life to keep him safe. Twenty-year-old Joey hopes to be a police officer and to get married and have children someday.

Perspective

Hundreds of millions of children around the world are victims of abuse, neglect, and exploitation, according to UNICEF reports. In the United States alone, more than 3 million children are reported to official agencies for severe maltreatment in any given year. U.S. Department of Health and Human Services (2013) surveys indicate that this figure grossly underestimates the true extent of the problem, as more than one-third of adults in the United States report having experienced physical abuse, sexual abuse, emotional abuse, and/or neglect as a child (Polonko, 2005).

According to the 2012 Child Maltreatment Report (National Child Abuse and Neglect Data System [NCANDS]), a yearly federal report based on submission by state Child Protective Services (CPS) agencies, more than a quarter of the victims were younger than three years old. The cases were substantiated as follows: More than 75 percent were neglected, 18.3 percent were physically abused, and 9.3 percent were sexually abused.[1]

While Joey's symptoms were more severe than those of many children who have suffered abuse and other early childhood trauma, the principles guiding his therapy can be applied to therapy with other children with a history of complex trauma.

Principles for Treating Children for Complex Trauma and Attachment

1. When you see healthy behavior, encourage and reinforce it with ABS.
2. When you see "unhealthy" behavior, think about underlying negative beliefs sustaining the detrimental behavior. Think of a corrective thought (positive cognition) that addresses the current behavior as well as the original trauma.
3. Provide educational interweaves during the course of EMDR.
4. Strengthen positive experiences and positive cognitions as they arise.
5. Use EMDR to support attachment and build trust in caregiving adults.

6. Use desensitization and reprocessing phases of EMDR to lift shame and anxiety that have resulted from traumatic experiences.
7. When you observe dissociation, work to establish safety and comfort before attempting trauma processing.
8. Develop a healing narrative about the child's life. Use the narrative to dispel the child's confusion about what happened to him and to help him distinguish between now (when he's safe) and then (when he was in danger).
9. Utilize creative opportunities for healing: Art, play therapy, drama, and sand tray work can be used to express feelings, as well as provide targets for desensitizing and reprocessing traumatic experiences.
10. Teach skills for calming and self-soothing, including mindfulness training.

The goals of Joey's therapy were to calm him so that he could cope with the typical day-to-day experiences of disappointment, to develop his trust in adults to help him and take care of him, and to integrate fragmented parts of his personality so that he could become more resilient, happier, and safe.

Joey's therapy proceeded through many phases, always following what was current for Joey as reported by his parents and confirmed by Joey. Initially, we worked only on circumscribed current fears and disruptive incidents and stayed very present-oriented (e.g., Joey's intense desire to have a particular parking space and the ensuing prolonged rage when he couldn't have the parking space he wanted). Every time, we made sense of his distressed behavior, but without condoning it. Our message to Joey was that his feelings were understandable but that his behavior could be calm because he was currently safe. EMDR was the ideal therapy for desensitizing memories and reprocessing beliefs to reinforce Joey's current safety. Focusing on relatively small but behaviorally significant incidents, such as tantrums over a parking space, made it easy for us to see and acknowledge progress.

We also addressed each of Joey's irrational fears, such as his fear that someone was in his closet. His irrational fears tended to dissolve quickly, sometimes with artwork, using the "folded paper" technique.

As Joey gave us clues that he was thinking about the past (i.e., when he came into my office and said, "She died," referring to his grandmother), we talked about experiences that had traumatized Joey early in life. We told stories to make sense of the confusion, which was always a trigger for Joey. Joey needed to hear over and over that what happened was not his fault and that he was good and lovable even though traumatic events had happened in his life.

Therapy with children with developmental and cognitive disabilities proceeds slowly. It is essential to target each incident individually and not to expect generalization of a sense of safety until dozens of incidents have been desensitized and reprocessed. Especially when working on traumatic early childhood memories, it may be necessary to revisit the same incident repeatedly, each time focusing on more detail.

With each step of trauma resolution, Joey felt closer to his parents and was more able to cooperate with them. Resolving trauma facilitates healthy attachment, and more secure attachment provides a holding environment for deeper trauma therapy. Parent participation in therapy, EMDR processing, cooperation games, and shared development of Joey's life story all contributed to improved relationships between Joey and his parents, professionals and other adults, and peers.

Note

1 See www.acf.hhs.gov/programs/cb/research-data-technology/statistics-research/child-maltreatment.

9

VIVIAN AND JENNY
Sisters' Different Expressions of Trauma

Children who spent their infancy in an orphanage generally display a range of "trauma-informed behaviors," including unrelenting attention seeking, the need for having "their own way," registering comments and corrections as criticism, distress at discarding anything, acute sensitivity to perceived unfairness, extreme mood fluctuations, and easily provoked anger or anxiety. This is the story of adopted sisters who were both challenging for their parents, but in very different ways.

Vivian and Jenny

Renee and Elliot adopted seven-year-old Vivian from an orphanage in China when she was 10 months old, and they adopted four-year-old Jenny from a different orphanage in the same country when she was 17 months old. Elliot was sweating just describing their home life: "The four of us have discovered an amazing ability to get on one another's nerves. I don't even know where to start . . ." Renee took over: "We need help with each girl individually and both girls together. The girls each have their own unique problems, and they're terribly jealous of one another." Elliot observed, "When Jenny gets attention from one of us, Vivian says, 'Send her back to the orphanage.' That makes it awfully hard for either of us to be with both girls. It's actually worse when the four of us are together because then Renee and I argue about how to handle them."

Renee and Elliot both worked full time. They tried to be home in time to put the girls to bed most evenings, and they were home on the weekends. They had a good babysitter who didn't have much trouble with the girls. As is typical for most adopted children, Vivian and Jenny seemed to save their most extreme rages for their parents.

Elliot admitted, "We're having a rough patch in our marriage. I get annoyed with how Renee handles situations with the girls, and Renee gets angry with me if I intervene. I'm stricter than she is, but I honestly don't think we should be bending over backward to do everything to make the girls happy every minute. No matter what we do, they seem

116

to want more." Renee looked exasperated: "When Elliott and I start arguing, the girls jump in and try to tell us what to do, and then they cry, and Elliott and I are left feeling guilty."

Renee sighed, "We've started couples counseling. I think that we can best use our time here if we get help with each of the girls, especially Vivian." Elliot concurred, "If they behave better, we'll fight less."

Renee started telling me about four-year-old Jenny: "She's very verbal about all of her needs and wants, but when she doesn't get her way, she hits and bites and screams." Renee paused for a moment and then reflected, "Even though Jenny becomes physically aggressive, at least we know what she's upset about because she tells us." Renee and Elliot agreed that Jenny was a "pleaser" and highly sensitive to any criticism. If they reprimanded her at all, she cried hysterically. Jenny was articulate. She expressed her feelings about her adoption: "I feel like somebody threw me out—like I was garbage." Jenny was easier for her parents to understand, and she responded well to their positive attention.

Elliot focused the discussion: "Let's talk about Vivian now because she has rages that are the most difficult to manage—right now they feel impossible to manage, and she is very controlling, insisting that everything be just the way she wants. She and Renee butt heads all the time." Renee frowned: "Her other response to stress is that she sulks and refuses to say what's bothering her, and I feel helpless. Nobody figured out what I needed when I was a kid, and I really don't know how to figure out what she needs. Maybe I identify with her. I find myself just trying to solve problems for her, but she doesn't accept my solutions."

Vivian often worried to her parents, "Are you going to send me back to China?" Renee looked perturbed: "Vivian is a perfectionist, and if she draws something she doesn't like, she scribbles over it, tears it up, and cries. One day she saw she had a spot on her blouse and said, 'If it doesn't come out, I'll kill myself.' It's really scary to hear your child talk like that."

Elliot scratched his head as he pondered the situation: "Vivian becomes distraught whenever we get rid of anything, even a used piece of scrap paper. That's really tough for Renee and me because we both want our home to be uncluttered." Renee sighed, "We don't have a lot of closet space, so we can't keep extra stuff, and there's no use for a lot of the stuff she wants to keep anyway. I've even found lots of candy wrappers in her closet."

Adoption was a difficult theme for Vivian. She was acutely aware that she looked different from her parents, and she didn't want to talk about adoption. Some of the children I see can't bear to hear the word "adoption," don't want to hear anything about their life story, and try to shut everything about adoption out of their awareness. Such avoidance of the idea of adoption or the sound of the word "adoption" indicates debilitating pain.

Here is what we know about Vivian's early history: She was one month old when she was left in a hospital in China. She was taken to an orphanage with 400 children. There were 6 to 10 women to care for 50 babies. Imagine one woman taking care of five babies (and sometimes as many as nine babies)! Imagine feeding so many mouths, changing so many diapers, and bathing and dressing so many bodies. There wouldn't be enough time to learn the communication signals of each infant. There wouldn't be much time left for cuddling or playing. Vivian had survived because her most basic needs were met, but barely.

We don't have any other history. From the first time Renee picked Vivian up, Vivian clung to Renee and didn't want her out of sight. Renee thought this meant that Vivian was well attached to her. Yes, Vivian was physically attached, but she had an insecure emotional attachment to Renee. Because of her early history of loss, Vivian still didn't trust that she could count on anyone she cared about to keep coming back to her.

Renee emphasized, "I want both girls to learn to deal with other children's mean comments and to stop tormenting one another with teasing." Whenever Vivian was teased at school, she cried, "I want to go back to China." Then Vivian came home from school and teased Jenny. Before long, both girls were crying.

In preschool, a little boy told Vivian that Renee was not her real mother. Vivian cried and cried and told her mother, "I wish I had white skin like you." Renee didn't hesitate to respond, "I wish I had skin like you." In kindergarten, Vivian passed on the insult to another girl, telling her that she wouldn't play with her because her skin was "too dark."

The first time I met with the whole family, I began by eliciting the parents' appreciation for their children. Renee said that Vivian was a good helper and that Jenny woke up happy in the morning. Both girls liked to play dress-up and play house. Elliot said that Vivian could be kind and cooperative and that Jenny shared her toys.

Vivian and Jenny didn't have anything nice to say about their parents. Vivian fiddled with her shiny, long, dark ponytail as she looked at me while pointing to her mother: "She's mean." Vivian turned to her parents: "You two don't understand me. You are disgusting. You are both weird. You two are boring, especially when you chat on the phone." I asked her to explain. "Mommy is mean—she got mad at Daddy and kicked him out of the car once. They argue. Mommy called Daddy a bad name."

I knew that Renee was already in individual therapy and the couple had started couple's therapy. My job was to see whether I could help the parents get along better by helping their children behave better and relieve their stress. Children tend to behave better when they are bonded more positively to their parents. Challenging children who cling, scream, and are chronically dissatisfied can stress even the best marriage.

118

When asked what she would like to have go easier, Vivian answered, "I want Mom and Dad to take a day off from work. I want Mom not to go to work at all." So maybe a lot of the girls' anger was kindled by their parents' long hours away from home. I was happy that Vivian was able to say that she wanted more time with her parents.

When I asked Elliott what he wanted to go better for his family, he looked at his daughters: "I want the girls to listen." Then Renee stated her wish: "I want to spend special time alone with each of the girls." Vivian agreed that she wanted both of those things—better cooperation and more time with her parents. Starting with a shared goal is a good start.

During my first visit with Renee and Vivian, I asked Vivian to imagine a "safe place." She pictured her backyard with her mom pushing her in the swing on a warm spring day, with fragrant flowers blooming. I taught Vivian and Renee the "butterfly hug."

After that, Vivian looked around the room and told me again that her parents argued a lot. We talked about a "no name-calling" rule. Seven-year-old children tend to respect rules, and both Renee and Vivian thought it was a good idea for their whole family.

Over the weekend, the family went to the mountains, where they played in a stream and picked wildflowers and hiked a little. They had a good time together. When they returned to my office, Vivian played in the sand tray. Renee and I sat with her, keeping her company and watching quietly as she chose toy figures, put them back, lined them up, then looked around for something else to put in the sand tray. She seemed undecided about which toys to choose and how to play. Afterward, Renee called to leave me a message: "It was really good to just be with Vivian while she played. At home, I would have interrupted Vivian's play to help her whenever she had a hard time deciding something."

Renee had gotten used to taking over play to avert conflict. Often, Vivian yelled at Jenny and broke her crayon, then Jenny got mad and broke Vivian's crayon, then Vivian pinched Jenny. Soon everyone was crying, and Jenny was screaming at her mother, "You love Vivian better!"

In another session, I wondered aloud how Vivian liked to be comforted and what helped her feel loved. Renee didn't really know because she had not been comforted as a child, and she had no idea what would comfort Vivian. I made some suggestions, Renee tried them, and before long we came up with a list of soothing resources for Vivian. She liked it when her mom held her, gave her a foot or hand massage, sang to her, or read her poetry. We had begun to develop a "tool kit" for comforting, soothing, and settling Vivian.

Over the next two years, I intermittently worked with Vivian and Jenny and their parents. We spent time helping the girls understand what adoption meant and figuring out and practicing what to say when kids asked, "How did you get adopted?" or "Why don't you look like your parents?" or said, "That isn't your real mom." We worked on developing ways that Renee could soothe her children and ways the girls could soothe themselves.

At the children's insistence, we often played a variation of hide and seek with objects they buried in the sand. They were so delighted every time we found their buried treasure. They beamed as if they themselves had been found after a long absence. This is very typical play for children with attachment issues. Everyone loves being found with an enthusiastic smile.

The girls each took turns cuddling with their mom and playing the lollypop game (see Chapter 12), which we used as an opportunity to strengthen Renee's bond with her daughters and their attachment to her. We played cooperation games—like the animal cracker game and the bubble game (see Chapter 12). Elliot came in with his daughters and got to know them better, listening to them talk about things that happened in the family.

Both parents learned to "partner" with their children instead of giving "time out." They learned to notice when their daughters were "miscuing"— acting as if they wanted distance when in fact they wanted their parent to be close to them.

Vivian often came into my office sulking, turned her back to her mother and me, and played in the sand tray. Renee said that Vivian often wouldn't respond to her and gave her the "cold shoulder treatment." I asked Renee how that made her feel. Renee replied, "Lonely and sad." I asked Vivian if she were feeling lonely and sad too. Vivian nodded slowly without looking at us.

I mentioned that I thought Vivian was giving us a tiny experience of how lonely and sad she felt sometimes. I wondered out loud if Vivian was doing it so Renee would have some idea of how she was feeling. Vivian nodded and looked shyly at her mother.

When Vivian didn't want to talk, she seemed to want Renee and me to guess how she was feeling and why. I taught Vivian to give thumb signals so that she would have a response even if she didn't feel like talking. Thumb up meant "yes." Thumb down meant "no." Thumb to the right meant "I don't know" and thumb to the left meant "maybe so."

We also figured out a system for Renee to follow when Vivian had strong negative feelings. First, Renee would ask or guess what happened, then she would identify what Vivian was feeling (and Vivian could use thumb signals if necessary until her mother guessed the right feeling). Then Renee would verbalize the feelings, and, finally, she and Vivian would figure out what her mom could do to help. Vivian was much happier once we had a procedure in place.

After Renee got pretty good at identifying what triggered Vivian's upset, we worked on helping Vivian to say what happened and how she was feeling. It became clear that Vivian wanted her mom to figure out how she felt. Then Renee could say either "Do you want to talk about what happened?" or "I want to talk about what happened." But if she gave Vivian the choice of whether or not she wanted to talk, she had to respect Vivian's choice. It drove Vivian crazy when Renee talked about it even after Vivian had said, "No, I don't want to talk about it."

I taught Renee and Vivian that it's a child's job to ask for what she wants, and it's a parent's job to give a "yes" or "no" answer. It's always OK to ask for what you want, but know that the answer will sometimes be "no." Vivian also learned to say, "I want some alone time with you, Mom."

Both parents came for a session with both girls to discuss what they were going to do about both girls' constant need for attention and jealousy if one girl momentarily got more attention than the other. For example, when Jenny had a fever and got to stay home from school, Vivian proclaimed, "Unfair!" and was furious that she didn't get to stay home too. Her parents tried to convince her that it was no fun to be sick, but that was beside the point. Vivian wanted a full day of her mom's attention, and she was willing to be sick if that was the way to get it.

I suggested that we work on helping each girl feel loved, even when their parents were paying attention to the other. I asked Elliot and Renee to hold and cuddle Vivian while Jenny and I were on the other side of the room, playing in the sand tray. I showed Renee and Elliott how to play the lollypop game with Vivian and asked them to give Vivian their full attention. While Jenny played with me and Vivian basked in her parents' attention, I asked Elliot and Renee if they were still thinking about Jenny and caring about her, even though they were with Vivian and weren't looking at Jenny. They responded in unison, "Yes!" Then I stood behind Jenny as she played and tapped her shoulders as I said, "Your parents are thinking about you and caring about you even though they're paying attention to Jenny."

Over the course of half an hour, while Jenny played in the sand tray, I used bilateral stimulation to strengthen Jenny's beliefs that she could be OK, even when her parents weren't paying attention to her; that she could feel them caring, even when she had her eyes closed; and that she was lovable and important, even when her parents paid attention to her sister. After half an hour, Jenny and Vivian switched places. Jenny got her parents' full attention, and Vivian played on the other side of the room. I used bilateral stimulation to strengthen Vivian's sense of well-being, even when her sister was getting attention.

After that, tension eased at home. When the girls began to squabble about the other getting more attention, Renee looked each one in the eyes and said, "Remember, you are still lovable and important to me even when I'm paying attention to her," while pointing to the other sister. Usually they all giggled when she looked at one girl and pointed to the other.

After about six months, Renee and Elliott and I met to discuss Vivian's progress and to outline our next goals. Renee said, "Vivian still likes things in order, but she doesn't have a meltdown if things are not lined up perfectly. She doesn't cry if we have to get rid of a candy wrapper after she's finished eating the candy." I was glad Vivian was less determined to be in control of everything all the time. Elliott catalogued some progress too: "Vivian rages less frequently and with less intensity. Her tantrums don't last as long as they used to. She uses words to express her feelings more." Renee said proudly, "And I know to give her more attention and to give her 'time in' instead of 'time out' when she misbehaves." Elliott smiled at his wife: "Now that the girls are doing better, Renee and I are getting along better too."

Renee and Vivian and I met the day before their family and friends got together to celebrate Vivian's "adoption day" anniversary. We practiced questions Vivian's friends from school might ask her so she could rehearse her answers. I asked Vivian, "If someone asks you 'Why do you look different from your mom?' what could you say?" Vivian stood up tall and said, "It doesn't matter; we're still family."

Perspective

Two girls adopted by the same family had different ways of expressing their distress, yet there were similar beliefs underlying their symptoms. Initially, both girls felt they were bad, that they desperately needed attention, and that they couldn't tolerate not having what they wanted. Jenny was very vocal about her feelings, needs, and wants. Vivian wanted her parents to figure out what she was experiencing, thinking, feeling, and needing.

Teaching the parents to "read" their children and to understand their needs, guiding them in discovering ways to soothe each child, and EMDR processing to take the charge off of distressing incidents helped this whole family. As Vivian became more confident that her parents "got" her experiences, she began to treat her little sister better. Working with both parents and both girls together provided the opportunity for each girl to have an experience of receiving all of both parents' attention, as well as the experience of feeling connected and loved even when both parents paid attention to the other sibling.

10

OLLIE

The Newborn Intensive Care Graduate

Half a million babies in the United States—approximately one in eight—are born prematurely each year.[1] Those that are born with respiratory distress or other physical problems are treated in the neonatal intensive care unit (NICU) until they are stable and no longer need life support or constant medical care. Ollie is a NICU graduate who survived through seven months of in-hospital care.

My own medical training familiarized me with the environment of the NICU, and this experience was invaluable for deciphering Ollie's mysterious behaviors. During my pediatric internship and residency, I found the NICU intimidating: I was met by surprisingly loud, cacophonous sounds from machinery, glaring lights, beeping monitors, alarms on ventilators and pumps, hanging bags filled with fluid and medications, and a flurry of doctors, nurses, and frightened parents. The urgency of impending disaster was omnipresent in the NICU, and at least several times a day a tight voice would announce, "The baby crashed," sending doctors and nurses hurrying to resuscitate a baby.

The NICU was full of babies the size of my hand. The sickest babies lay on warming beds that would accommodate respirator equipment and were easily accessible for medical procedures. When babies became more stable, they were housed in individual Isolettes—clear, Plexiglas containers with two round portals on each side so that nurses, doctors, and parents could access the baby. Each baby was connected to at least one machine, and usually more, to provide life support and monitoring of vital signs such as heart rate, respiration, and temperature.

The most premature babies, with their translucent skin and tubes and wires everywhere, looked like little aliens—almost unrecognizable as human babies. No wonder their parents had stunned expressions on their faces. This was not the baby they had dreamed would be theirs. Grief was palpable in the air.

Numerous articles have been written about parents (especially mothers) who develop posttraumatic stress disorder (PTSD) as a result of having premature babies requiring intensive care. Yet there is very little written about the effects of that early trauma on the infants themselves. NICU graduates—that is, babies who are finally strong enough to go home—are sometimes given medical diagnoses that are really part of a posttraumatic stress disorder. For example, it is not uncommon to see a diagnosis of "oral aversion" in a baby who has spent time on a respirator. Recognizing this behavior of intolerance of anything touching the mouth as a posttraumatic symptom rather than a sensory processing disorder indicates the need for trauma therapy, not just eating therapy or occupational therapy. Yet most NICU graduates with posttraumatic symptoms never receive the benefit of trauma therapy.

Ollie

Ollie was a very wanted baby, born to a healthy, loving single mom with a substantial support system of family and friends. His mother ate well, exercised, and received prenatal care from conception. She never used drugs or alcohol. She did everything right. Like most babies born prematurely, there was no known cause for Ollie's early arrival. Nobody knows how many premature babies go on to develop posttraumatic symptoms stemming from their time in the NICU. But Ollie's story indicates that the procedures and experiences that babies undergo in the NICU can have profound effects on their development and on their behavior.

Ollie was born at 27 weeks' gestation by emergency Cesarean section, and he required hospitalization for seven months. For the first three months of Ollie's life, he required a ventilator, a machine that mechanically forced oxygenated air into his lungs to allow him to breathe. He needed tape all over his cheeks to hold the ventilator tube and a nasogastric tube in place. He had breathing disorders (respiratory distress syndrome and bronchopulmonary dysplasia), problems that were not surprising for an infant born so early. He required heart surgery to make his underdeveloped heart function properly. He had multiple cardiac arrests requiring resuscitation. Nurses drew blood from the heels of his feet so many times that his heels were covered with scars. He was unable to suck, so he was given food through a tube threaded through his nose to his stomach, which was later replaced with a gastrostomy tube surgically inserted into his stomach.

Veronica brought her son Ollie to me at age three and half because he refused to eat. Despite a year of "eating therapy" focused on getting Ollie to chew, he still wouldn't even touch food or look at it. He received 80 percent of his nutrition through a gastrostomy tube, a feeding tube inserted directly through his abdomen into his stomach. The other 20 percent he received by being spoon-fed baby food while being distracted by a video or book.

Veronica, who was a computer programmer, worked at home so that she could spend every free minute with her son. The strain of taking care of a medically fragile child, as well as working, was visible on Veronica's face. She looked much older than her 30 years could account for. Veronica obviously had a lot of experience explaining Ollie's medical problems to healthcare professionals. She recited, "Ollie has been diagnosed with lung damage called bronchopulmonary dysplasia, a surgically repaired heart defect called patent ductus arteriosus, ataxic cerebral palsy (a term for brain damage that causes poor coordination and decreased muscle tone), gastroesophageal reflux, an eye problem called retinopathy of prematurity, oral defensiveness, and sensory avoidance." The list of diagnoses was long, but I noticed that it did not include posttraumatic stress disorder or any other label that connected any of his symptoms to early trauma.

Ollie was discharged from the hospital with a list of diagnoses and an astounding 26 daily medication doses, supplemental oxygen, a gastrostomy tube, and daily home visits from a nurse. He had poor feeding and severe gastroesophageal reflux, which caused him to vomit so frequently that his mother had to accompany him everywhere with a bucket.

Veronica had read Francine Shapiro's first book, *EMDR: The Breakthrough Eye Movement Therapy for Overcoming Anxiety, Stress, and Trauma* (Shapiro, 1998): "I read that book because I felt so stressed and wanted something to help me. I read the section about your work with children. I thought about Ollie's stress and trauma. I wondered whether Ollie's reluctance to eat was a posttraumatic symptom related to the first three months of his life when he required a ventilator in order to breathe, and needed a nasogastric tube so he could receive his nourishment in liquid form."

Meeting Ollie

When I first met Ollie, he lay on the floor of my office and silently moved a toy car back and forth in front of his face. He didn't seem to notice anyone or anything else around him. He didn't respond to my greeting or my offer of a toy truck, even though I sat on the floor beside him and looked directly at him. I could understand why his mother was so concerned about him!

But not eating was just one of many behavioral issues. Ollie barely talked. When he did talk, he usually whispered, "What is it?" or "What's happening?" or "Crash." Veronica enumerated some of his troubles: "Ollie screams when he has a T-shirt pulled over his head, when the car window is open, when he sees fluorescent lights, when he hears any mechanical noises, and when he doesn't get his way." Veronica continued to tell me that Ollie appeared afraid of toys and wanted her to touch a toy first and then hand it to him. He didn't seem to notice any of his own body sensations, and he didn't seem to feel pain. I was astounded to see

125

that he could lie on my office floor on top of a pile of little metal cars and airplanes with their sharp wings without wincing.

When I met Ollie, my initial reaction to him was one of despair. How could I help a child with so many overwhelming problems? Over the years, I have learned to pay attention to my initial emotional reaction when I meet a new patient. When I meet someone in my office, my job is to listen deeply, with all of my senses, to learn about the person who has come to see me, to follow his lead like a dance partner, to connect his current symptoms with earlier experiences, and then to use everything I know to help him solve problems. The sense of despair I felt upon meeting Ollie seemed to be a visceral indication of his feeling of helplessness.

Veronica told me sadly, "He's like a kernel hiding deep inside himself." Veronica had also had a very difficult time during Ollie's stay in the NICU. Ollie's birth coincided with Veronica's mother's sudden death, leaving Veronica depressed and distraught. When describing Ollie's behavioral problems, Veronica realized that she must have transmitted her deep sadness and despair to her infant son. She acknowledged that his life-threatening condition terrified her: "He was so tiny and fragile, and he kept almost dying. He was resuscitated many times, and I just didn't know whether he would make it."

At age six months, Ollie had a procedure called direct laryngoscopy that involved inserting a tube with a light into his throat so that the doctor could view his vocal cords directly. The procedure, done without anesthesia, is an experience adults have described as terrifying because they are uncomfortable, can't move, and can't talk. Veronica remembered that Ollie was petrified when the laryngoscopy tube went down his throat: "I was in the room with him, and his eyes were wide open and bulging. The doctor was nice about explaining to me what he was doing, but I'm not sure that helped Ollie. He must have felt like he was suffocating. Afterward, he looked like a person who has just been mugged."

When I saw Ollie for the first time in my office, I got down on the floor and lay in a position that was the mirror image of Ollie's position. I started imitating Ollie by moving a toy car back and forth in front of my face. In a few minutes I felt more relaxed and realized that Ollie was giving himself the kind of eye movement we use for soothing during EMDR. His ability to self-soothe was a good starting place for his treatment. I wanted to help this frightened little boy develop his ability to calm himself.

I observed what Ollie was doing and decided to reinforce any behavior that was normal. When Ollie looked at toys, I alternately tapped his feet or knees or shoulders while saying, "It's OK to play," to strengthen his positive feelings. What Ollie was doing was repetitive movement— not normal play for a three-year-old, but rather a hallmark of an unresolved trauma. I wanted to help Ollie play and use his imagination in a

126

way that would help him resolve his trauma, and EMDR was the tool I used to do so.

It's OK to Play; It's OK to Talk

I saw Ollie once a week, and I spent the first three months following him around the room tapping his hands or knees or feet whenever he did something appropriate. I just wanted Ollie to know that he was alive! The positive beliefs I wanted to strengthen initially were "It's OK to talk," "It's OK to touch things," and "It's OK to play with toys." I wanted to let Ollie know that it was safe for him to come out of hiding.

When he did begin to touch toys, Ollie swept them off the shelf onto the floor and quietly said, "Crash." I recalled that Ollie was born by "crash" C-section. "Crash" is the term that doctors use for a life-threatening emergency. "Crash" is also used in the NICU when a baby's condition has deteriorated rapidly and an immediate response is necessary. Ollie must have heard the word "crash" frequently when he was in the NICU. I was beginning to understand the many aspects of trauma that Ollie had experienced in his first seven months.

One day, I reinforced everything that Ollie said with the words "It's OK to talk." That next evening, I received an excited call from Veronica: "Ollie slept on the way home from your office, and when he woke up he started talking and talked for 45 minutes without stopping!" That caught our attention! We were clearly making important progress with EMDR. That was the breakthrough that convinced me that EMDR "resource enhancement" could be one of the therapeutic modalities that could help, even without targeting traumatic memories.

Overcoming the Fear of Food

Since Veronica had brought Ollie to me specifically to help him to eat normally, I decided to bring in a lunchbox with some food that Veronica said he might taste. Ollie looked at the lunchbox curiously: "What is this?" I opened the lid and offered a choice: "It's a lunchbox, and I'll show you what's inside. Do you want to see the Coco Puffs or the Cheerios?" Ollie made fearful whining sounds and tried to close the lunchbox lid. I held the lunchbox open as I tapped his knees and said, "It's safe to look at food. It's OK to say what you want. It's OK to look." Ollie visibly relaxed.

I began to open the bag of Cheerios: "How about I'll start it, and then you pull it the rest of the way open? You open it the rest of the way. Good job. You're getting the Cheerios. Will you put them in the bowl, please?" Ollie poured the Cheerios in the bowl and then immediately dumped them on the floor. Though he made a mess, at least he was taking control of the food instead of being fearful at the sight of it.

I offered food on several subsequent visits. After Ollie became comfortable looking at food, the next step was to encourage him to touch food. We used the same process, and I repeated, "It's OK to touch food." After a few sessions, Ollie reached for a pretzel I offered him, and he snapped it in two pieces.

At last, Ollie began to taste food. One day he came into my office and lay on his back with a faraway expression, holding a small pretzel near his lips. Finally, he rubbed the salty pretzel on his tongue. I wanted him to notice when he tasted the pretzel. In the past, he had dissociated completely from all bodily sensation; he didn't appear to know when he urinated, when he hurt himself, or when he tasted anything in his mouth. I commented, "How's that feel on your tongue? Can you feel the little bumps? How does it taste? Does it taste salty? Or does it taste sweet like sugar? Does it have sugar?" Ollie said quietly, "No."

I didn't know if Ollie even knew the difference between something sweet and something salty. A normal three-year-old would know that a pretzel was salty, but he/she might think it was funny that I had suggested that it was sweet. I decided to treat Ollie like a normal three-year-old and see how he would respond. I confirmed, "No, it's not sweet. I'm teasing you. Does it have salt?" Ollie still looked dazed when he said, "No." I responded with a smile, "No? What does it have? Are you teasing me now? I teased you so now you're teasing me?" Ollie began to smile. It was the first time he had ever joked or teased playfully. He was smiling for the first time!

Ollie began to lick the pretzel. I wanted him to be really present to notice the texture and taste of the pretzel. He had spent so much of his life protecting himself from feeling that he was still reluctant to notice food, even if it felt or tasted good. He was often dissociated, or residing in a gray universe where he wasn't really present as a way of avoiding more trauma. I asked, "Does it feel good on your tongue? Taste good? It feels so good to do it by yourself." I wanted him to understand that he didn't have to be a passive victim anymore, now that he was physically capable of eating on his own. Ollie began to break the pretzel with his hands. I pointed out that he was in control of his food. "Oh, you can break it. You did it!"

Ollie was reclining in an awkward position across my lap, with his feet in the lunchbox. He was in an awkward position reminiscent of an infant tethered to machines by wires, as he had been for months in the intensive care nursery. Part of my job was to separate Ollie's past in the NICU, when he was immobilized and helpless, from his present, where he could move and express himself with words, gestures, and physical action.

128

I asked, "Are you comfortable? Is your head comfortable? You can sit up. You want to sit up?" Ollie sat up, looking surprised at his ability to move. I continued to narrate his present situation: "That's it. You can swallow. You're fine. You can sit up and move."

Then I began to tease Ollie: "What? Feet in the lunchbox?" He laughed, then began to hiccup and laughed again. I smiled: "You're being silly . . . You got the funny hiccups. They're pretty funny. Can you feel them? They're funny. They sound like hiccup laughs." Ollie laughed at himself—another great sign. And becoming aware of his hiccups was a sure sign that he was beginning to tune in to his body's sensations.

Tolerating Transition: Changes Won't Hurt Me

Frequently, children who have experienced trauma have trouble trying new things and experience distress with almost any kind of transition or new experience. When Ollie was in the NICU and someone approached, he didn't know whether he would receive a gentle touch or whether he would be subjected to a painful procedure. Through play, I worked to show him that most change is OK, and that even if something breaks or is unexpected, he is safe. The car that could break and be repaired was a good metaphor for demonstrating that "breaking" is not necessarily dangerous. It might even be funny.

I picked up a toy car and wondered aloud, "What happened? Uh-oh. That car got broken. Looks like it's bouncing around. Is it jumping? Jump jump jump jump jump jump jump." (I used the toy car to "jump" repeatedly from one of Ollie's knees to the other.) "Hey, I think it's playing."

Ollie walked toward me as I sat on the floor, and he began to push me backward. "Ahh! It's attacking me! It's playing but it hurt me. I don't know what to expect. I don't know whether it's going to play with me or hurt me. I didn't know that was going to happen!" I fell backward in mock surprise: "You knocked me over and I didn't even know that was going to happen."

Ollie began to laugh excitedly. He glanced at me, rolled backward on the floor, and laughed again. This was one of the first times his mother or I had ever heard him laugh. Laughter represents a turning point. Just as young children don't think potties are funny before they know how to use one, a child who is potty trained finds potty talk hysterically funny.

The Open Window

One day, Ollie came into my office and pointed to the open window. He said, "Can we close this window?" I remembered that Veronica had told me that Ollie could not tolerate open windows in the car or at home.

I wondered whether Ollie objected to open windows because he remembered the feeling of the breeze on his delicate skin in the NICU when someone opened the portals on his Isolette to reach for him. The breeze might have signaled that something was about to happen, and the baby had no way to anticipate whether the touch that was coming would be gentle or painful.

All of Ollie's symptoms pointed back to his early traumatic experiences and made sense in that context. I wanted to give Ollie the experience of control over the window and its worrisome breeze: "Would you like to go to the window and close it?" Ollie promptly and anxiously answered, "Close it." He still seemed present, not distant or glazed over, so I decided to use the opportunity to teach him that an open window is "safe."

"You know what? I will close the window, but I want to tell you something. You know when you were a little tiny baby, and you could feel the breeze and the window was open? That was when you were in a special place, and sometimes the people would have to come in and do things to you that maybe hurt, and *now* . . . nobody's going to do that. Do you remember how the window was open? Could you feel the breeze? Is it scary to have the window open, or is it OK? Do you want me to close the window or is it OK to have it open?"

Ollie had been walking around a circular chair near the window, pausing in front of me to receive my taps on his shoulders for a few seconds at a time. Sometimes he easily allowed me to tap his shoulders, and other times he passed me quickly. Children have their own ways of pacing therapy. These brief interludes of EMDR were apparently enough to decrease the fear associated with the breeze through the window. Suddenly, Ollie ducked behind the chair. This seemed like impromptu "peek-a-boo," so I said, "Where's Ollie?"

Ollie jumped up gleefully and exclaimed, "Right here!" I acted surprised, as if a jack-in-the-box had sprung up. "There he is! There you are." I knew that Ollie played peek-a-boo as a way of saying, "I'm here! I'm alive." He sometimes played it when he was in the process of putting his painful early experiences into past memory and becoming more present for life unhampered by terrifying memories. My joy at "finding" him was my way of saying, "You're alive, and you were meant to be here."

I gave Ollie another choice—the option to make a decision is a powerful possibility: "And you can have what you want when you ask about the window." He disappeared behind the chair for a second, and I playfully wondered, "Where are you?" Ollie popped up. I let him know that I was delighted to see him again: "There you are!" I added, "It's OK to say what you want. Do you want the window open or closed?" Ollie asserted himself: "Open." I was pleased and amazed: "Open!"

For Ollie, EMDR disconnected the current open window with the visceral memory of danger associated with the breeze when the window was open to the Isolette, his warm, temperature-controlled home in the NICU. After that, Ollie was always content to have the window open—in the car, at home, in my office—anywhere!

Tales of the Baby Panda

During our time together, Ollie had developed an interest in hearing my stories about himself as a baby through stories about the baby panda, the tiny quarter-inch ceramic panda in my miniature Zen rock garden. I used these stories as a metaphor for Ollie's life to help put words to his early, preverbal experiences.

I offered, "Do you want to hear the story about the baby panda?" Almost before I was finished asking, Ollie went across the room to sit on a chair and said, "I remember when he was on a little bed." I was surprised that he chose his story so quickly.

"Oh! On a little bed. OK. I'm going to tell you—you see the little panda? You can watch the little panda. Remember the story of when you were—when the little panda was on the bed." I was going back and forth between talking about the little panda and talking about Ollie himself because I was unsure how much reality Ollie could handle. I soon found out.

Ollie began to talk in a storytelling voice: "He was a little scared." I repeated, "He was a little scared. Can you point to where in his body he felt scared? Can you point to the scary feeling?" Traumatic experiences are stored in the body as physical sensations, and directing mindful attention to the sensations helps to process the trauma. Ollie's voice sounded a little stressed: "I'm scared." I didn't know why he switched to talking about himself; the trick with treating young children is to know when to talk about them personally and when to use story characters to represent their experiences. Children love to hear stories about others' adventures and scary experiences because it helps them to face their own challenges in a nonthreatening way.

Ollie suddenly shifted his attention to a clock on the wall. "There's a plate clock." When children are stressed, they often dissociate from the stressful topic. Ollie began to use a more normal voice: "There are numbers on it!"

Several times, children have pointed to the unusual clock when they are stressed, and I use that as a prompt to say, "That was a long time ago." Part of the goal of trauma therapy is to put past memories in their proper place in the past. Commenting, "That was a long time ago" is one of the strategies for helping someone who has slipped too far into the memory and is abreacting—that is, behaving as if the trauma were happening in the present. The idea is to distinguish whatever frightening event happened in the past from the safety of the present in my office.

I reassured Ollie, "Yes, that's right, there are numbers on it. But that was a long time ago that the baby panda was lying in the bed and feeling a little scared. What happened to him?" I wanted Ollie to choose the direction of the story—he seemed to have an event in mind.

Ollie's voice became strained again: "He was dying." I wanted Ollie to believe the obvious truth that he did not die: "He was scared that he was dying. Was he really dying?"

Ollie whispered, "He was dying." I noticed that he talked about himself in the third person, signifying that the emotion was so intense that it was too much for him to acknowledge as his own experience. I continued using the third person in the story. "He was scared; he *thought* he was dying," I reminded him. I wanted him to recognize the truth that he had survived that terrifying experience. I kept kneeling behind him and tapping his shoulders, hoping to help him process the physical sensation of feeling scared to death.

Ollie was abreacting now: "I'm dying." I wanted to keep him in the feeling enough to tap into it for processing, but I wanted to maintain the story format to make it feel as safe as possible: "He thought, 'I'm dying.' Was he really dying?"

At that point, Ollie had extended his neck backward, and I realized that he had exactly the position of someone positioned for direct laryngoscopy, the insertion of a tube deep into his throat to have a view of his vocal chords. He croaked, "Mommy, I'm dying," his voice strained with extreme distress. I put Ollie's statement in story format: "He was trying to say to his mommy, 'I'm dying!'" Ollie continued to repeat, "I'm dying. Mommy, I'm dying."

Then Ollie shifted into an urgent but more regular voice: "Mommy . . . Mommy, please come." Veronica came over to kneel in front of him: "I'm coming. Mommy's coming." Ollie looked into his mother's eyes and said, "Mama, I'm dying." His mother responded earnestly, "No, you're OK." I interjected, "That's what the mommy was saying."

Ollie stretched into the extended position as if there were a rigid tube in his throat: "Mommy, I'm dying." I reassured him as I tapped his shoulders, "He was scared that he was dying. That was a long time ago." Ollie persisted, "Mommy I'm scared." His mother responded tenderly, "I know you were scared you were dying, but you're alive." Ollie repeated, "I'm dying." And Veronica replied, "Oh, you're so scared of that."

Once again, Ollie said, "Mommy, I'm dying," but his voice was beginning to sound more normal again. His mother said, "I know, it felt like you were dying. I know it did."

Ollie exhaled with a long sigh, "Ahh." I gave him a minute to relax, then said, "Now where does the little panda feel the scary feeling?"

Ollie sat up and spoke in a strong voice: "Mommy, the doctor, the doctor's taking out the tube." I repeated, "The doctor's taking out the tube" as I tapped his shoulders. Even Ollie seemed surprised by what happened next, when he said, "I feel it in my throat." His mother confirmed, "That's what happened."

Ollie surprised us again when he said, "Mama, please hug me." His mother hugged him, and as I tapped his shoulders she said, "That's what you wanted to say when you were a little baby, but then you couldn't because you had to sit in a little chair and have a doctor look down your throat." Ollie said in a dreamy voice, "The doctor was looking down my throat."

"Yes," I confirmed.

Ollie pointed to his abdomen: "My stomach's down here." His mom nodded: "That's right, that's your stomach down there." Next, he pointed: "That's my esophagus. And that's my stomach . . . and those are my legs." I repeated, "Those are your legs." Ollie's mother commented, "You know a lot of things."

I asked Ollie, "Tell me, how does it look now when you remember the baby in the seat?"

Ollie settled back in the chair and said, "Mommy, I'm in a little seat." I noticed that Ollie had begun to use the pronoun "I," claiming the experience as his own. I was curious: "You're in a little seat. And what's happening?"

Ollie sounded jubilant and almost incredulous, "I'm OK." His mom nodded and smiled: "You're OK." Ollie became serious again: "I don't like it." And I inquired, "You don't like it?" Ollie said, "I want to jump out of here."

I thought it was great that Ollie no longer felt he was stuck in the little chair—he finally felt free to move. I gave my permission enthusiastically: "You want to jump out of here? You can jump out of there!" Ollie announced, "I'm going out of here, Mommy . . . Momma! Hug me." Ollie leaped into his mother's arms. Both of them were smiling and laughing. "You did it!" I said, and I smiled too.

Ollie had a new awareness of himself—he finally felt it was safe enough for him to actually feel his body and be present. It was as if "remember" really meant to *re-member*—to bring the body parts back together into a whole again. By fulfilling his desire to jump out of the seat, he had released himself from one of the old painful memories that had bound him to the terrifying past.

Baby Ollie's Photos and Story

One day, Veronica brought in an album with pictures of Ollie as a baby. We sat close to one another as we looked at a picture of Ollie shortly after birth, when he was on a ventilator. One of the issues that was "up" for Ollie was that he hated having anything touch his face—food, a spoon, a toothbrush, or a shirt pulled over his head. I decided to use the photos as an opportunity to desensitize the memory of discomfort and pain associated with anything touching his face.

I pointed to the picture: "Oh, look. Here's a tiny newborn baby. He's got tape on his cheeks. Here, let me show you where. He's got tape on his cheeks right here. See it? He's got tape on his cheeks right there. And there's the tube for the oxygen to help him breathe." I tapped on Ollie's cheeks as he looked at the picture of himself with wide bands of tape holding the tube in place. When Ollie was finished looking at the photo album he said to me, "Please, tell me a story of the baby panda before he was born."

I thought about what Ollie might need to hear and understand. I wanted him to know that he was normal while he was in his mother's uterus. I started making up my story and began to tap Ollie's feet as he lay on the floor. "OK," I began. "Once there was a baby panda who was born very little. And even though he was born early and very little, he was a perfect baby panda." Ollie was listening intently as he lay on the floor silently moving a toy ambulance back and forth. With the movement of the ambulance and my alternate toe tapping, Ollie visibly relaxed.

"The baby panda formed so he had a perfect head, and perfect brain, and perfect face, and perfect body, and perfect arms that moved, and legs that moved, and perfect insides. Everything was perfect. His throat was perfect, and his mouth was perfect, and, in fact, even before that baby was born, he was able to bring his thumb up to his mouth, and to suck his thumb, and to swallow. He was all safe and warm inside his mommy.

"He liked to bring his thumb up to his mouth and to suck. And he'd go suck, suck, suck, and whenever he'd suck, he'd swallow." I wanted him to know that he was capable of eating. I continued, "He'd suck and swallow, suck and swallow, suck and swallow, make little movements with his mouth, and it felt so good. He was doing it just perfectly. And it was so easy, it felt just right. He'd put his thumb in his mouth, and swallow some of the amniotic fluid, and everything worked totally fine."

I turned to his mom and asked, "Is there more you want to tell about the baby panda before he was born?" Veronica thought a moment and then added, "Before the baby panda was born, the mommy already really loved the baby panda." I checked with Ollie, "Can you feel the mommy loving the baby panda?" Ollie had a pleasant, dreamy expression on his face. Veronica stroked his cheek and told him that she always loved him. He didn't flinch from her touch as he previously had. The story had worked.

Perspective

Posttraumatic symptoms often stem from medical trauma that occurred early in life and involved painful treatment that was frightening to the parent as well as the child. The following is a quote by neonatologists Gardner, Garland, Merenstein, and Lubchenco (1993, p. 604), who acknowledged that hospitalization in a neonatal intensive care unit can be traumatic: "From the infant's perspective, the altruistic pain of lifesaving care is indistinguishable from the pain of child abuse."

Furthermore, these neonatologists outlined the factors that contribute to the risk that NICU infants may be unattached:

> The infants have multiple caregivers; the parents are not always present and after a prolonged stay of the baby, may be "strangers" to the baby; the needs of the multiple caregivers and baby may be asynchronous (e.g. it is "care time," but the baby is asleep); lifesaving care in the NICU is intrusive, noxious, and painful; and these experiences give the baby a history independent of his or her parents.
>
> (Gardener et al., 1993)

We often equate trauma with intentional abuse; yet even "excellent care" in a newborn intensive care unit can cause trauma and attachment problems in babies. Not only did Ollie have the easily understandable avoidance strategies of PTSD and behaviors indicating the source of his distress, he also had some explicit memories of what had actually happened to him when he was an infant. Yet PTSD is a diagnosis that is rarely given to NICU graduates who are seen in neonatal follow-up clinics.

When I was a pediatric intern and resident in the late 1970s, I was told that babies could not feel pain and that, even if they did feel pain, they couldn't remember it. I was taught that anesthesia was risky for newborns. It was not until 1986 that the American Pediatric Surgery Association developed guidelines for giving anesthesia to neonates during surgery. Prior to that time, it was not unusual to do surgery, including cardiac surgery, with paralytics but not analgesic medication. In other words, newborns were paralyzed during surgery but did not receive any pain medication. Because Ollie was born after 1986, it is likely that he had anesthesia during his heart surgery. However, he did not have anesthesia or medication to help him relax when he underwent direct laryngoscopy, and his body remembered the painful experiences even if he couldn't articulate his memory in words.

My experiences with Ollie reaffirmed my belief that infants have profound emotional experiences and that they remember those experiences on a visceral level. In this context, many of Ollie's abnormal behaviors made sense. When he was stressed, Ollie walked on his toes to avoid pressure on his heels where he had so much blood drawn. He tilted his head to the side, recalling his months of reclining on his side in the NICU. He expressed distress when a breeze from an open window reminded him of the uncertainty about whether a touch would be painful or gentle when the portal to his NICU Isolette was opened.

Mechanical sounds, clothes pulled on over his head, and even food in his mouth triggered panic, indicating that these normal sounds and activities of daily living made him recall painful experiences in the intensive care unit. It became evident to me that his early experiences set a template for his future behavior, even when the danger had passed.

Ollie demonstrated that trauma interferes with attachment and that resolution of posttraumatic symptoms facilitates healthy attachment. In the beginning of our work, Ollie spontaneously hit his mother frequently, even though she was loving, gentle, competent, reassuring, and understanding with him. By the end of the first year, Ollie spontaneously called out, "Mama, please hug me," and after that he became more connected and responsive to his mother. Trauma resolution opens the possibility for trusting, loving relationships.

Follow-up

I saw Ollie weekly for about a year and a half. When Ollie was six, I got a note from Veronica saying that Ollie was enrolled in a special education "transitional kindergarten" and that he showed "delight and keen interest in spelling, drawing, singing, and rhyming." His teacher told her that Ollie was very social and kind, saying things to his peers like, "It's OK, it just takes practice." Later, he transitioned to a regular kindergarten with the help of an aide. By the time Ollie was 10 years old, he was doing well in school with the help of an aide to help him make transitions from one activity to another, to refocus his attention as needed, and to help with social skill building, especially at recess. He had friends and play dates, and he was invited to birthday parties. He was affectionate and empathetic and had a warm relationship with his mother.

During the course of treatment, Ollie did get his feeding tube out. Later, he had to have surgery to repair the site in his abdomen where the tube had been connected. When he told me about that experience, he asked, "When they give you pain medicine for a stomachache, why does the medicine go to your head instead of just your stomach?" I felt proud of Ollie for talking in complete sentences about what had happened to him, and for touching on an idea about the nonspecific action of pain medication that has eluded medical researchers. For the first time, I could envision Ollie growing into a functional, productive adult. I responded, "Great question, Ollie. Maybe when you grow up you'll be able to figure out how to make pain medicine that just goes where it's supposed to go." Ollie smiled.

Note

1 In 2011, 11.9 percent of babies born in the United States were premature (www.huffingtonpost.com/2012/11/13/us-preterm-birth-rate-hit_n_2118244. html).

Part II

CULTIVATING POSITIVE EMOTIONS

11

STRATEGIES FOR ENHANCING
A CHILD'S STRENGTHS

Helping children resolve trauma and develop a secure attachment with their parents requires balancing the work of trauma resolution with the layering of positive experiences of intimacy. Trauma resolution focuses on desensitizing and reprocessing distressing experiences to remove obstacles to children's natural inclination to trust adults to take care of them, and parent-child activities can give children the opportunity to experience joy in relationships with others. Cultivating positive emotions in children who have suffered PTSD and complex trauma is crucial.

Encourage parents to cuddle their distressed child daily, preferably at the beginning of the day to fill their "love tank" for the day. Babying is the cornerstone of treatment. Cuddling is a way of recognizing and gently tending the "inner baby." The parent can enjoy holding, rocking, nurturing, cooing, and appreciating the preciousness of the child. Daily nurturing holds, eye contact, and baby play are all valuable for children, especially if they have missed out on attentive babying early in life.

Children have to learn to recognize and articulate their needs and wants, learn how to make requests in order to have needs understood, and learn how to tolerate it when someone says "no" to what they want. It's helpful for children to learn to distinguish between needs and wants and know that a parent's job is to provide for their needs, but that a good parent does not always give what the child wants.

This chapter focuses on enhancing the strengths a child already has and qualities he/she can develop by using his/her imagination. It details games and activities that are fun ways for children to learn the skills required for communicating what they want and need. It also provides exercises to teach children to comfort themselves and believe that they are still lovable and good even if they can't have what they want.

Some of these exercises are original and others have been adapted from Theraplay activities and ideas contributed by Debra Wesselmann, MS, LIPHP, and other therapists.

Calm, Safe, Peaceful, Special, or Fun Place

Imagine a special place where everything would be exactly as you'd like it to be. Anything or anyone real or imaginary could be there with you to help you feel safe and calm. When you imagine that you are there, what do you see? Would you like to call the place a safe place or calm or peaceful or special or fun place or . . .?

For a child who cannot imagine a safe place or for a child who has intruding feelings of impending disaster when imaging a safe place, suggest that the child "imagine a place where nothing happens and everything stays the same."

What do you see that helps you feel especially calm?

What do you hear that helps you feel calm?

What do you smell?

What are you doing?

How do you feel?

Point to where you feel the safe feeling in your body.

Now imagine that you are there in that safe place. As you breathe in, breathe in more of the safe feeling. As you breathe out, let go of any stress your body feels ready to let go of.

Where in your body do you feel the safe, relaxed feeling?

Now you can practice going on a short vacation by imagining your safe place. I'll time you for 20 seconds while you go on vacation.

Remember to picture your safe place with all of the sights and sounds and smells that remind you that you're safe. Notice the safe feeling in your body. As you breathe in, breathe in the good, safe feeling, and as you breathe out, let out any stress your body feels ready to let go of.

Butterfly Hug

The butterfly hug was originated and developed by Lucina Artigas during her work performed with the survivors of Hurricane Pauline in Acapulco, Mexico, 1998 (Jarero & Artigas, 2012). Here is the way I teach the butterfly hug:

I start by saying, "Now I'm going to show you a special hug you give yourself. Please start by putting your arms all the way open as I am."

I stretch my arms out horizontally, and as I bring my arms together and cross them across my chest, I say, "Now imagine that you are bringing in all the safe (or calm or relaxing or comforting or peaceful) feelings that you need." I go through the safe place exercise as described above.

There are three important parts of the butterfly hug:

1. Get a picture of a safe place in your mind.
2. Notice the safe feeling in your body.

142

3. Tap your hands alternately on your shoulders like this (right hand to left shoulder and left hand to right shoulder).

There are three ways to do the butterfly hug:

1. Cross your arms across your chest, placing your hands on your shoulders, to form the wings of a butterfly.
2. Hold your hands so that your palms face your chest and then slide your hands across one another until your thumbs can hook together. Now put your hands (the wings of the butterfly) on your chest, and you can tap that way.
3. Instead of using your hands, tap your feet. So get the picture of the safe place in your mind, notice the calm feeling in your body, and tap your toes alternately inside your shoes.

A parent can also do a butterfly hug with a young child by holding the child on his/her lap, with the child facing the parent or facing outward. Then the parent crosses his/her arms across the child's chest or back, puts his/her hands on the child's shoulders, and taps the shoulders alternately while saying calming things in a soothing voice.

A Learning Experience

The learning experience exercise offers a metaphor for the whole thera-peutic process: "Remember something that used to seem hard or impos-sible for you, but now you can do it and it feels easy." The therapist guides the child to recall a personal challenge and the steps involved in attaining mastery, including the motivation to accomplish the task, the helpers involved, and the persistence and practice required.

You may introduce this activity by saying, "I am interested in how people learn to do things that are hard for them. Can you think of something you have learned that seemed difficult or impossible before you could do it, but now you can do it easily?" (For example, ride a bike, drive a car, use a computer; for therapists, learning to use EMDR successfully!)

"Do you remember how you felt about it before you could do it?"

"How did you learn?"

If the child says he or she wanted to do it, that indicates motivation that facilitates the process. If the individual does not mention wanting to do it, you can say, "If it seemed that hard, you must have really wanted to do it." Nothing happens unless the client wants it to happen. If the child learned the skill (like multiplication tables) even if he/she didn't really want to, you can say, "Think about how you learned that even though you didn't want to and now you feel glad that you can do it."

Learning might involve watching, listening, asking questions, visualizing being able to do it, practicing, etc. Perhaps a parent or teacher helped, or perhaps the child observed and then figured out what to do by herself/himself.

Write the list of steps and read them back to your client. ("Wanted to do it" or "agreed to" should be at the top of the list.)

"How did you feel when you had learned how to do it well? Where in your body do you feel that?"

"Now, would it be OK with you if I tap your hands (or whatever bilateral stimulation the client prefers) while you remember how it was before you learned _____, the feeling in your body then, the steps you went through to learn to do it, and finish with how you feel now that you can do it easily (or well or competently). You can imagine it's a movie and you are watching."

"Let me know when you have finished remembering all of it."

"How do you feel now?" (Usually the answer is "proud" or "good" or "happy.")

"Where in your body do you feel that proud feeling? May I tap your hands while you notice that proud feeling you have because you accomplished something that used to seem very hard for you?"

Overcoming a Fear

You may also ask the child how he/she overcame a fear and use the same procedure outlined above (A Learning Experience) to review the process of achievement and to strengthen the positive emotion associated with the accomplishment.

A Special Person Who Believes in You

"Think of someone who believes in you" (a parent, grandparent, friend, teacher, therapist, doctor, coach, clergy, etc.).

"Who was that? Can you remember a situation that told you that he or she believed in you?"

"What feeling do you get, knowing that he/she believed in you?"

"Where in your body do you feel it?"

"Would it be OK with you if I tap your hands (or whatever form of ABS the child prefers) while you remember the situation (or the person) that helps you remember the feeling of someone believing in you?"

A "Yes!" (Success) Experience

"Remember the first time you kicked a goal in soccer/rode a bike/got 100 percent on a math test, and notice the 'Yes!' feeling in your body."

A Proud Feeling

"Remember a time when you worked hard to do something and, with perseverance, you were able to accomplish it" (learning to drive, finishing a report, learning to do math, swimming the length of the pool, etc.).

A Protector

"Think of someone real or imaginary who can help you feel really protected and safe."

A Nurturer

"Think of someone real or imaginary who can help you feel loved and comforted."

Love for a Pet

"Imagine petting your dog/cat. How do you feel? How do you imagine your pet feels?"

A Fun Time With a Parent, Sibling, or Friend

"Remember a good time you had with _____."

A Fun Time Alone

"Remember a time when you enjoyed being by yourself."

The Power Wheel

Whenever I evaluate a child, and sometimes for adults, I make a "power wheel" (sometimes called a "resource wheel") so that the individual's strengths are visible on paper.

I ask the child and parents to help me make a power wheel. First, I draw a big circle on a piece of paper and make spokes for the wheel by putting in a few dotted lines from the center to the perimeter of the circle. I ask the parents to name some of their child's resources or strengths, and as they tell me, I write a resource on each spoke of the wheel. The list can include qualities like sense of humor, kindness, patience, or perseverance. I ask for a specific example for each quality.

Powers or resources can also include people (family members, teachers, coaches, neighbors, clergy), pets, authors, or even characters in books or movies. They may include love of nature, specific books or movies, or

Power Wheel

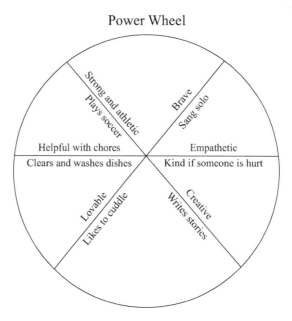

Figure 11.1 The power wheel shows the child's strengths and resources

religious beliefs. The idea is to show that the individual has many strengths and many things that help him/her in life.

Then I read the list to the child and ask which qualities he/she likes about himself/herself. Parents bring their children to me because of problems. I think the resource wheel is one indication that I see the child as a whole person, with strengths that can be helpful in overcoming problems.

Sometimes parents list the child's talents and accomplishments. That's fine, unless it's the whole list. If it's the whole list, I ask questions to elicit qualities.

Sometimes I make a resource wheel for a teen or adult who doesn't have much good to say about himself/herself. I add strengths to the wheel as the individual tells me about himself/herself. It can be a resource to recognize the need for help and to seek out therapy. One adult chose the father in the old TV show *Father Knows Best*. Another chose Bob Marley and Alice Walker because they transformed their suffering into art.

I initially make the spokes of the wheel dotted lines so that, if I used the strengths listed for resource installation with alternating bilateral stimulation (ABS), I can turn the dotted line into a solid line. Making the lines solid is a way of showing that the resource has been reinforced.

12

GAMES FOR PROMOTING CONNECTION AND COOPERATION

These games can be effective in promoting a child's cooperation with a parent or in encouraging siblings to enjoy working together. Before you begin, tell the child that if he/she doesn't follow directions, you understand that he/she doesn't want to play by the rules and that you will put the game away. These games should only be played "by the rules" if the goal is to teach cooperation. The games were adapted from work by Debra Wesselmann, MS, LIMHP, and Theraplay.

Animal Cracker Game

This game can be played with a parent and child or by siblings to model cooperation.

With Parent

The parent chooses the animal cracker and is in charge.

The parent is instructed to make eye contact and say: "You may eat the head."

The child then eats the designated part. (Let the child know that if he eats any more than the designated part, that is a signal that he wants to end the game for the day.) The therapist instructs the parent to say, "Good job cooperating!" or "Thank you for following directions" or "Thank you for doing what I asked."

The therapist instructs the child to look at the parent and say, "You're welcome."

Repeat the steps above, designating parts of the cracker to be eaten (e.g., mane, front legs, last half).

With Siblings

One child holds an animal cracker and instructs his/her sibling:

"You may eat the head."

When the sibling cooperates, the therapist instructs the child to say, "Thank you for doing what I asked" or "Thank you for playing with me" or "Thank you for listening to me."

If using EMDR, the therapist taps the hands of the child who is cooperating and says, "Good job cooperating!"

Repeat instructions, designating parts of the cracker to be eaten (e.g., head, front legs, etc.).

The children take turns feeding and eating.

Bubble Games

Explain the rules of the game to the parent and child.

For the Child Who Needs to Practice Cooperating

The therapist gives the parent soap bubbles and a wand ("bubble stuff" may come in a "bubbler bear" or "bubble rocket"). The parent blows bubbles with "bubble stuff."

The parent gives instructions to the child: "You may pop the bubbles with your hands" (or with your elbows, or right hand, etc.).

After the child has done as asked, instruct the parent to look the child in the eyes and say, "Thank you for following directions."

The therapist taps the child's shoulders while the parent praises the child.

You can ask the child to look at his/her parent and say, "You're welcome."

For the Child Who Needs to Practice Asking
for What He/She Wants

Instruct the child to look at his/her parent and ask, "May I pop the bubbles with my thumb?" (feet, etc.).

The parent says, "yes" and blows bubbles with "bubble stuff."

After the child has asked, instruct the parent to look the child in the eyes and say, "It's OK to ask for what you want."

The therapist taps the child's shoulders and repeats, "It's OK to ask for what you want."

For the Child Who Needs Practice Tolerating "No"

Tell the child that the rules are that he/she may request how he/she would like to pop the bubbles (by clapping, by stomping, with elbows, etc., and that the parent will say "yes" two times and that the third answer will be "no," then the fourth "yes" again, etc.

If the child tolerates "no," tap his/her shoulders and say, "You can be OK even if your mom/dad says 'no.'" If the child doesn't tolerate "no," ask the parent to say, "I still love you and you're important to me, even when I say 'no.'"

Face Painting

The face painting activity can improve attunement and closeness between parent and child.

Ask the parent and child if they would like to paint faces with imaginary paint. The child gets to choose the imaginary colors for his/her own face. For example, the child may say, "I want purple eyebrows," and the parent dips a finger in the imaginary paint and traces the child's eyebrows.

The parent continues to paint the child's face until the child has had enough.

Then the child is invited to "paint" the parent's face.

Lollypop Game

The parent holds the child, as if cradling a baby, so that the parent and child are face to face. The child chooses a lollypop, and the parent opens the wrapper. Tell the parent that this game is about the parent reading the child's signals. The parent must hold the lollypop all of the time. This game is useful for helping children with attachment issues learn to trust that they can allow the adult to be in charge.

For the Child Who Likes Eye Contact

The child gets to suck on the lollypop while looking at his/her parent.

When the child wants the parent to take the lollypop out, the child opens his/her mouth.

When the child wants the lollypop back in, the child opens his/her mouth and nods.

For the Child Who Avoids Eye Contact

The child gets to suck on the lollypop with his/her eyes closed.

When the child wants the parent to take the lollypop out, the child opens his/her mouth.

When the child wants the lollypop back in, the child opens his/her eyes and makes eye contact with the parent.

When you see that the parent is reading the child's signals well, ask the child, "Is your mom/dad getting your signals?"

If doing EMDR bilateral stimulation to strengthen positive experiences:

If the child can acknowledge that the parent is getting his/her signals correctly, tap the child's feet and say, "You can count on your mom/dad to do her/his best to figure out your signals."

Magic Cord or Magic Ribbon

The "magic cord" exercise can reinforce a sense of object constancy—the sense that the parent is always connected with the child even when they are sleeping or in different locations. It is particularly helpful for children who experience separation anxiety and children who feel they need constant attention.

While the parent is holding the child in the face-to-face position, and only if you feel the parent loving the child, say:

"There is a magic cord connecting your heart with your mom's/dad's heart. And your mom/dad is sending you love through that cord all the time. The cord can stretch anywhere and can never be broken, no matter what. Even if you are at school and your mom/dad is at work, that cord can stretch anywhere. That cord is even connecting you while you are asleep."

You can ask the child what color his/her cord is and encourage the child to visualize it. Sometimes parents like to draw their picture of the connection with their child. Sometimes the child likes to draw the magic cord.

Alternating bilateral stimulation (ABS) can be used to reinforce the positive feelings associated with the parent's drawing or the child's drawing.

Tell the child to close his/her eyes and feel the magic cord.

Alternating bilateral stimulation can be used to strengthen the feeling of connection between parent and child.

13

ADDITIONAL THERAPEUTIC OPTIONS

The child's therapist must be comfortable developing a relationship with a child, assessing the child's developmental level, playing with the child, and finding out what motivates each child. It's essential to have a variety of ways to work because there is no one therapy or therapeutic approach that works for every child.

The following aids to therapy with children are some of many strategies for helping children identify and reinforce their strengths, bring their intense emotions into a tolerable zone, and find nonverbal ways of expressing their experiences.

Artwork and EMDR

A drawing of "the worries" or a nightmare can serve as a target for EMDR.

Using a modification of Philip Manfield, PhD's, "dyadic resourcing," the drawing of a protector can be used as a resource for helping the child imagine both how he/she feels being protected and helping the child imagine how it feels to be the protector.

This adopted child's drawing of his baby self (Figure 13.1) was a basis for discussion of what babies need and how they feel when their needs are not met. Alternating bilateral stimulation (ABS) was used to process the distressed feelings the child imagined the baby had when he didn't get what he needed. Next, I encouraged the boy's mother to talk about what she would have done for him if she had been taking care of him when he was a baby. During ABS, the child imagined that his adoptive mother was meeting his baby self's needs. The boy then drew a picture of the same baby, but this time he was wearing brightly colored clothes and was smiling. Next, ABS was used to reinforce how he imagined the baby felt when his needs were met. Finally, ABS was used to strengthen beliefs that the baby was good and lovable.

Figure 13.1 A seven-year-old child's drawing of himself and his worries

Figure 13.2 An 11-year-old child's drawing of his imagined protector

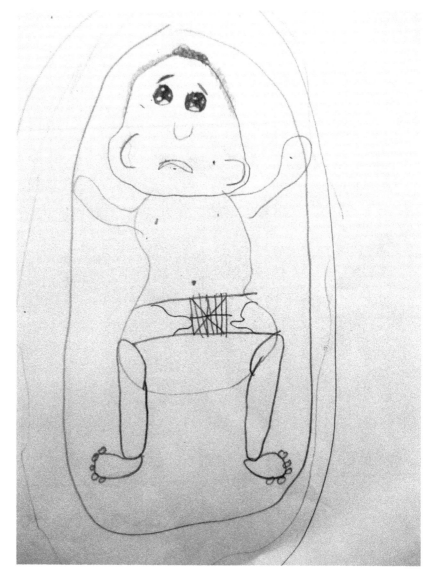

Figure 13.3 An 11-year-old child drew a picture of his "baby self" who was neglected

Artwork can be used for resource installation as well as for focusing on a target that can be desensitized and reprocessed. I often ask children if they would like to draw their safe place, their protector, and the magic cord that connects the child and parents. Then ABS is used to install the feelings of being good, lovable, and safe.

The Folded Paper Method

A technique for screening and treating groups of traumatized children that was developed by the HAP team in Mexico can be used for targeting a traumatic memory or for targeting an irrational fear or nightmare.

Fold a paper into four equal sections. Ask the child to draw the scariest part of the memory, fear, or dream in the upper left corner of the paper. Ask for an emotion, a SUD rating, and the location of a physical sensation, then give ABS until the child is ready to draw the next picture. Repeat this process until all four sections have been filled. If the SUD rating has not reached zero by the fourth square, the child may continue drawing pictures, identifying the SUD rating, and receiving ABS until the SUD rating is zero. Then draw a positive picture and install positive cognitions.

Below is a drawing by a child who used the folded paper method to overcome her fear of germs.

Square 1 (upper left):
The germ says, "You're going to get sick and die." SUD = 8
Square 2 (upper right):
The child and the germ are now the same size. SUD = 6

Figure 13.4 Folded-paper drawings for overcoming fear of germs

155

Square 3 (lower left):
The child is much larger than the germ and the germ is crying. SUD = −10,000,000
Square 4 (lower right):
The child is much larger than the shrunken germ and is crushing it with her foot. SUD = −10,000,000

I sometimes use a modification of the procedure called "Slaying the Monsters," developed by D. Spindler-Ranta (1999).

1. Fold a paper in half and ask the child to draw herself/himself on one half of the page and, on the other side, to draw the fear, perpetrator, or whatever you have chosen for a target.
2. Cut the paper down the middle and put the picture of the child in a safe place.
3. Ask the child to make up a story of how he/she and two helpers overcome the fear or monsters. Many children are unable to think of a story to go with their drawing. That's OK.
4. Instruct the child to color back and forth horizontally over the target until it is not visible. (Crayons are usually the best tools for covering a drawing.)
5. Encourage the child to tear the paper into tiny shreds while saying the positive cognitions "I am taking my power back," "It's over," "It's gone," "It will never happen again," or whatever positive cognitions are appropriate.
6. Use ABS to install the positive cognitions.

Some children draw a picture of their traumatic experience, and that picture can be the target for desensitization and reprocessing. One five-year-old girl, who was preoccupied with worries about illness and physical aches and pains, immediately drew a picture of herself vomiting and having diarrhea that was so severe that she thought she was going to die. We targeted the memory of that illness several times, until she believed that it was over and she was well. Then she spontaneously drew a picture of a rainbow.

Mindfulness: Feeling Safe and Calm in Your Body, Here and Now

Mindfulness involves paying attention to one's experience through the senses and the mind to enter a state of calm. Mindfulness is a way for a child to feel embodied and safe in the present. Here, I describe activities that can be used as part of a child's daily routine or can be used in the therapist's office to anchor a child who is hyperaroused or distressed by trauma processing.

Even young children can learn to calm themselves by noticing what is happening in the moment. Physical activity, like rolling or tossing a ball back and forth with another person, directs the child to pay attention to what his/her body is doing "now." I have squishy, squiggly balls that light up when in motion that children love to toss back and forth at the end of every session. Gently tossing a pillow back and forth can have the same calming effect of bringing the child into present awareness.

Playing a type of "I spy" game is another way to become more oriented to the present. Ask the child to pick three items in the room that are a particular color or shape. Focusing outward to locate the designated item helps the child to concentrate and become calm in the present.

Some children like to use their breath to calm themselves. I have seen children as young as three enjoy breathing in to fill their "balloon belly" and then breathing out to let the air go slowly out of their "balloon belly." Help the child notice how controlling his or her breath is soothing.

Blowing bubbles with "bubble stuff" is a good way for children to become calmer and more present. Encourage the child to blow slowly and steadily until he or she can make a stream of bubbles. Learning to control the breath is a skill that can be taken anywhere!

Singing, especially songs that involve hand movements (like "Eensy, Weensy Spider," "The Wheels of the Bus," and "Little Man by the Window") utilize breath and touch, both of which help to connect the child with his/her body and the sense of being safe in the present.

Some children can visualize two doors—one where the thoughts lead to scary feelings and one that is right now, right here, where everything is safe. They can imagine choosing the door to the "present" and clearly visualize what is around them when they choose the door that leads to a safe place.

Babies love to play peek-a-boo and are especially delighted when the finder smiles and says, "I see you!" But some children, especially if they have experienced attachment trauma, love to play the game when they are as old as five or six. Older children love to play hide-and-seek. Both games give the child the opportunity to be "present" and experience a parent's delight when they are "found." These games help to reinforce an experience of object constancy.

Another activity that draws children into the present is rubbing two textures simultaneously. The child can put one hand on his/her clothes and another on his/her chair and rub both textures at the same time, noticing the difference. Many people notice that their breathing becomes slower and deeper and that they feel more relaxed.

Making saliva (or spit) is a way to stimulate the parasympathetic nervous system and activate a natural calming effect. Many school-aged children enjoy making saliva and then swallowing it or spitting it out.

All of these activities can be taught to parents so they can work with their child to find which mindfulness practices appeal to their child. Teenagers may enjoy using mindfulness and meditation tutorials online as well as meditation apps on their phones.

Strong Feelings Rod

The "strong feelings rod" is useful for helping children discharge frustration, anger, or disappointment. A physical experience of pushing the rod with the feet while pulling the rope with the hands allows total body engagement in releasing strong physical sensations. Only use the strong feelings rod if the child feels ready to get over a stuck negative emotion. Never use the strong feelings rod if you are concerned that the child might use it as a weapon.

Nancy Joyce, MFT, taught me about the strong feelings rod and how to make one:

1. Buy a piece of 2-inch-diameter PVC pipe at a hardware store.
2. Cut the pipe to a length of 2 feet.
3. Take a strong rope (about three-quarters of an inch in diameter) that is about 6 feet long and thread it through the rod two times. Tie a knot on the ends of the rope.
4. The child who wants to get over intense negative feelings can push his/her feet into the rod while pulling up on the two ends of the rope.
5. You can ask the child to tuck the buzzers into his/her pockets or under his/her thighs.
6. Instruct the child to think of a situation that angers or frustrates him/her, and get a SUD rating.
7. Tell the child to push the strong feelings through the rod with his/her feet while simultaneously pulling the rope with his/her hands at the same time. Notice the strong feeling, push and pull, with buzzers going.
8. Determine the SUD rating and continue to process the feelings until the SUD equals 0.

Parenting for Connection and Cooperation

All children need to feel confident that an adult knows them well, cares about them, protects them, and teaches them to behave appropriately. The recommendations for "parenting for connection and cooperation" are especially useful for adoptive parents and parents who need direction as they practice connecting with their child and eliciting cooperation.

Here is a list of parenting advice I gave to Amy's parents.

Catch Her Doing Things Right

The rule is six compliments for every correction:
 "I like the way you put on your shoes when I asked."
 "I like the way you stayed close to me at the grocery store."

Give Positive Instructions

Whenever you tell her what you don't want her to do, be sure to tell her in a positive way:
 Instead of "Don't bang the door," say, "Close the door quietly."

Give Her a Chance to "Re-do"

Give her a chance to correct her mistakes and be praised for doing things correctly.
 "You get a re-do. It's not OK to slam the door, so you get a chance to do it the way I show you." If necessary, add in "Let's do it together . . . That's it. This is the way to close the door quietly." Help her be successful!

Make Sure You and Your Child Are Safe

Never allow your child to injure you or herself physically.
 Stop the behavior as soon as it begins.
 Stay calm and clear about your obligation as a parent to do your best to keep your family safe.

Teach Her to Express Feelings in Words

Children need to learn to identify the physical sensations associated with feelings and the words that identify feelings, and to use words to communicate feelings in an acceptable way.

Mirror Her Feelings With Your Intensity Matching Hers

"I hear you telling me that you hate spinach!"
 "It sounds like you really want that toy, and you're feeling angry that you can't have it right now."

Model What You Want to Hear

"I'd like to hear you say, 'No thank you,' when I offer you spinach, even if you don't like it."

Make Eye Contact

Let your eyes smile at her eyes when you make requests and when she does what you ask. Other times too!

Play Peek-a-Boo and/or Hide-and-Seek

It's a game that teaches object constancy.

Be delighted to find her and see her. "There you are! I see you!"

Have an Ongoing Narrative Explaining What's Happening

"It looks like the baby in the dollhouse isn't getting what she needs. What do you thinks she needs? A baby needs attention, milk, clean diapers, lots of cuddles, and rules to keep her safe. Let's pretend to give her what she needs."

Give Her Structure So She Knows What to Expect

"We can play now for a while, and then we will clean up."

"We can cuddle for five minutes, and then it's time to get up, dress, and have breakfast."

Set Limits

"Stop means stop now."

"We don't put our shoes on people's sofas."

"We don't touch people's belongings without asking."

"It's not OK to open drawers in someone's desk without asking."

"When it's time to stop and clean up, we say, 'OK' and we clean up."

"Name calling is not OK."

If your child's behavior is unsafe, stop it right away and, if possible, don't allow it to happen again.

Never let her hurt herself, you, or anyone else physically. Children who are allowed to hit or hurt anyone get the idea that they can't trust themselves and that adults can't keep them safe. Restrain the child firmly and safely if anyone is in danger, and agree to let go as soon as the child can be calm.

Call on the Rules

Following certain rules of being respectful, polite, helpful, and cooperative makes everyone feel happier.

When appropriate, say, "The rule is . . ." and then make sure that you follow through.

Consequences

Some children respond to a frown, a request, or a brief warning to stop inappropriate behavior. Others respond to a consequence.

Never punish a child by taking away something that is necessary or good for her, like food or a bedtime story.

Only Give a Choice When It's a Real Choice

Do not ask, "Do you want to put on your shoes?" or "Do you want to hold my hand when you cross the street?" Do not say, "It's time to go, OK?" When you give a child a choice by beginning with "Do you want to?" or by tacking on "OK?" at the end of a request, or you use a tone of voice that goes up at the end of the sentence like a question, most of the time the child will ignore you or answer, "No."

Instead, state in a matter-of-fact way, "It's time to put on your shoes."

Give Age-appropriate Choices

Give choices rather than a command or an ultimatum when a reasonable accommodation is possible.

"Do you want to hold my right hand or my left hand while we cross the street?"

"Do you want to put on your shoes or your sweater first?"

Scoop Her Up

Snuggle her when possible and if she likes it, during a nap, reading, or getting dressed.

Give massages—figure out how she likes you to massage her back, feet, and hands.

Teach Her to Recognize Her Needs and State Them

"I'm hungry. I need a snack."

Teach Her to Make Requests

Not only "I'm hungry" but also "May I have something to eat?"

Teach her that it's always OK to ask for what you want, and it's a parent's job to say "no" sometimes.

"When I say 'no,' you're still lovable and good and important to me."

Partner With Her Verbally

Stay connected verbally if she clamors for constant attention when you want her to do something and you're busy doing something else—e.g., if you're busy preparing dinner and she wants you to come in another room to do something with her.

"I'm making dinner. I can't leave the kitchen right now. I'd like to have you come to the kitchen to help me stir or look at books and keep me company . . . or you can stay in there and know I'm thinking about you." Or "I can't watch you right now, but we can sing together while I make dinner."

Children's books like *The Kissing Hand* by Audrey Penn and *The Invisible String* by Patrice Karst are great for helping children feel more secure and connected to their parents even when they can't be with them.

Or, tell her you will listen and give her your full attention for five minutes and then it's time for her "quiet free choice time" while you do what you want/need to do.

Give Her Meaningful Tasks and Supervise as Much as Necessary

For example, you could say, "You get to tear up the lettuce for our salad." If necessary, have your hands on her hands to make sure you get the size of lettuce pieces you want. Praise her for learning to help.

Partner With Her through Touch

For example: "I'm talking on the phone, so I can't talk to you right now, but you can sit beside me quietly and snuggle up while I talk."

Notice What Triggers Her Distressed Behaviors

Share your list with her therapist. Observe whether she has an extreme reaction when she doesn't get her way, when she has a disappointment, when she doesn't know what's going on, when a plan changes, when she has to make a transition, when she needs full attention, etc.

Use Humor and Silliness

To diffuse tension and to avert power struggles.

For example: "I see you're not putting your socks on your feet. I'll put them on my head! Hey, they fell off. They want to be on your feet."

Play, Following Your Child's Lead

Spend some time every day playing with your child, following her lead. For suggestions on how to play, look at Theraplay videos on YouTube and read the article, "The Importance of One-on-One Time" by Tamara Eberlein.

Do Something Nice for Yourself Every Day! Eat Well, Exercise, and Get Enough Rest

You can take better care of another person (especially a challenging little person) if you take care of yourself!

162

If your child is triggering your own feelings of being a helpless child, get the help you need to stay in your competent adult self while you are helping your child become self-regulated.

Circle Breathing for Attunement

Rest the child's left arm on the inside surface of your left arm. Match your breathing to the child's breathing.

Put your right hand palm facing your child's forehead, with about an inch between your palm and your child's forehead. Continue matching your breathing to his/hers.

Now place your right hand on top of your child's left hand. Continue to match breathing for as long as it feels good for both of you.

EMDR Can Help Change Basic Belief Systems

In the left column of Table 13.1 below, there are some common beliefs that arise from traumatic experiences and go along with the theme of

Table 13.1 Negative cognitions, educational interweaves, and positive cognitions

Trauma and Shame	Clinician's Message	Trust
Negative Cognition	Educational Interweave	Positive Cognition
I am alone.	You have others in your life who care about you.	I belong.
Everything bad is my fault.	It's not your fault.	I am a good person.
I shouldn't be alive.	You were meant to be.	I am valuable.
I'm not safe.	It's safe to play. It's safe to relax.	I am safe.
I'm helpless.	You can ask for what you need and want.	I am worthy of help. I can ask for help.
No one can help me.	Others can help you.	I can trust adults to help.
It's not safe to trust.	You can trust when someone is trustworthy.	I can trust my parents.
I'm worthless.	You're valuable.	I am valuable.
I must have attention.	You are safe even if you're not getting attention.	I'm connected even if I'm not getting attention.
I am not lovable.	You can give love and receive love.	I am lovable.
I have to control everything.	You're safe even if you don't get your way. It's safe to let adults be in charge.	I'm safe even if I don't get my way. I can let adults be in charge.
I have to be the boss.	You can be OK even when someone else is the boss.	I can relax and take turns.

(Continued)

163

Table 13.1 (Continued)

Trauma and Shame	Clinician's Message	Trust
Negative Cognition	Educational Interweave	Positive Cognition
If I love, I'll lose.	It's worth the risk to love.	I can love.
I am bad.	You are a good person.	I am good at heart.
My feelings are bad.	Your feelings are normal.	It's OK to feel.
Feeling bad means I am bad.	You are good even if you feel bad sometimes.	I am good at heart regardless of how I feel.
If I feel good, something bad is sure to happen.	Feeling good is good. It's safe to feel good.	I can enjoy the good times.
I cannot tolerate feelings.	You can learn to tolerate your feelings.	My feelings are OK. Feelings come and go.
It's not safe to need adults.	It's OK to need your mom and dad.	It's OK to have needs.
I don't belong.	You do belong. It's safe to belong.	I belong.
It's too scary to hear nice things.	You deserve to hear nice things.	I deserve good things.
It's too scary to have fun.	You can have fun and you will be OK.	It's OK to have fun.
It's too scary to try new things.	You are safe even if you do something new.	It's safe to try new things.

profound, prolonged ruptured of sense of safety, trust, and self-worth. In the middle column are messages the clinician can offer the child when this cognitive information is current, appropriate, and true. The clinician's messages can be given silently, verbally, or, when appropriate, along with bilateral stimulation. The column on the right consists of positive cognitions the clinician may suggest and install.

Deb Wesselmann and I compiled the list in Table 13.1 of negative cognitions, cognitive interweaves, and positive cognitions.

Thumb Signals

Sometimes children who come to see me don't want to talk. There can be many reasons for remaining silent. A child might be shy, angry, or afraid of repercussions from parents, or they may have been threatened by a perpetrator and convinced that harm will come to them or their family if they tell a secret. Sometimes a child simply doesn't know how to put thoughts and feelings into words.

If the child is silent and I want to have answers to questions, I think of ways to word the questions so that they could be answered with a "yes" or "no." Then I tell the child that they can give me thumb signals. A child taught me the system, and I've found it very useful.

Thumb up means "yes."

Thumb down means "no."

Thumb to the right means "I don't know."

Thumb to the left means "Maybe so."

Sunglasses and Cell Phones

I always keep sunglasses and three inactivated cell phones in a basket in my toy cupboard. Children who don't feel comfortable talking about themselves or their problems will often be willing to talk as someone else (the person wearing sunglasses) or to listen as their parents and I discuss their situation on the phone. One ingenious five-year-old pretended that he was a teenager driving a car as his mother and I had a "phone conversation" about how, when he was five, he used to get upset if she said "no" to him, even about little things—like that he had to wait until after dinner to have dessert. Now that he was a teen, he always remembered that his mother loved him and he was important to her, even when she said "no." He could trust that she was making a good decision for him. Another five-year-old chose to wear sunglasses while he talked on the phone, expressing his feelings using words he knew were not acceptable for him to use when talking to his mother. Puppets can also speak for the child. A degree of anonymity can make honesty easier!

Part III

WRITING THE NEW STORY

14

A HEALING NARRATIVE
What? Why? How?

Children naturally come up with explanations for why things happen. Children who were traumatized by scary or dangerous events, in which they felt helpless, try to make sense of their confusion. Given their young age and developmental stage, they tend to come to the conclusion that they were bad and that what happened was their fault. They may conclude that they can't tolerate anything unless they have constant attention or that they are not safe unless they have control of whatever is happening. The result is posttraumatic behaviors that reflect their distorted beliefs about themselves and the world.

A healing narrative is a tool to address a child's confusion and distorted beliefs about the trauma he/she has experienced. The narrative, which can be a story of a single event or a life story, provides objective information, a developmentally appropriate explanation, and a positive resolution. The therapist and parents collaborate to write the story, providing parents with a chance to understand how trauma distorts beliefs and misguides their traumatized child's current behavior, to empathize with their child, to consider carefully what changes they want for their family, to clarify their role as parents, and to help their child recover. Collaborative story writing provides the therapist with an opportunity to evaluate the parents' degree of trauma resolution, to learn language that is familiar to the child, and to understand the family's belief systems about why trauma happens and how it can be resolved. Through the process of working with the parents, the therapist can develop a case formulation and treatment plan.

The story can be written at any point in the course of treatment and for any patient. Optimally, a child can tell his or her own story, explaining what happened and why. However, many children cannot tell their own story.

The story format is well suited for the developmental needs of young children who are unable to articulate what happened, who don't want to verbalize what happened, or who experienced preverbal trauma and do not remember the events. Young children, especially those too young to read, often cannot consolidate the memory of a traumatic event into a representative image, and the story can serve to guide them through the "frame-by-frame" sequence of what happened. Young children, who naturally do not have the "adult perspective," may depend on "educational interweaves" in order to process trauma and come to an adaptive resolution. The parents can supply the cognitive information and emotional understanding their child may need to make sense of what happened.

Parents, as well as their children, may have been affected by the same traumatic event. Even if the parents were not present at the time of their child's traumatic experience, they may feel guilty that they were unable to protect their child and helpless because they could not help their child get over the trauma. Parents may feel overwhelmed with thoughts of their child's traumatic early life and exhausted from trying to respond to their child's extreme behaviors. Participating in writing the story for their child gives parents an opportunity to resolve their own trauma with regard to the events and assists them in developing or regaining confidence in their ability to parent and raise a resilient child.

During the course of writing the story collaboratively with the parents, the therapist asks the important question: "What do you want your child to think about himself/herself, given he/she had this experience?" Parents who have been distressed and may have viewed their child as an innocent victim begin to reevaluate their assessment. Instead of seeing the child as injured and abandoned, they may want the child to see himself/herself as someone who is resilient, who can overcome trauma, and who can take advantage of the help and love they offer.

Healing narratives can also be used with adults who want to formulate a helpful story (for their "child self") about an early childhood event that was confusing at the time and has remained too frightening to process. One adult client who had written a story initially described her own "light as so bright" that it burned her mother and caused her mother's mental illness. In reworking the story with me, the adult woman began to realize that her own "bright light" had not caused her mother's illness and that it could serve as a beacon of hope for the rest of the family as she led the way to a healthy life. Developing a coherent, cohesive life story empowers an adult to behave like an adult (instead of a hurt child) and widens the possibility of healthy attachment to others.

Writing the therapeutic story encourages the therapist to understand the family belief systems regarding the traumatic incident, focus the therapeutic work, and identify elements in the history that cause confusion for the patient. It is important for the therapist to pay attention to the parents' belief system and choice of language, as they help formulate a resolution for the traumatic experiences. For example, some parents may want their child to believe that adoption was God's plan, or that the loved one who passed away is "alive in heaven" and that they will meet again someday, or that things happen for the best. Other parents may want their child to understand that sometimes things just happen and we will never know why, that while we can't see the loved one who is no longer alive, he/she lives on in our hearts and minds, or that bad things happen and we have to learn to deal with them. When the healing narrative is complete, the clinician can think in terms of the child's empowering life story and can weave these family belief systems and insights into the child's play and conversations.

Giving a child a coherent life narrative itself may contribute to the development of a secure attachment. Mary Main (1996) and her colleagues developed the Adult Attachment Interview to help determine "retrospectively the nature of the parent's own early attachment experiences, assuming that the better the experiences of the parent, the more secure the parent, the more securely attached the child would be" (Mitchell, 2000, p. 85). The researchers learned that it was not whether the parent had been deprived or nurtured as a child, but the degree of coherence of a mother's narrative about her childhood that was the most important predictor of attachment style (e.g., Main, 1995; Main & Solomon, 1986; Mitchell, 2000; Siegel & Hartzell, 2003). Perhaps writing a coherent life story for a child will send him/her on the path to earned secure attachment!

What Are Some Elements of a Good Healing Narrative?

A good story "rings true." Even if some of the details of the story are omitted (such as a discussion of a parent's extramarital affair), the pain and confusion caused by the experience should be acknowledged.

A good story has a beginning, a middle section, and an ending. The story starts with a setting of safety and describes strengths and resources. The middle section relays one or two significant events, including some sensory information accompanying the events that can be useful targets in EMDR processing. The story ends in a way that offers the possibility of trauma resolution, personal empowerment, and trusting relationships.

An effective story has a neutral tone. It leaves out a description of known or presumed emotional expression, and repeated readings offer an opportunity for the young listener to add feelings, thoughts, and information about his/her own experience.

The story includes cognitive interweaves or educational interweaves, information that serves to fill in the gaps in the child's understanding. Cognitive interweaves can provide information about safety, responsibility, or choices that the child couldn't have known at the time of the traumatic event. They could also elicit the adult perspective or encourage the patient to imagine giving his/her younger self what he/she needed at the time of the trauma. A good story provides positive cognitions, which are beliefs about the self that are true, useful, and self-enhancing.

171

The story differentiates between "then" and "now." "Then" the child was truly in danger. "Then" the child was powerless and helpless. "Now" the emergency is over. "Now" the child can begin to trust others to take care of him/her and can continue to learn to take care of himself/herself.

If the healing narrative is about problems like a long history or abuse or a complicated medical situation, or if the child dissociates easily, the initial story should be brief, emphasizing the child's current safety. As the child is able to tolerate remembering more, more information or additional chapters can be added to the story.

How to Use a Healing Narrative

The healing narrative can be written out and read to the child, preferably with both parents present to emphasize the importance of the child's story. Some children like to hear their story multiple times over a number of visits. The story does not have to be read aloud, but rather may be used informally, with parts of it woven into the child's play. Some children may like to have toy figures act out the story so that they can visualize what happened. Sometimes parents turn the story into a book with photos or their own illustrations or the child's drawings.

Before you read the story to the child, let the child know that there will be a good ending.

Read the story all the way through, while giving alternating bilateral stimulation (ABS). After reading the story, ask the child if there is a part of the story that he/she likes. Reinforce the part of the story the child likes with ABS, drawing attention to the physical location where he/she feels the happy, good, or loved feeling.

The second time you read the story, ask the child to help you make the story better. Read the story, this time asking the child what he/she thinks the child in the story thought, felt, and wondered at each of the upsetting parts. Use ABS to desensitize and reprocess distressing memories and install positive cognitions. If the child recognizes and talks about the story as his/her own, talk about the child in the room instead of the child in the story.

Ask the child what he/she thinks the child in the story needed when he/she felt sad, etc., and imagine giving the child what he/she needed. Add in ABS as the child imagines getting what he/she needed. Ask the child how the baby feels after getting what he/she needed. Reinforce or desensitize that feeling with ABS.

Consider adding a paragraph that includes the description of a current problem that you think is the consequence of earlier trauma. Desensitize and reprocess the current situation. Desensitize current triggers.

If the SUD rating does not go down to zero, ask the child what is keeping the memory upsetting. Consider targeting whatever stands in the way of trauma resolution. You might say, "Notice what still makes it hard for the child in the story to trust that his/her parents will make sure the child has the food he/she needs . . ."

Find out if there is still a part of the trauma or the current situation that is confusing. If so, give information (cognitive interweaves) that will help the child make sense of the confusing experience. If the experience cannot be understood, label it "confusing." For example, confirm that divorce is confusing. A child can accept that he/she will understand divorce better when he/she grows up. Likewise, it may help to tell the child that there are some mysteries we can't understand, like why a person dies young. Then add ABS to desensitize or "clear" the feeling of confusion.

Imagine the future with the problem resolved. Add in ABS as the child imagines the future when he/she is safe and free from posttraumatic problems.

If the healing narrative is a story of loss of a loved one and grief, be sure to include a way to hold the beloved person's memory and love safe in the child's heart. Discuss loyalty and give the child permission to have fun even though the loved one is no longer alive.

Guidelines for Developing a Healing Narrative to Resolve Trauma and Promote Attachment

1. Identify the issues you want to address and resolve in your story.

   People often come to therapy because of an issue that repeatedly stimulates an exaggerated emotional response or distress, which can take the form of extreme irritation, anxiety, frustration, anger, sadness, or low self-worth.

   Consider: What issues are important to resolve?

Table 14.1 Examples of issues and negative cognitions

Issues	Negative Cognitions
Trust	I can't trust anyone.
Unfairness	I can't tolerate it if anything seems unfair.
Perfectionism	I am not good enough.
Fear	I am not safe.
Distrust	I can't be intimate because I might be hurt.
Disappointment	If I don't get something I want, I am a loser.
Control	I have to be in control and get my way, or I am in danger.
Confusion	I can't tolerate something I don't understand.
Sadness	I can't go on.
Survivor guilt	I can't enjoy my life because he/she doesn't have his/hers.
Transitions	I can't tolerate change.
Rejection	I am unlovable.
Abandonment	I am not worth caring about.

2. Identify strengths and resources.

Each person has a unique set of attributes, abilities, and support that can help his/her overcome issues.

Consider: What are the personal qualities (sense of humor, compassion, health, perseverance, creativity), tangible resources (family, religious beliefs, friends, therapist, financial assets, education, a pet), or other nurturing resources (a favorite character in a book or movie, a favorite piece of music, journaling, artwork) that help the individual?

3. Identify key events, critical incidents, or experiences that contributed to the limiting "story."

There are usually one or more specific events that "taught" the person distorted or negative beliefs. (For example, the depressed patient may believe that it's not safe to relax or be happy because something terrible happened while he/she was having a good time.)

Consider: What is the memory of a moment in a real experience that represents the worse part of the trauma? What sensory information goes along with the memory? Does a "float back" (see Glossary) reveal an earlier underlying traumatic experience?

4. Identify the confusion.

Confusion accompanies all traumatic events. The traumatic experiences happened too fast or inexplicably or unfairly, or are beyond the child's developmental scope. Later, new experiences that seem confusing or hard to understand may continue to trigger excessive anxiety.

Consider: What are the recurrent, swirling (and sometimes unanswerable) questions?

For example: Why didn't my mom keep me? Why did my dad hit me? Why did someone break into my house? Why did my brother die? Why do people use drugs? Why did the accident happen?

It can be helpful to label these considerations as confusing or mysterious. The sense of confusion can be a target for EMDR processing.

5. Address issues of fault.

Young children tend to believe that everything that happens is someone's fault.

Consider: What is wrong with me that makes bad things happen to me? This becomes very sticky and confusing—e.g., If it's not his fault that his mother left him, why do people become angry and leave when he behaves in hurtful ways? Remember the word "and." It is possible that it is not his fault that his mother left, "and" hurtful behavior is not OK.

6. Identify current triggers for exaggerated emotional responses or distress.

> Parents can keep a log of their child's disturbing behaviors and notice what preceded the upset.
> Consider: What triggers excessive upset? Being ignored? Physical contact? Teasing? Certain noises? Being excluded?

7. What problem behaviors and feelings are triggered by exaggerated emotional responses or distress?

> Children who have been traumatized may exhibit excessive anger, anxiety, sadness, frustration, or despair.
> Consider: Does the child show his/her distress by hitting, hiding, aggression, crying, screaming, stealing, or lying?

8. Identify negative cognitions.

> Sometimes negative cognitions may have been true at the time of the trauma, but they are not currently helpful and impede normal life.
> Consider: Is the child letting you know, either through words or actions, that he thinks he is bad, helpless, unlovable, or can't tolerate it when he doesn't get what he wants right away?
> Ask yourself, "Is there a way that the negative beliefs were useful or helpful at the time of the trauma?" If so, is it appropriate to acknowledge and thank the "self" for using that successful strategy for survival? For example, if a child was punished or shamed by an angry parent every time she asked for something, it makes sense that the child learned to suppress her needs and not ask for anything she wants. The strategy of needs suppression limited the amount of damage to the sense of self. When the child is out of the dangerous situation, it may be important for her to speak up and ask for what she needs.

9. Identify positive cognitions.

> It is important to identify the true, useful, and self-enhancing beliefs that fit the current situation and are useful in moving forward in life.
> Consider: Does this child need to know that he/she is important and lovable even when his/her parents say "no" to something the child wants? Does the child need to know that he/she is safe even if the parent feels upset?

10. Identify cognitive interweaves or additional information that might be necessary to resolve the trauma.

> Consider: Does the child need additional information or the adult perspective? For example, "It's never a child's fault if a parent is abusive." Or "A child's angry feelings can't make someone die."

11. What is different about the patient's life now that makes it possible for a change in "story"?

> Babies can't talk, get their own food, or change their own diapers. They are truly dependent on adults for their well-being.
>
> Consider: What is different now that the child is able to talk and say what's happening and ask for help? What is different now that the adults in his/her life know how to take care of children? What can the child understand now that he/she couldn't understand when he/she was younger?

12. What does the child have to learn or practice?

> It may be necessary for the child to have new experiences in order to develop judgment and resolve the trauma.
>
> Consider: Would it be valuable for him/her to practice sharing how he/she feels with a trusted adult? Does he/she need more experience with an adoptive parent to trust that the parent can take care of him/her?

13. How can the child cope or manage an ongoing difficult situation?

> Clearing the distress of traumatic memories may be only the first step in healing. Some children need to develop tools for self-soothing or for asserting themselves effectively.
>
> Consider: What strategies does the child have or need to soothe himself/herself when he/she is stressed?
>
> Does he/she know how to approach an adult to ask for help?
>
> Does the child have a safety plan to help him/her know what to do if his/her parents are arguing or not available?

14. Are there any transitional cognitions that would be helpful?

> Transitional cognitions are beliefs that are "stepping-stones" that offer encouragement on the way to mastering new skills.
>
> Consider: Does the child know that everyone makes mistakes while they are learning? Does the child know when it's OK to ask for help or comfort?

15. Are there any quotes by important people that might offer support, encouragement, and confidence?

> Parents, teachers, therapists, religious figures, action figure heroes, and characters in books can offer important advice and encouragement.
>
> Consider: Who appreciates the child or can offer words of encouragement? Who can provide developmentally appropriate information and explanations?

16. What is the hope for the future?

Everyone needs hope, everyone needs to dream, and everyone needs to believe that a better future is possible after trauma resolution.

Consider: What can this child look forward to in the future? Can the child expect his/her family to look out for him/her and do what they can to keep him/her safe? Can the child expect the family to come together every year to celebrate his/her birthday? Can the child look forward to going to school and making new friends and learning new things?

Story for Resolving Trauma and Enhancing Attachment Potential in a Child: The Basic Framework

1st Section: establishes a current safe place; include information about strengths and resources, positive experiences.

Once upon a time there was a girl/boy (current information, e.g., a little boy, a girl, a teen) who lived with _____.
He or she enjoyed _____.
He or she loved _____
(include information about strengths and resources, the child's special interests, what the family appreciates about the child, etc.).

2nd Section: describes the circumstances; critical incidents with sensory information.

Just like everyone else in the world, the girl/boy had some things in his/her life that were lucky/blessings/wonderful and some things that were _____ (choose one or two: sad/difficult/confusing/unfair/hard to understand, etc.).
One lucky/blessing/wonderful thing was that she/he was born good and lovable and _____ (choose one or two: strong/caring, etc.).
One sad/difficult/hard to understand/confusing thing was that _____
_____ (issue or incident).

(If helpful . . . Sometimes, when sad/difficult things happen, they can be confusing and hard to understand. Little children sometimes wonder whether it is their fault or think they are bad.)

Explain what was confusing and what the child is supposed to think about it. Use educational interweaves as needed.

Or, if appropriate:

If his/her parents had known him/her then, they would have been right there to help.

Or

If his/her parents had known, they never would have let . . .

His/her mother says, "_____."

His/her father says, "_____."

3rd Section: understandable resolution with educational interweaves, positive cognitions, words of wisdom from parents, and future template.

> Now that he/she is older, he/she can understand some things that he/she couldn't understand when he/she was a baby (or young child).
> Or
> Now his/her parents want him/her to know some things that are important. They want him/her to know that _____.
> Or
> Now it is time for him/her to _____.
> He/she can understand that _____.

Examples:

> it was nobody's fault/it was not his/her fault
> he/she is lovable
> he/she can be OK even if things don't go his/her way
> now he/she can express his/her feelings and _____ will understand
> he/she can have feelings and calm himself/herself enough to control his/her behavior
> we can be OK even if we can't understand exactly why something happened; the world is full of things we can't understand
> everyone deserves to be treated kindly and so does he/she
> he/she can trust _____ to _____
> he/she is safe even if others are in control, like when he/she does what the teacher or his/her parents tell him/her to do
> he/she is safe, even if something is unfair, like when he/she plays a game and the kids change the rules
> Now she can _____.
> Or
> Now she is free to _____.
> Or
> Now she can begin to _____.

Story Template for Resolving Trauma and Promoting Attachment in a Child Adopted From a Foreign Country

1st Section: establishes a current safe place; includes information about strengths and resources, positive experiences.

Once upon a time there was a boy who lived in a cozy house with his
_____. They loved to _____.
His parents especially appreciated that _____.
The family liked to _____ together. (Include
some information about the child's important place in his extended
family.)

(Optional: He loved having his very own bed and his very own clothes
and his very own toys.)

2nd Section: describes the circumstances; tells the history.

Like everyone else in the world, some things in the child's life were
wonderful and some things in his life were_____
(hard to understand, confusing, sad). One wonderful thing was
that the child was born lovable and good and _____.
Another important thing was that he had his own forever mommy
and daddy to take care of him and family and friends who loved
him.

Like everyone else in the world, the boy had some things in his life
that were sad. One sad thing was that when he was born, his birth
parents could not take care of him. He was a very lovable baby,
but they could not take care of babies, so the lovable little baby
was taken to an orphanage, a place where babies wait for their
forever parents/family. Each caregiver in the orphanage had a lot
of babies to take care of, and they were too busy to spend enough
time to get to know each baby well. While the boy was in the
orphanage waiting for his forever mother, he had to try hard to
get the attention of the busy caregivers so that he could get fed or
picked up or get his diaper changed. He was too little to talk. He
sometimes needed to work hard to get his way so he could get fed
and cuddled and clean, dry clothes.

Alternatively: He figured out that he could get the best care by being
a "good" baby who pleased his caregivers by not showing that he
had any needs at all.

Or

The caregivers were so busy that they didn't hold the baby's bottle.
The bottle was propped on a pillow, and he had to stay very still
so he wouldn't lose it—or he had to hold it himself.

Sometimes the caregivers were too busy taking care of so many
babies, and every baby had to wait for attention. Sometimes he
couldn't get what he needed, but that was not his fault.

While he was waiting he felt _____.

He thought _____.

He wondered _____.

The little baby was too little to talk and didn't know any English then, but if he could have talked, he might have said _____.

If his forever parents had known about him then, they would have been right there to _____ (give him food and cuddles and clean, dry clothes and whatever else he needed).

Then one day something changed. One day his forever parents, who knew how to take good care of a baby, came to the orphanage to take him home to _____. They put clean clothes on him and gave him his very own _____. They took a plane and flew to _____.

There were so many new things to get used to!

At first everything was new and hard to understand and confusing for the baby because he had new parents and heard a new language, and food was different, and there was so much new to see and hear and feel!

He felt _____.

He thought _____.

He wondered _____.

The baby was too little to talk and didn't know English, so he couldn't explain what he was thinking or ask questions or say how he felt.

If he could have talked, he would have said _____ _____.

3rd Section: understandable resolution with educational interweaves, positive cognitions, words of wisdom from parents, and future template.

Now that he is older, he can understand some things he couldn't understand when he was a baby. He can understand that now he has his very own forever mommy and daddy to take care of him and love him and keep him safe. Even when his mommy and daddy are not paying attention to him, they remember him and will give him what he needs—like food or cuddles. He may have to wait a little while, but he is OK and he can relax because they will take care of him.

Here is a sample of the parent's words to the child, but it's just a sample. The parents (or other trusted adults) can say whatever they want:

His mom says, "I love you. I always remember you and think about what you need, even if I'm away from you. I'll do my best to make sure that you are safe and that you will get what you need. You're safe and loved even if you have to wait. I will love you and take care of you forever."

His dad says, "I will do my best to protect you. Now you're safe and you can learn and do new things. It's not your fault the sad things happened. I love you, and I want you to be happy and know I will always be your very own dad."

Now, he can trust his parents (or other trusted adults) to be in charge. He can try new things and say how he feels. He can learn new things. He can play and take turns and know that if he waits, he will get a turn. He can play and he can share his toys. There will always be something for him. Now, he is free to love and know that he is safe and good and lovable and smart. He can begin to _____

_____.

SAMPLE STORIES

Molestation by a Family Friend

Between the ages of 4 and 8, this 11-year-old girl was molested by her father's best friend, who was the family's next-door neighbor. When she began therapy, her dominant symptoms were confusion, fear, frustration, and anger. She frequently asked why the man had molested her if he was her father's best friend. She wanted to know why her parents had let the molestation happen.

She was afraid of seeing the perpetrator and fearful of new men, certain doorways, dogs, cancer, asthma, snakes, and movies. She generally seemed anguished and confused and had a sensitive stomach. She was fearful at night, woke nightly, and slept in her parents' bed. She was held back a year in school because of learning disabilities and difficulty concentrating.

The girl's mother and I wrote the following story. The italicized portions of the story are the words that the girl provided when asked, "What did the girl think? What did she wonder? How did she feel?"

The challenge: How would you explain the molestation by a family friend to an 11-year-old girl and help her get over her fears and trust her parents again?

Angelina

Once upon a time there was a girl who lived with her younger brother and her mom and dad. The girl loved sports and books and dogs.

When she was born, the girl was lovable and good and smart and lots of fun. Like everybody else in the world, the girl had some things in her life that were wonderful and some things that were scary and confusing. One wonderful part is that she had a family that loved her.

The scary, confusing part started when she was four years old and a man moved in next door with his family. The man was very friendly and helpful. The scary part was that sometimes the man touched her body by putting his hand inside her underpants. The confusing part was that the man was so friendly and nice and fun to play with. The man was strong, and the girl loved to play with him. The next-door neighbor was a close friend of her parents, and he was especially close to her dad.

When the man touched her, she thought *that maybe a lot of people do that.*

She thought *let go of me.*

She felt *curious.*

Sometimes when these things happen, children want to tell their parents but they feel afraid.

The girl felt *surprised at what he was doing.*

One day during summer vacation, near the start of school, the girl was with her mom, and her mom asked her "What's your secret password for someone to pick you up? And who should be allowed to pick you up?" The girl said, "Anybody, but not our next-door neighbor." Then the girl told her mom that the man had been touching her inappropriately around her private parts.

As soon as her mom knew, she went into action to protect her daughter. When they got home, her mom called the police. The girl was scared that the man would come to get her and maybe hurt her. The mom assured her that she would be OK. They went to a special police station and told the officers what happened and answered their questions. The man's daughter told the police that her dad molested her too. He also molested other kids. The police believed all the kids and put the man in jail.

The neighbor wrote a letter saying he was sorry about what he had done and that he wouldn't do it again. It was good he wrote the letter apologizing. Even though he apologized, what he did was wrong.

The man was in jail for nine months. But then he got out. The girl was afraid he would be angry with her and try to hurt her family since he went to jail. Her mom assured her that he couldn't harm her anymore because the police were watching him and because he wanted to get on with his life.

The man was a pedophile—an adult who touches children in inappropriate ways. That is against the law. It isn't OK for anyone to touch a child's private parts.

Sometimes the girl remembers what happened and wonders *who and what she can trust.*

She thinks *she can trust her mom.*

She feels *happy she can trust somebody.*

Her parents want her to know that even though there are some pedophiles in the world, most people are OK.

Now that she's older, she can understand some things that she couldn't understand when she was younger.

Her mom and her dad want her to trust her own judgment and to trust them.

They want her to know that she is safe and loved and that she can express her feelings and thoughts.

If her mom and dad had known that the neighbor was a pedophile, they never would have been friends with him or left her alone with him. Everybody learned a lot from what happened. Her parents want her to be cautious, but not fearful.

She is safe now and can feel free to enjoy her body and trust that she will be able to decide whether someone's touch is inappropriate or OK. If she's not sure, she can ask her mom.

Molestation by a Babysitter; Molestation by a Child

This nine-year-old boy was molested by his babysitter. Later, the boy touched other children inappropriately.

The challenge: How do you explain sexual molestation to a nine-year-old boy and help him trust his parents? How can you help him forgive himself for touching other children inappropriately and help him behave appropriately?

Mick

Once upon a time there was a boy who lived in a house with his family and pet rabbit. The boy loved to read adventure stories and play with Legos. He had lots of friends in his neighborhood, and he especially liked riding bikes, playing video games, and playing catch with his friends.

Like everybody else in the world, this boy had some things in his life that were wonderful and some things that were sad and hard to understand. One wonderful thing was that the boy was born good, lovable, and intelligent.

One sad and hard-to-understand thing in his life happened when he was four years old. He had a babysitter who sometimes touched him in ways that no one should touch a child. For example, while the babysitter was playing and wrestling with him, the babysitter put his hand on the boy's penis and rear end. The babysitter sometimes put his hand on the boy's crotch while he flew him around like an airplane. One time the babysitter took the boy into the bathroom and closed the door. Then the babysitter said, "Do you want to see my secret weapon?" Then the babysitter exposed his penis to the boy and asked if he wanted to touch it.

Sometimes when people expose themselves to a child or touch them inappropriately, the child feel confused and wonders if it's OK for someone to touch his private parts. It is especially confusing if the child likes and trusts the person. The child might feel guilty knowing that it's wrong, but he doesn't need to feel guilty even if it was something that felt good. No matter what the child does or feels, it is never a child's fault if he is molested.

Sometimes children who have been molested experiment with touching other children's private parts. It is not their fault that they experimented, but it's not OK to touch other people's private parts. It is only OK to touch your own private parts while you're a child.

Sometimes children are scared to tell their parents what happened. The babysitter threatened that if the boy told his parents, he would kill the rabbit the boy loved so much.

A few months later, while on vacation, the little boy told his mother about the babysitter showing him his penis and asking him to touch it. Telling his mother was a very brave thing for him to do. The boy's parents were very upset about what the babysitter had done. If they had known that the babysitter was a child molester, they never would have let him babysit for their son EVER.

This was the first time the boy's parents knew that the babysitter had molested the boy. They reassured their son that it was not his fault. The parents called the police and reported the babysitter because child molestation by an adult is a crime.

The parents wanted to do everything they could to help the boy. They took him to see a therapist who helps children who've been molested.

The parents talked to the babysitter and told him never to come near their children again.

The babysitter apologized for what he had done, and he moved out of the area.

Now that the boy is older, he can understand some things that he couldn't understand when he was little.

He can understand that what the babysitter did was wrong. Nothing that happened was the little boy's fault. Now he can understand that his parents were upset about the babysitter, not about anything the boy did.

Child molesters are adults who have something seriously wrong with them. They choose young boys and girls for inappropriate sexual behavior. Any child can be a target for a child molester. The children they molest are innocent.

The boy can also understand that is important to respect people's bodies, and it is not OK for children to touch anyone else's private parts.

When he was four he was too young to understand about appropriate and inappropriate kinds of touching. Now he is old enough to say "no" if anyone tries to touch him inappropriately and to tell his parents right away if somebody tries. He can also ask his parents when he's not sure what is appropriate.

His mother says, "You can tell us about anything that anyone does or says, especially if that person does or says something that makes you uncomfortable or if you're not sure what is OK. It's never OK for anyone to tell you to keep a secret from your parents. We'll always listen to you and help you."

His father says, "Now you understand that it's not OK to touch anyone else's private parts, and I trust that you will respect other people's bodies. I'll always do my best to take care of you and protect you. You can always come to me with any problem. I love you."

Now the boy knows that his parents would never have let that babysitter stay with him if they had known what he was doing. The boy can trust his parents and tell them if he's unsure if something is right or wrong.

Adoption Complicated by Divorce

Ashley was a woman in her early 20s who was adopted from an orphanage in Asia at age three. When she was five, her adoptive parents divorced. Ashley came to therapy because she found it very hard to make decisions. She was always worried that her choices would hurt someone's feelings.

The challenge: How do you help an adopted young adult whose adoptive parents divorced make sense of her indecisiveness and begin to make decisions about her life?

Ashley

Once upon a time there was a young woman who lived with her parents. She loved animals and she loved her friends.

Like everybody else in the world, some things in the woman's life were lucky and some were hard. One lucky thing was that she was born good and lovable and she had an eye for beauty. One hard thing was that it felt hard for her to make decisions for herself about what she wanted to do in her life.

She wanted to make computer programs, but she didn't seem to really get into it. She sort of wanted to be a nurse, but sort of not. She wanted to learn Spanish, but she didn't sign up for Spanish class. She wanted to travel, but she didn't make plans to do it. She wanted to leave her job in a store, but she didn't want to tell the manager that she wanted to leave. She wanted to learn to play chess, but she didn't sign up for a class because she thought she might not follow through.

All of that wanting to do things and not doing them took a lot of energy!

When the young woman was a young girl, wanting to do things and at the same time not wanting to do things made sense. If she chose one thing to do, she displeased her mother. If she made another choice, she displeased her father. The fog of indecision blunted the pain of the feeling that she couldn't please anybody enough to make them truly happy.

Now that she is an adult, she is in a very different situation. Through her actions, she has demonstrated that she is capable of making good decisions.

Despite feeling that she was stuck in her life, the young woman accomplished many things. She persisted in organizing and arranging for her GED, and when she took the exam, she passed.

Despite her fears about traveling, she went on a trip to another state with her family and enjoyed it.

Despite not feeling 100 percent connected to her friends, she persisted in contacting them and maintaining some of her high school friendships. Even though she had fears about applying for jobs, she got a job at a card shop, a job babysitting, and a job helping a disabled person.

Despite her fears that any decision she made would disappoint someone or result in loss, the truth is that she didn't disappoint anybody or lose anything. Every time she did something new, she felt afraid that she would lose something, but instead, every time she tries something new, she gains new experience.

The young woman knows that this is a time in her life for exploring and experimenting. As she does this, mistakes and disappointments are inevitable, but the mistakes don't hurt anybody, and she as well as others can tolerate the disappointments.

It is OK for this young woman to try things, even if she's not sure she wants to do them, or even if she thinks she might quit. It is OK for this young woman to try new things, even if she feels scared. As she looks back at her accomplishments over the past year, she can realize that she can still make progress in her life, even if she feels scared or uncertain. Over time, she will reject some paths and choose others. She can trust that over time, she will discover her own passions and that her parents care about her, even when she makes a decision that doesn't please them.

Preverbal Trauma and Sleepless Nights

Rachel was a three-year-old child with loving parents. Although Rachel was a late talker, her parents knew that she was very smart. Her mother affectionately described her daughter as a mute adult inside a baby's body. Until she was 18 months old, Rachel was a pleasure during the daytime and slept like a dream at night.

We don't know what happened the night the babysitter was there. At the time, Rachel was only 18 months old, and she was not yet able to talk. Her mother reported that the next day, Rachel refused to get in her crib. She cried a lot and had trouble getting to sleep, and she was very unhappy. Before the night when the babysitter came, Rachel had sucked on her pacifier to comfort herself to sleep for every nap and bedtime. After that night, she refused to suck on her pacifier at all, and she slept fitfully and woke and cried many times every night.

Rachel's parents found it hard to believe that the babysitter would have done anything to hurt their little girl. The babysitter was a teenager who lived in the neighborhood, and all of the families in the neighborhood loved her. She had babysat several times before, and everything had gone fine.

Rachel's parents tried to figure out what could have happened the night the babysitter was there. They knew that Rachel had already had two naps that day and that she probably wasn't tired. They noticed a thumbprint-sized bruise on their daughter's thigh and thought that the babysitter probably had had to hold her down to change her diaper. They didn't think much about it until later, when the little girl continued to have trouble falling asleep, and when she did sleep, she woke frequently, crying.

When Rachel was two years old, she began to talk. One day she told her mother that the babysitter had hit her. She pointed to a spot on her cheek. By then Rachel's nights were nightmarish. She either sat awake most of the night staring or crying, "Help me, Mommy," or she sobbed for hours while she was asleep, sometimes crying out, "No, I don't want it. I don't need it." She became tired and cranky during the day.

The challenge: How do you help a three-year-old child get over a preverbal experience that happened when her parents were not with her? How could you help her sleep again?

I made the decision to write two stories for Rachel—the first one was written to help the three-year-old distinguish between "then" and "now" and to see that she was so much more competent now than when the traumatic incident happened. The second story was written to address the parents' attempts to help Rachel through play. This strategy had backfired, as Rachel thought the toy babysitter was real, and she became even more upset, waking from fitful sleep every hour all night long.

Rachel's parents had asked their precocious daughter what they should do to help her at night. Both Rachel and her parents were at a loss to figure out what would help. After we worked with the stories, Rachel's parents were able to tell their daughter with confidence that she was safe at night and that they were big and strong and could protect her. The stories, and EMDR, combined with a slight change in parenting style helped Rachel and her parents sleep through the night.

Story 1 for Rachel

Once upon a time there was a girl who lived in a house with her mommy and daddy and somebody who took care of her while her mommy and daddy were at work. There were a lot of people who loved the little girl: Her mommy and daddy and her grandparents and aunts and uncles and cousins loved her so much.

Like all the other girls and boys in the world, some things in the girl's life were wonderful and some things were hard. One wonderful thing was that the girl was born lovable and good and happy. Another good thing was that as the girl grew up she was able to do more and more new things.

When she was a baby, she could only crawl. She tried over and over until she could stand up and walk. One day she walked from her mommy to her daddy.

Then she learned to walk downstairs. At first she could only walk downstairs holding somebody's hand. Then she learned to walk all by herself. Now that she is a big girl, she can hop and jump.

When she was a baby, she liked when someone blew bubbles, but she couldn't do it herself. Now that she's bigger, she can blow bubbles all by herself.

When she was a baby, she couldn't talk.

When she wanted something, she had to point.

When she was tired, she rubbed her eyes.

When she didn't like something, she cried.

When she was a baby, some adults couldn't always understand what she wanted or needed.

Now that she is a big girl, when she feels tired, she can say, "I'm tired."

Now that she's a big girl, when she wants something, she can say what she wants or ask for help.

Now that she's a big girl, when she feels hurts, she can say, "I have a boo-boo."

Now that she's a big girl, when she doesn't like something, she can say, "No, I don't like that."

Now people can listen to her and understand what she needs.

Now adults can try to make it better when she doesn't like something or needs help.

Now the big girl can have lots of fun playing and learning new things every day and relax at night because she knows that she can use her voice and her words to help herself.

Story 2 for Rachel

Once upon a time there was a girl who lived in a house with her mommy and daddy. Lots of people loved the little girl, especially her mommy and daddy and grandparents.

Like all other girls and boys in the world, some things in the girl's life were wonderful and some things were hard. One wonderful thing was that the girl was born lovable and good and happy.

After the little girl's scary night with a babysitter, the little girl had a hard time sleeping. The girl's parents wanted to help their little girl feel better. They made up a pretend babysitter named Agatha. Agatha was just a doll. The girl's mom pretended that the doll babysitter named Agatha came to take care of a doll little girl. Her mom thought that it would help the real girl feel better if she could tell the babysitter, "Go away and never come back." Maybe the little girl was too little to understand that the doll Agatha was just a made-up babysitter—Agatha is not a real person.

Now that the girl is a big girl, she is learning that some things are real and some are just pretend. Dolls and movies are all pretend. They can't hurt anybody. The girl is safe and OK even if someone pretends that they hit. It's just play. Everybody is safe and OK.

Dreams are not real either. Even if someone has a bad dream, they are still safe. Dreams are just something that happens when we sleep. They can't hurt anybody. All dreams are safe and OK.

Now when the big girl goes to bed, she can relax. If she's in bed and awake, she can just relax or sing to herself. When she is asleep, it's OK if she dreams or if she doesn't dream. Everybody is still safe. It's OK to relax and sleep all night long. Her mommy and daddy are loving her and thinking about her all night, and they help keep her safe, even while she sleeps.

Adoption After Physical Abuse

Lucas was a five-year-old boy who was adopted when he was three. His birth mother had neglected him, and he was found wandering around a shopping center alone, dirty, and hungry. The police took him to a foster home, where he was beaten when he soiled his pants. He was moved to an emergency shelter and was adopted at an adoption fair. His adoptive parents brought him to me because he was stealing food, and he was very depressed, anxious, and afraid to try new things. His kindergarten teacher described him as the saddest boy she had ever seen.

The challenge: How do you help an adopted five-year-old believe that he wasn't "bad" even though he was neglected by his biological mother and beaten in foster care?

Lucas

Once upon a time there was a little boy who lived with his mommy and daddy and brother. They lived in a neighborhood that had lots of children. The boy and his brother liked to play together in the sandbox in their backyard. The whole family liked to go camping and fishing together. The boy's parents appreciated that he was nice with the family dog and that he enjoyed listening to books.

Like everybody else in the world, the little boy had some things in his life that were lucky and some things that were very sad. Luckily, the boy was born good, lovable, and caring. The sad part was that even though his birth parents cared about him, they couldn't take care of children, and they didn't keep the little boy safe. His birth mother loved to hug him and kiss him, but she couldn't take care of him, and sometimes he was left outside all alone. When he was left all by himself,

he wondered _____.

he thought _____.

he felt _____.

One day the police, whose job it is to keep people safe, found him outside all by himself. The police and the judge decided that they had to move the good little boy to a safe place. They chose a nice man and woman to take care of him for a while, until they could find a foster home.

Next the police and the judge chose a foster mommy and daddy who seemed nice at first, but they didn't know how to take care of children. The judge and the police didn't know that the foster mommy and daddy would be mean, or they never would have chosen that family for the little boy. That foster mommy and daddy had never had children before. They didn't know that little children sometimes poop in their pants, especially if they are scared or sad. They spanked the little boy with a belt sometimes.

The little boy wondered _____.

He thought _____.

He felt _____.

A nice neighbor saw that the little boy was all alone—all by himself outside, and they called the police for help. The police came and decided to put the foster daddy in handcuffs, and then they took him to jail. He's out of jail now, but the police and the judge will never let that foster mommy or daddy take care of children again.

The police and the judge decided that the little boy should go back to the emergency shelter while they looked for the right family for him. The little boy was too little to understand what was happening.

He wondered _____.

He thought _____.

He felt _____.

The police and the judge worked hard to find a forever family for the lovable little boy. They wanted to make sure that the family would keep him safe and love him and take care of him forever. And they finally found the right family. The parents already had a grown-up daughter and a son a few years older than the boy, and they knew about children. The new family chose the little boy over all the other adoptable children in the world.

It took a while for the little boy to get used to his forever family. Sometimes, especially when he didn't get attention right away, he felt sad or angry or scared.

When he didn't get attention right away,

the boy wondered _____.

he thought _____.

he felt _____.

He did whatever he could to get attention so he wouldn't feel all alone again.

His mom said, "I want you to know that what happened to you will never happen again. It's not your fault your birth mother and old mommy and daddy couldn't take good care of you. You deserve to feel good, and we will keep you in our family forever."

His dad reminded him, "I love you. You are a caring, smart boy, and now it's safe for you to learn to do new things."

Now that he's older, the boy can understand some things that he couldn't understand when he was little.

Now he can understand that he didn't do anything wrong. It's not his fault that his birth mom and foster parents couldn't take care of children.

Now that he's older, he knows that his forever family will always love him and make sure that he has food and take care of him and keep him safe.

The little boy can always feel his mommy and daddy loving him, and he can hold their love in his heart. Even when he is not with them, he can remember their love and feel it in his heart and know that he is lovable, good, and safe.

Child With Hearing Problems

Eduardo was a hearing-impaired five-year-old boy who was adopted from South America when he was three. His parents couldn't cope with his screaming, which sometimes lasted for hours. Sometimes they punished him by spanking him or putting him outside until he stopped screaming.

The challenge: How to explain to a young child why his parents punished him by spanking him or putting him outside and how to help him gain trust in his parents.

Eduardo

Once upon a time there was a boy who lived together with his mommy and daddy in their apartment near a park. They had a dog and two birds. The boy had a playroom full of art supplies and toys especially for him.

The mommy and daddy had waited a long, long time to have a child. They decided to adopt a boy because they had love in their hearts and a home to share. The mommy and daddy chose a boy from South America to be their son, and they went to South America to bring him home. The parents loved and cherished their son.

The boy was athletic and loved to play ball. He was strong and loved to climb in the climbing gym. He loved to have his mom and dad read to him. His parents appreciated that he had a kind and compassionate heart. He was strong too. He liked to climb and swing across the monkey bars at school. He loved playing outside, running and climbing, making up games, and riding bikes.

Every day the boy's parents cuddled him and read to him and fed him and played with him and prayed with him.

Like everybody else in the world, some things in the boy's life were lucky and some were difficult. Luckily, the boy was born good and lovable.

One thing that was both lucky and difficult was that the boy was adopted. Luckily, he was adopted by parents who loved him and were grateful to have him. The boy was a joy to his parents, and they were proud of him.

One difficult part of the boy's life was that his birth parents could not take care of him. It's mysterious why some birth parents can't take care of their children. It can be confusing.

Another difficult thing was that the boy couldn't hear with his right ear, and he had a hard time hearing some sounds with his left ear. At first no one realized how hard it was for him to hear.

When the boy was three and a half years old, his mother said, "I don't think he can hear." Then his parents took him to have his hearing tested, and they learned he needed a special device called a hearing aid to help him hear.

When he got the hearing aid, everything suddenly seemed different. Some sounds were way too loud. The audiologist adjusted the computer in his hearing aid. When it was adjusted just right, the boy began to hear beautiful sounds, like birds singing and music. His hearing aid was very important to him, and he learned to take care of it.

Now that he could hear music, he wanted to listen to all kinds of music, and the hearing aid made that possible.

At school his hearing aid helped him hear the teacher and the other children.

Sometimes the boy came home from school and screamed and screamed and screamed. At first, the boy's parents and his teacher didn't realize what was going on. His parents didn't know why he was screaming. When the screaming was too loud and went on for too long, the boy's parents sent him outside.

Sometimes his parents even spanked him. Everybody was upset.

His parents did their best to figure out what was going on. It took a while for them to realize that sometimes the hearing aid wasn't adjusted right and the boy was hearing loud screeching noises that made him feel like screaming.

Also, the boy's teacher discovered that there were some unfair things happening at school. She figured out that sometimes at school, a child would pull off the boy's hearing aid and run away with it and not return it until the end of the day. As soon as the boy's parents knew there was a problem at school, they went into action to take care of their son to keep him safe. The parents were so sorry they had spanked their son and punished him for his screaming behavior.

They talked to the teacher, the principal, and the other parents. They wanted all the adults to look out for their son and keep him safe. Once his parents understood what he was experiencing and how he was feeling, they knew what to do.

Now when the boy is upset, his parents check to see whether he is being treated unfairly at school or if the sound in his hearing aid is too loud. Sometimes it takes a while to figure out what the problem is.

The boy is learning what to do to help himself too. He is beginning to recognize when something is bothering him and to use his words.

His mom says, "I love you forever and for always, even when I'm upset with your behavior."

His dad says, "I love you always and will do everything I can to take care of you and protect you."

The boy can learn from the hard experiences he has had. Now, he can practice telling how he feels and saying what he needs. He can trust that his parents will do their best to understand and will make decisions that they think are best for him and their family.

"Scared Speechless" Following a Hospitalization

April was a three-year-old girl who was literally scared speechless by an incident that occurred when she was hospitalized for appendicitis. Until that time she had been happy and talked quite well. Weeks after the incident, she still hadn't spoken again.

The challenge: How would you help a three-year-old child get over a hospitalization that had been so frightening for her and her parents?

April

Once upon a time there was a little girl who lived with her mommy and daddy and her big sister and big brother. Her mommy and daddy and sister and brother loved her very much. They all had fun playing and going to the park. The girl liked to snuggle up on the couch and listen while her brother and sister read stories to her.

Like all other girls and boys in the world, some things in the little girl's life were nice and some things were scary. One nice thing was that the little girl was born good and lovable.

The scary thing that happened one day was that the girl got a tummy ache and had to go to the hospital. Some of the things that happened to her were upsetting.

First she had a tube put in her hand.

Next she had to lie on a hard table.

Then she had to lie very still while her bed moved into a machine with moving lights. The machine made noise like this . . .

Then a doctor gave her medicine to make the pain go away.

A nurse gave her a teddy bear to help her feel better.

The doctor fixed her tummy. When she woke up, her mommy and daddy were right there. The medicine made her feel nauseous. Sometimes that medicine makes it hard to talk for a while.

Soon she went to another room with curtains and beds. The nurses moved her onto a bed. For the next few days she stayed in the hospital for her tummy to get better. Her mommy and daddy were with her all the time.

Sometimes the girl's mommy and daddy were upset. They were not upset with their little girl. They were upset that she had to be in the hospital. They were upset that she hurt. They were not upset with their girl. They knew that it was not her fault. She was and is a good girl.

The nurses took her temperature under her arm and checked her blood pressure on her leg and gave her medicine through the tubes. Sometimes they had to wake her up to do things to make sure she was getting better.

Her mommy was checking on her all the time. One night her mommy noticed that one of the tubes was leaking and there was a lot of blood all over the little girl's pajama top. Her mommy was very upset and looked scared. She called the nurse, who came and fixed the tube, and her mommy changed her into clean pajamas. Then the girl went back to sleep.

After that she felt better and better. She was able to walk to the playroom and to eat dinner in the cafeteria with her parents.

Finally, when she was better, she got to go home. It was great that her body knew how to get better so quickly! Everyone was really happy to have the good, lovable girl back home.

Her mommy and daddy say, "It's all over. Now you are all better. You can play and laugh and talk and have fun doing new things. You are a good girl. We love you so much, and we are so glad you're all better and home again."

Detachment Therapy: Separating the Mother From the Painful Experience

Sam was a five-year-old boy who described himself as "bad." He didn't make eye contact with anyone, and he was especially uncomfortable if anyone complimented him. His mother felt that he didn't trust her because she had held him during painful and scary medical procedures during treatment for his clubfeet.

The challenge: How do you explain clubfeet to a five-year-old and help him love and trust his mother, who held him through painful procedures?

Sam

Once upon a time there was a boy who lived in a house with his mommy, his daddy, and his big brother. He enjoyed building with Legos, and he loved to play in the sandbox at school. He was beginning to learn to write his name and to read.

Like everybody else in the world, some things in this boy's life were lucky and some things were hard. One lucky thing is that the boy was born good and lovable. One hard thing that happened was that the boy was born with crooked feet that are called club-feet. When he was a little baby, the boy had to have casts on his feet to help straighten them out so that when he grew up, he would be able to walk and climb and jump and run and ride a bike.

Every week, the doctor used a special machine to take the cast off. The machine made a lot of noise. Every week, the boy's mom held him while the doctor took off his cast and put on a new one to help his feet grow straight. The boy's mom felt sad and upset that her baby had to have uncomfortable, scary things done to him, but as she held him and looked in his eyes, she smiled to let him know that she loved him so much.

One day, the doctor had to make little cuts at the back of the boy's heels to help stretch his tendons. The mommy and daddy were upset. They were not upset with the little boy. They were just upset that what the doctor had to hurt their lovable little boy.

Sometimes, when a baby has something wrong with his feet, he feels bad, or he thinks it is somehow his fault. We know that it is not a baby's fault if he is born with clubfeet. It is not his mommy's fault. It is not his daddy's fault. It is not anybody's fault. If his mommy and daddy had known how to have their baby be born with straight feet, they would have made it happen. His parents knew they loved him just the same whether he had straight feet or crooked feet.

With all of the doctors' help, and all of the mommy and dad-dy's help and care and love, the baby's feet began to straighten out. The baby grew up and turned into a little boy. He learned how to do many new things. He learned how to walk when he was only one year old. He learned how to talk and to say what he thought and how he felt. Then he learned how to run and jump and play with Legos. He is a normal boy who is smart and capable and is good at learning new things.

One of the boy's feet is still a little bit turned in. Every night, his mommy massages his foot and kisses his foot and tells him that she loves him. She is doing everything she can to help his foot get all better. And with some more help, it will get better. When he grows up, his feet will be just fine.

Now that he's older, the boy can understand some things he couldn't understand when he was a baby.

He can understand that clubfeet are nobody's fault. Some kids are just born that way.

He can understand that even the things that the doctor did that were uncomfortable or scary still helped him.

He can understand that his mommy and daddy love him no matter what.

Now that he is bigger, he is free to walk and jump and climb and run and play and learn to ride a bike and do lots of other new things too.

At night, his mommy says, "I love you, Sam."

Now, this boy can listen to his mommy and feel all the love she has for him, and he can love her back. The boy is a good person, and he can love himself too.

Follow-up: After listening to the story and EMDR processing, Sam exclaimed, "My mommy *is* my mommy!" That night his mother awoke to find him stroking her cheek and saying, "I love you, Mommy." After that he was able to look at her and enjoy compliments.

EMDR combined with the story helped achieve "detachment" of the parent from the frightening and painful medical procedures.

Severe Physical Abuse and Neglect

Elijah was a nine-year-old boy adopted at age five. When he was three years old his birth mother's boyfriend punished him by dipping him in a bath of scalding water. Although the burns were severe, his mother didn't take him to the hospital. When he finally got medical attention, Child Protective Services intervened and removed him from his home. The boy was hospitalized for several months while he received care for the burns. Reunification with his mother failed because she continued to live with the boyfriend who had scalded her child. Then the boy was in a series of foster homes and, after two years, adopted by a loving, religious family.

The boy was depressed, sad, and anxious. Although he could be sweet and helpful, frequently he was angry, uncooperative, and belligerent, and he had trouble learning in school.

The challenge: How can you explain to a nine-year-old boy why his mother and her boyfriend abused him and that it was not his fault they punished him. How can you help him trust his adoptive parents?

Elijah

Once upon a time there was a boy who lived with his mother and father and brother. They liked to play games together and go to church together. His mom and dad and brother all loved him very much. He also had grandparents who loved him very much and liked to play with him. He had cousins who liked to play with him and a lot of other people who cared about him, like his teacher and friends at school. He enjoyed bikes and scooters. His parents liked to do sports with him. They appreciated that he wanted to do the right thing and that he was brave enough to speak out about what's right and brave enough to learn to swim.

Like everybody else in the world, some things in the boy's life were blessings and some things were hard. One blessing was that the boy was born lovable and good and caring.

One hard thing was that his birth dad didn't live to see him grow up to be such a lovable boy. The birth dad had died when the boy was just a little baby. His mom loved the boy and cared about him, but she didn't take care of him and keep him safe. She didn't know how to take care of him and keep him safe because she never had a mom and dad who could take care of her or keep her safe.

The boy's mom started living with a man who got very angry sometimes. The man didn't know a safe thing to do when he felt angry. He didn't know that it's normal for little children to poop in their pants, especially if they're scared.

Instead of helping the little boy, the man hurt him by putting him in scalding hot water. That was the wrong thing to do. It's never OK for any adult to whip or burn a child. It's against the law. That's why people who whip or burn children should be in jail. The man and the boy's mom had to go to jail because they hurt the little boy instead of protecting him or taking him to the doctor when he got hurt.

The little boy had to go to the hospital to get help for the burns. He had to be in the hospital for a long time. The doctors and nurses all helped the good, lovable little boy get better.

After he left the hospital, the boy stayed in several different houses until the social workers could find a safe home for him. He also sometimes had supervised visits with his birth mom after she got out of jail. She couldn't understand that children just need to be taught. She didn't learn how to teach him. She still didn't make her home safe for children.

The law said it was time for the social workers to find a forever family to take care of the little boy. They were looking for a family who understood that children are good. Children are just learning, and it's the parents' job to take care of them while they learn. They chose parents who wanted their children to be happy because they know how to make good choices. When children make choices that aren't good, the parents help them learn how to fix it. Good parents show children what to do and teach them how to make good choices by giving them consequences and rewards. No matter what, the parents always love their children.

His mom says, "I will always love you and do my best to take care of you. You are a special boy. I love your sense of humor, I love watching you play and learn, I love when you help me, and I'm excited to watch you grow up to become a wonderful man."

His dad says, "I love you. I believe in you. I will always be there for you."

The boy's parents want him to know very deep down inside that he is good, that he is loved more than he knows, and that he can do whatever he needs to do because he is strong, he is smart, he is kind, and he is capable. He can trust that all of his family and friends and God are behind him to support him, to love him, and to cheer him on.

As the boy grows up he can understand that the adults around him care about him and love him and that he's a child of God.

CONCLUSION

15

IMPLICATIONS FOR HEALTH

Treating childhood trauma and facilitating attachment between children and their parents is challenging work. Nonetheless, it's important work because the future prospects for untreated traumatized children are even more daunting. The Adverse Childhood Experiences (ACE) study, an ongoing collaboration between Kaiser Permanente and the Centers for Disease Control and Prevention, compiles data on adults' exposure to adverse childhood experiences and links the number of these traumatic experiences with poor health outcomes in adulthood. The study focused on 10 types of childhood trauma, including sexual, verbal, and physical abuse; family dysfunction caused by a mentally ill or alcoholic parent; a mother who is a victim of domestic violence; an incarcerated family member; loss of a parent through divorce or abandonment; and emotional and physical neglect.

Research from the ACE study, based on data from over 17,000 Kaiser patients, indicates that significant childhood trauma is common. Two-thirds of study participants were exposed to at least one type of adverse experience in childhood. The study shows a direct link between childhood trauma and adult onset of chronic disease, mental illness, incarceration, and work issues such as absenteeism.

One in six study participants had experienced four different types of adverse childhood events (an ACE score of 4 out of a possible 10). Those adults with an ACE score of 4 were twice as likely to be diagnosed with cancer and twice as likely to have heart disease as those with an ACE score of 0. They had a 240 percent increased risk of hepatitis, were 390 percent more likely to have chronic obstructive pulmonary disease, and had a 240 percent greater risk of sexually transmitted disease. They were twice as likely to be smokers, 12 times more likely to have attempted suicide, 7 times more likely to be alcoholic, and 10 times more likely to have injected illicit drugs (Felitti et al., 1998; Dube et al., 2001; Edwards, Holden, Felitti, & Anda, 2003; Dube et al., 2003; Dong et al., 2004; Chapman et al., 2004; Anda et al., 2002; Dong, Dube, Felitti, Giles, & Anda, 2003; Hillis, Anda, Felitti, Nordenberg, & Marchbanks, 2000).

Severe, chronic childhood trauma mobilizes an emergency hormonal stress response, flooding the brain with hormones like cortisol and adrenaline that raise heart rate and blood pressure and cause clammy hands and dry mouth. The stress response also focuses the mind on the threat (or perceived threat) facing a person, diverting attention from everything else. (High stress levels make it very hard for a child to focus on schoolwork.) The emergency stress response releases inflammatory proteins into the bloodstream and can affect the cardiovascular system, immune system, and metabolic regulatory systems. In a true emergency, this response can be life-saving. But when normal daily experiences trigger or maintain this extreme stress response, it can be crippling.

If a child's emergency response system is overwhelmed by trauma, high levels of stress hormones can cause changes in the structure and function of children's developing brains and bodies (Teicher et al., 2003). The prefrontal cortex—a part of the brain that is essential in doing math or learning grammar—becomes inhibited, and learning is compromised. According to pediatrician Nadine Burke Harris, founder and CEO of the Center for Youth Wellness, children who have an ACE score of 4 or above have a 32 times higher risk of having learning or behavior problems in school than children who have not experienced an adverse childhood experience (Tough, 2011).

Research indicates that a nurturing, responsive caregiver can help buffer a child from a toxic stress response by providing a supportive environment in which the brain and other systems can recover (Schore, 2001). Attachment to a supportive caregiver can help prevent and ameliorate the effects of stress, as well as facilitate recovery from trauma.

Some research suggests that changing the behavior of parents or caregivers can help calm the excessive stress response of children who have experienced chronic stress. One study in Oregon and another in Delaware taught foster parents to be more responsive to the emotional cues of their foster children. In both studies, researchers measured the children's cortisol levels at various points in the day and compared those cortisol patterns with a control group of foster children whose foster parents were not in the intervention program. In both studies, the children whose foster parents participated in the intervention to promote more secure attachment showed cortisol patterns similar to those of children brought up in stable homes (Fisher, Stoolmiller, Gunnar, & Burraston, 2007; Dozier et al., 2006).

The children featured in stories in *Trauma-Attachment Tangle* are all currently fortunate to belong to families that protect and nurture them. Despite being in a safe environment with caring adults, these children all exhibited effects of significant adverse childhood experiences prior to therapy. A loving home is sometimes not enough to help children overcome the effects of trauma, and therapy can make an immense difference.

While children do have the neurological capability for linking memories to adaptive memory networks for trauma resolution, they do not have the experience, information, and judgment that compose the "adult perspective." Treating children for trauma requires an active role on the part of the therapist and parents, who have to provide a new repository of understanding and trust for a developmentally immature child. Often, the traumatic events that have created obstacles to normal development are truly beyond the understanding of a child. Traumatic preverbal experiences form a template for future memory input. In children, "adaptive resolution" may be possible only if a context for understanding early experiences is provided through an attuned relationship with a caring adult and a cohesive narrative.

Many different types of therapy are being used to help children recover from trauma and develop loving relationships. This book highlights EMDR, along with storytelling, activities for promoting attachment, mindfulness, and creative expression through play and artwork as effective therapeutic modalities for treating complex developmental trauma. In addition, treating childhood trauma removes some of the obstacles to normal social, emotional, intellectual, and physical growth and development, and it enhances attachment potential.

From my work with many children who endured adverse childhood experiences, I have seen therapy transform the lives of traumatized children. Children are naturally motivated by a developmental directive compelling them to experience the world and to grow physically, emotionally, socially, and intellectually. The plasticity of the brain favors adaptation. With appropriate therapy, traumatized children can improve and lead fulfilling lives with loving relationships.

BIBLIOGRAPHY

Adler-Tapia, R. L., & Settle, C. S. (2008). *EMDR and the art of psychotherapy with children*. New York: Springer.

Adler-Tapia, R., & Settle, C. (2009). Evidence of the efficacy of EMDR with children and adolescents in individual psychotherapy: A review of the research published in peer-reviewed journals. *Journal of EMDR Practice and Research*, 3(4), 232–247.

Adler-Tapia, R., & Settle, C. (2012). Specialty topics on using EMDR with children. *Journal of EMDR Practice and Research*, 6(3), 145–153.

Adúriz, M. E., Bluthgen, C., & Knopfler, C. (2009, May). Helping child flood victims using group EMDR intervention in Argentina: Treatment outcome and gender differences. *International Journal of Stress Management*, 16(2), 138–153.

Afifi, T. O., Mota, N. P., Dasiewicz, P., MacMillan, H. L., & Sareen, J. (2012). Physical punishment and mental disorders: Results from a nationally representative US sample. *Pediatrics*, 130(2), 184–192.

Ahmad, A., Larsson, B., & Sundelin-Wahlsten, V. (2007). EMDR treatment for children with PTSD: Results of a randomized controlled trial. *Nordic Journal of Psychiatry*, 61(5), 349–354.

Ahmad, A., & Sundelin-Wahlsten, V. (2007, September). Applying EMDR on children with PTSD. *European Child & Adolescent Psychiatry*, 17(3), 127–132.

American Academy of Child and Adolescent Psychiatry. (2011). *The adopted child*. Retrieved April, 26, 2014, from www.aacap.org/aacap/Families_and_Youth/Facts_for_Families/Facts_for_Families_Pages/The_Adopted_Child_15.aspx

American Psychiatric Association. (2004). *Practice guideline for the treatment of patients with acute stress disorder and posttraumatic stress disorder*. Arlington, VA: Author. doi:10.1176/appi.books.9780890423363.52257

Anda, R. F., Whitfield, C. L., Felitti, V. J., Chapman, D., Edwards, V. J., Dube, S. R., & Williamson, D. F. (2002). Adverse childhood experiences, alcoholic parents, and later risk of alcoholism and depression. *Psychiatric Services*, 53(8), 1001–1009.

Beer, R., & Bronner, M. B. (2010). EMDR in paediatrics and rehabilitation: An effective tool for reduction of stress reactions? *Developmental Neurorehabilitation*, 13(5), 307–309.

Boel, J. (1999). The butterfly hug. *EMDRIA Newsletter*, 4(4), 11–13.

Brand Flu, R. L. (2012). P-267—Tap, tap tap the usefulness of EMDR on kids on the autism spectrum. *European Psychiatry*, 27(Supplement 1), 1.

Bureau of Consular Affairs, U.S. Department of State, Intercountry Adoption. (2013). *Statistics*. Retrieved from travel.state.gov/content/adoptionsabroad/en/about-us/statistics.html accessed online October 10, 2014

California Evidence-Based Clearinghouse for Child Welfare, The. (2010). *Trauma treatment for children*. Retrieved from www.cebc4cw.org/program/eye-movement-desensitization-and-reprocessing/detailed accessed October 10, 2014

Chapman, D. P., Whitfield, C. L., Felitti, V. J., Dube, S. R., Edwards, V. J., & Anda, R. F. (2004). Adverse childhood experiences and the risk of depressive disorders in adulthood. *Journal of Affective Disorders*, 82(2), 217–225.

Chemtob, C., Nakashima, J., & Carlson, J. (2002, January). Brief treatment for elementary school children with disaster-related posttraumatic stress disorder: A field study. *Journal of Clinical Psychology*, 58(1), 99–112.

Constantine, L. L. (1978). Family sculpture and relationship mapping techniques. Journal of Marital and Family Therapy, 4(2), 13–23.

de Jongh, P. J., Andrea, H., & Muris, P. (1997, June). Spider phobia in children: Disgust and fear before and after treatment. *Behaviour Research and Therapy*, 35(6), 559–562.

Department of Veterans Affairs and Department of Defense (2004, 2010). VA/DoD Clinical Practice Guideline for the Management of Post-Traumatic Stress. Washington, DC. www.oqp.med.va.gov/cpg/PTSD/PTSD_cpg/frameset.htm accessed online October 11, 2014

de Roos, C., & de Jongh, A. (2008). EMDR treatment of children and adolescents with a choking phobia. *Journal of EMDR Practice and Research*, 2(3), 201–211.

de Roos, C., Greenwald, R., den Hollander-Gijsman, M., Noorthoorn, E., van Buuren, S., & de Jongh, A. (2011). A randomised comparison of cognitive behavioural therapy (CBT) and eye movement desensitisation and reprocessing (EMDR) in disaster-exposed children. *European Journal of Psychotraumatology*, 2, 1–11.

DiPasquale, L. I. S. B. E. T. H. (2000). The Marschak interaction method. Theraplay: Innovations in attachment-enhancing play therapy, 27–51.

Discovery of an insecure-disorganized/disoriented attachment pattern. Main, M & Solomon, J. Brazelton, T. Berry (Ed); Yogman, Michael W. (Ed), (1986). Affective development in infancy. , (pp. 95–124). Westport, CT, US: Ablex Publishing, v, 161 pp.

Dong, M., Dube, S. R., Felitti, V. J., Giles, W. H., & Anda, R. F. (2003). Adverse childhood experiences and self-reported liver disease: New insights into the causal pathway. *Archives of Internal Medicine*, 163(16), 1949–1956.

Dong, M., Giles, W. H., Felitti, V. J., Dube, S. R., Williams, J. E., Chapman, D. P., & Anda, R. F. (2004). Insights into causal pathways for ischemic heart disease adverse childhood experiences study. *Circulation*, 110(13), 1761–1766.

Dozier, M., Manni, M., Gordon, M. K., Peloso, E., Gunnar, M. R., Stovall-McClough, K. C., & Levine, S. (2006). Foster children's diurnal production of cortisol: An exploratory study. *Child Maltreatment*, 11(2), 189–197.

Dube, S. R., Anda, R. F., Felitti, V. J., Chapman, D. P., Williamson, D. F., & Giles, W. H. (2001). Childhood abuse, household dysfunction, and the risk of attempted suicide throughout the life span: Findings from the Adverse Childhood Experiences Study. *Journal of the American Medical Association*, 286(24), 3089–3096.

208

Dube, S. R., Felitti, V. J., Dong, M., Chapman, D. P., Giles, W. H., & Anda, R. F. (2003). Childhood abuse, neglect, and household dysfunction and the risk of illicit drug use: The adverse childhood experiences study. *Pediatrics*, 111(3), 564–572.

Eberlein, T. (1977, August). The Importance of One-on-One Time. *Child*. Retrieved from www.wolfe411.org/Parenting%20Resources/Docs/childart.htm accessed online October 10, 2014 (no page numbers given).

Edwards, V. J., Holden, G. W., Felitti, V. J., & Anda, R. F. (2003). Relationship between multiple forms of childhood maltreatment and adult mental health in community respondents: Results from the adverse childhood experiences study. *American Journal of Psychiatry*, 160(8), 1453–1460.

Engelhard, I. M., van den Hout, M. A., Janssen, W. C., & van der Beek, J. (2010). Eye movements reduce vividness and emotionality of "flashforwards." *Behaviour Research and Therapy*, 48, 442–447.

Erikson, E. H. (1963). *Childhood and society*. New York: Norton.

Federichi, R. (1996). *Help for the hopeless child: A guide for families (with special discussion for assessing and treating the post-institutionalized child)* (2nd ed.). Gaithersburg, MD: Mosby.

Felitti, V. J., Anda, R. F., Nordenberg, D., Williamson, D. F., Spitz, A. M., Edwards, V., Koss M. P., & Marks, J. S. (1998). Relationship of childhood abuse and household dysfunction to many of the leading causes of death in adults: The Adverse Childhood Experiences (ACE) Study. *American Journal of Preventive Medicine*, 14(4), 245–258.

Fernandez, I. (2007). EMDR as a treatment of post-traumatic reactions: A field study on child victims of an earthquake. *Educational and Child Psychology*, 24(1), 65–72.

Fernandez, I., Gallinari, E., & Lorenzetti, A. (2004, Spring-Summer). A school-based EMDR intervention for children who witnessed the Pirelli Building airplane crash in Milan, Italy. *Journal of Brief Therapy*, 2(2), 129–136.

Field, A., & Cottrell, D. (2011, November). Eye movement desensitization and reprocessing as a therapeutic intervention for traumatized children and adolescents: A systematic review of the evidence for family therapists. *Journal of Family Therapy*, 33(4), 374–388.

Fisher, P. A., Stoolmiller, M., Gunnar, M. R., & Burraston, B. O. (2007). Effects of a therapeutic intervention for foster preschoolers on diurnal cortisol activity. *Psychoneuroendocrinology*, 32(8), 892–905.

Fleming, J. (2012). The effectiveness of eye movement desensitization and reprocessing in the treatment of traumatized children and youth. *Journal of EMDR Practice and Research*, 6(1), 16–26.

Gardener, S. L., Barland, K. R., Merenstein, S. L., & Lubchenco, L. O. (1993). The neonate and the environment: Impact on development. In G. B. Merenstein & S. L. Gardener (Eds.), *Handbook of neonatal intensive care* (3rd ed., pp. 564–608). St. Louis, MO: Mosby Year Book.

Gauvry, S. B., Lesta, P., Alonso, A. L., & Pallia, R. (2013). Complex regional pain syndrome (CRPS), Sudeck's dystrophy: EMDR reprocessing therapy applied to the psychotherapeutic strategy. *Journal of EMDR Practice and Research*, 7(3), 167–172.

Gillies, D., Taylor, F., Gray, C., O'Brien, L., & D'Abrew, N. (2012). Psychological therapies for the treatment of post-traumatic stress disorder in children and adolescents (Review). *Evidence-based Child Health: A Cochrane Review Journal*, 8(3), 1004–166.

Gómez, A.M. (2007). *Dark, bad . . . day go away: A book for children about trauma and EMDR*. Phoenix, AZ: Author.

Gómez, A.M. (2009). *The thoughts kit for kids*. Phoenix, AZ: Author.

Gómez, A.M. (2012a). *EMDR therapy and adjunct approaches with children: Complex trauma, attachment and dissociation*. New York: Springer.

Gómez, A.M. (2012b). Healing the caregiving system: Working with parents within a comprehensive EMDR treatment. *Journal of EMDR Practice and Research*, 6, 136–144.

Grandison, P. (2007). A combined approach: Using EMDR within a framework of solution focused brief therapy. *Educational and Child Psychology*, 24(1), 56–64.

Gray, D. D. (2002). *Attaching in adoption: Practical tools for today's parents*. Indianapolis, IN: Perspectives Press.

Green, J., Whitney, P., & Potegal, M. (2011). Screaming, yelling, whining, and crying: Categorical and intensity differences in vocal expressions of anger and sadness in children's tantrums. *Emotion*, 11(5), 1124–1133. doi:10.1037/a0024173

Greenwald, R. (1998, April). Eye movement desensitization and reprocessing (EMDR): New hope for children suffering from trauma and loss. *Clinical Child Psychology and Psychiatry*, 3(2), 279–287.

Greenwald, R. (1999). *Eye movement desensitization and reprocessing (EMDR) in child and adolescent psychotherapy*. Northvale, NJ: Jason Aronson Press.

Helen. (2011, February). Child abuse and voice hearing: Finding healing through EMDR. *Psychosis*, 3(1), 90–95.

Hensel, T. (2009). EMDR with children and adolescents after single-incident trauma: An intervention study. *Journal of EMDR Practice and Research*, 3(1), 2–9.

Hillis, S.D., Anda, R.F., Felitti, V.J., Nordenberg, D., & Marchbanks, P.A. (2000). Adverse childhood experiences and sexually transmitted diseases in men and women: A retrospective study. *Pediatrics*, 106(1), e11.

International Society for Traumatic Stress Studies. ISTSS Treatment Guidelines for PTSD.Guideline 8. Eye Movement Desensitization and Reprocessing www.istss.org/AM/Template.cfm?Section=PTSDTreatmentGuidelines&Template=/CM/ContentDisplay.cfm&ContentID=2328 accessed online October 11, 2014

Jaberghaderi, N., Greenwald, R., Rubin, A., Zand, S.O., & Dolatabadim, S. (2004, September-October). A comparison of CBT and EMDR for sexually abused Iranian girls. *Clinical Psychology and Psychotherapy*, 11(5), 358–368.

Jarero, I., & Artigas, L. (2012). The EMDR integrative group treatment protocol: EMDR group treatment for early intervention following critical incidents. *Revue Européenne de Psychologie Appliquée/European Review of Applied Psychology*, 62(4), 219–222.

Jarero, I., Artigas, L., & Hartung, J. (2006). EMDR integrative group treatment protocol: A postdisaster trauma intervention for children and adults. *Traumatology*, 12(2), 121–129.

Jarero, I., Roque-López, S., & Gomez, J. (2013). The provision of an EMDR-based multicomponent trauma treatment with child victims of severe interpersonal trauma. *Journal of EMDR Practice and Research*, 7(1), 17–28.

Jarero, I., Roque-Lopez, S., Gomez, J., & Givaudan, M. (2014). Second research study on the provision of the EMDR integrative group treatment protocol with child victims of severe interpersonal violence. *Revista Iberoamericana de Psicotraumatología y Disociación*, 6(1), 1–24.

Jayatunge, R. M. (2008). Combating tsunami disaster through EMDR. *Journal of EMDR Practice and Research*, 2(2), 140–145.

Karst, P. (2000). The invisible string. DeVorss Publications.

Keck, G., & Kupecky, R. (1995). *Adopting the hurt child: Hope for families with special-needs kids: A guide for parents and professionals*. Colorado Springs, CO: Pinon Press.

Keck, G., & Kupecky, R. (2002). *Parenting the hurt child: Helping adoptive families heal and grow*. Colorado Springs, CO: Pinon Press.

Kemp M., Drummond P., & McDermott B. (2010, January). A wait-list controlled pilot study of eye movement desensitization and reprocessing (EMDR) for children with post-traumatic stress disorder (PTSD) symptoms from motor vehicle accidents. *Clinical Child Psychology and Psychiatry*, 15(1), 5–25.

Korn, D. L., & Leeds, A. M. (2002). Preliminary evidence of efficacy of EMDR resource development and installation in the stabilization phase of treatment of complex posttraumatic stress disorder. *Journal of Clinical Psychology*, 58(12), 1465–1487.

Kristof, N. (2013, November 13). When children are traded. *The New York Times*, A35.

Levy, T. (2000). *Handbook of attachment interventions*. San Diego, CA: Academic Press.

Lewis, D. B. W., & Lee, C. (Eds.). (1930). The stuffed owl: an anthology of bad verse. New York Review of Books.

Lovett, J. (1999). *Small wonders: Healing childhood trauma with EMDR*. New York: The Free Press.

Main, M. (1996). Introduction to the special section on attachment and psychopathology: 2. Overview of the field of attachment. *Journal of Consulting and Clinical Psychology*, 64(2), 237.

Main, M., & Solomon, J. (1986). Discovery of an insecure-disorganized/disoriented attachment pattern.

Mehrotra, S., & Geng, W. (2011, February). EMDR in India. *Journal of Xihua University* (Philosophy & Social Sciences). doi:CNKI:SUN:CDSF.0.2011-02-000

Mevissen, L., Lievegoed, R., Seubert, A., & de Jongh, A. (2012). Treatment of PTSD in people with severe intellectual disabilities: A case series. *Developmental Neurorehabilitation*, 15(3), 223–232.

Mitchell, S. (2000). *Relationality: From attachment to intersubjectivity*. Hillsdale, NJ: The Analytic Press.

Mol, S. S. L., Arntz, A., Metsemakers, J. F. M., Dinant, G., Vilters-Van Montfort, P. A. P., & Knottnerus, A. (2005). Symptoms of post-traumatic stress disorder after non-traumatic events: Evidence from an open population study. *British Journal of Psychiatry*, 186, 494–499.

National Institute for Clinical Excellence (2005). Post traumatic stress disorder (PTSD): The management of adults and children in primary and secondary care. London: NICE Guidelines. www.nice.org.uk/guidance/CG26/chapter/key-priorities-for-implementation accessed online October 11, 2014

Nickerson, A., Bryant, R., Aderka, I., Hinton, D., & Hofmann, S. (2013). The impacts of parental loss and adverse parenting on mental health: Findings from the National Comorbidity Survey-Replication. *Psychological Trauma: Theory, Research, Practice, and Policy*, 5(2), 119–127. doi:10.1037/a0025695

Oras, R., de Ezpeleta, S. C., & Ahmad, A. (2004, June). Treatment of traumatized refugee children with eye movement desensitization and reprocessing in a psychodynamic context. *Nordic Journal of Psychiatry*, 58(3), 199–203.

Pellicer, X. (1993). Eye movement desensitization treatment of a child's nightmares: A case report. *Journal of Behavior Therapy and Experimental Psychiatry*, 24(1), 73–75.

Penn, A. (1993). The kissing hand. Regnery Publishing.

Pocock, D. (2011, November). The promise of EMDR in family and systemic psychotherapy: A clinical complement to Field and Cottrell. *Journal of Family Therapy*, 33(4), 389–399.

Pollack, S., & Sinha, P. (2002). Effects of early experience on children's recognition of facial displays of emotion. *Developmental Psychology, 38*(5), 784–791. Retrieved on April 28, 2014, from http://web.mit.edu/bcs/sinha/papers/effects_early_experience_devpsych.pdf

Polonko, K. (2005). Child abuse and neglect: The need for courage. *Quest, 8*(2), p26–30. Retrieved from http://al.odu.edu/sociology/isoc/pdfs/ChildAbuseandNeglect.pdf accessed online October 12, 2014.

Puffer, M., Greenwald, R., & Elrod, D. (1998). A single session EMDR study with twenty traumatized children and adolescents. *Traumatology-e*, 3(2), Article 6.

Purvis, K., Cross, D., & Sunshine, W. (2007). *The connected child: Bring hope and healing to your adoptive family*. New York: McGraw-Hill.

Ribchester, T., Yule, W., & Duncan, A. (2010). EMDR for childhood PTSD after road traffic accidents: Attentional, memory, and attributional processes. *Journal of EMDR Practice and Research*, 4(4), 138–147.

Rodenburg, R., Benjamin, A., de Roos, C., Meijer, A. M., & Stams, G. J. (2009, November). Efficacy of EMDR in children: A meta-analysis. *Clinical Psychology Review*, 29(7), 599–606.

Rodenburg, R., Benjamin, A., Meijer, A. M., & Jongeneel, R. (2009, September). Eye movement desensitization and reprocessing in an adolescent with epilepsy and mild intellectual disability. *Epilepsy & Behavior*, 16(1), 175–180.

Schore, A. N. (2001). The effects of early relational trauma on right brain development, affect regulation, and infant mental health. *Infant Mental Health Journal*, 22(1–2), 201–269.

Schubert, S. J., Lee, C. W., & Drummond, P. D. (2011). The efficacy and psychophysiological correlates of dual-attention tasks in eye movement desensitization and reprocessing (EMDR). *Journal of Anxiety Disorders*, 25, 1–11.

Shapiro, F. (1998). EMDR: The breakthrough eye movement therapy for overcoming anxiety, stress, and trauma. New York: Basic Books.

Shapiro, F. (1989). Eye movement desensitization: A new treatment for post-traumatic stress disorder. *Journal of behavior therapy and experimental psychiatry*, 20(3), 211–217. Accessed online October 11, 2014 www.sciencedirect.com/science/article/pii/0005791689900256

Shapiro, F. (2001). *Eye movement desensitization and reprocessing: Basic principles, protocols and procedures* (2nd ed.). New York: Guilford Press.

Shapiro, F. (2007). EMDR, adaptive information processing, and case conceptualization. *Journal of EMDR Practice and Research*, 1, 68–87.

Shapiro, F. (2012a). *Expert answers on E.M.D.R. New York Times Consults: Experts in the front line of medicine.* Retrieved May 29, 2014, from http:// consults.blogs.nytimes.com/?s=Expert+answers+on+EMDR

Shapiro, F. (2012b). *Getting past your past: Take control of your life with self-help techniques from EMDR therapy.* New York: Rodale.

Shapiro, F. (2012c). *The Evidence on E.M.D.R. New York Times Consults: Experts in the front line of medicine.* Retrieved May 29, 2014, from http://consults.blogs. nytimes.com/?s=The+Evidence+on+EMDR

Shapiro, F. (2014). The role of eye movement desensitization and reprocessing (EMDR) therapy in medicine: Addressing the psychological and physical symptoms stemming from adverse life experience. *The Permanente Journal*, 18(1), 71–77. Retrieved May 29, 2014, from http://dx.doi.org/10.7812/TPP/13–098

Shapiro, F., Kaslow, F., & Maxfield, L. (Eds.). (2007). *Handbook of EMDR and family therapy processes.* Hoboken, NJ: Wiley.

Shapiro, F., & Maxfield, L. (2002). Eye movement desensitization and reprocessing (EMDR): Information processing in the treatment of trauma. *Journal of Clinical Psychology*, 58(8), 933–946.

Shapiro, F., & Solomon, R. (2008). EMDR and the Adaptive Information Processing Model. *Journal of EMDR Practice and Research*, 2(4), 315–325.

Siegel, D. J., & Hartzell, M. (2003). *Parenting from the inside out.* New York: Penguin.

Siegel, D. S. (Ed.). (2013). *Healing moments in psychotherapy: Mindful awareness, neural integration, and therapeutic presence.* New York: W.W. Norton.

Spindler-Ranta, D. (1999). Slaying the monsters. *EMDRIA Newsletter, Child and Adolescent Issue, Special Edition*, 4(4), 9–10.

Stallard, P. (2006, November). Psychological interventions for post-traumatic reactions in children and young people: A review of randomised controlled trials. *Clinical Psychology Review*, 26(7), 895–911.

Struwig, E., & van Breda, A.D. (2012). An exploratory study on the use of eye movement integration therapy in overcoming childhood trauma. *Families in Society*, 93(1), 29–37.

Taylor, R.J. (2002, September). Family unification with reactive attachment disorder: A brief treatment. *Contemporary Family Therapy*, 24(3), 475–481.

Teicher, M.H., Andersen, S.L., Polcari, A., Anderson, C.M., Navalta, C.P., & Kim, D.M. (2003). The neurobiological consequences of early stress and childhood maltreatment. *Neuroscience & Biobehavioral Reviews*, 27(1), 33–44.

Tinker, R.H., & Wilson, S.A. (1999). *Through the eyes of a child: EMDR with children.* New York: W.W. Norton.

Tough, P. (2011, March). The poverty clinic. *The New Yorker*, 25–32.

Tufnell, G. (2005, October). Eye movement desensitization and reprocessing in the treatment of pre-adolescent children with post-traumatic symptoms. *Clinical Child Psychology and Psychiatry*, 10(4), 587–600.

U.S. Department of Health & Human Services Administration for Children & Families http://scholar.google.com/scholar?hl=en&q=US+Department+of+Health+and+Human+Services+%282013%29+Child+maltreatment+2012&btnG=&as_sdt=1%2C5&as_sdtp=accessed October 10, 2010

van der Kolk, B. (2005, May). Developmental trauma disorder: A new rational diagnosis for children with complex trauma histories. *Psychiatric Annals*, 35(5), 401–408.

Wadaa, N. N., Zaharim, N. M., & Alqashan, H. F. (2010, April). The use of EMDR in treatment of traumatized Iraqi children. *Digest of Middle East Studies*, 19(1), 26–36.

Wanders, F., Serra, M., & de Jongh, A. (2008). EMDR versus CBT for children with self-esteem and behavioral problems: A randomized controlled trial. *Journal of EMDR Practice and Research*, 2(3), 180–189.

Wesselmann, D. (1998). *The whole parent: How to become a terrific parent even if you didn't have one*. Cambridge, MA: Da Capo Press.

Wesselmann, D., Davidson, M., Armstrong, S., Schweitzer, C., Bruckner, D., & Potter, A. E. (2012). EMDR as a treatment for improving attachment status in adults and children. *European Review of Applied Psychology*, 62, 223–230.

Wesselmann, D., & Potter, A. E. (2009). Change in adult attachment status following treatment with EMDR: Three case studies. *Journal of EMDR Practice and Research*, 3, 178–191.

Wesselmann, D., Schweitzer, C., & Armstrong, S. (2014a). *Integrative parenting: Strategies for raising children affected by attachment trauma*. New York: W. W. Norton.

Wesselmann, D., Schweitzer, C., & Armstrong, S. (2014b). *Integrative team treatment for attachment trauma in children*. New York: W. W. Norton.

White, M., & Epston, D. (1990). Narrative means to therapeutic ends. WW Norton & Company.

Wizansky, B. (2007). A clinical vignette: Resource connection in EMDR work with children. *Journal of EMDR Practice and Research*, 1(1), 57–61.

World Health Organization (2013). *Guidelines for the management of conditions specifically related to stress*. <http://apps.who.int/iris/bitstream/10665/85119/1/9789241505406_eng.pdf p.1>. Accessed online October 10, 2014

Yu, H., Wier, L. M., & Elixhauser, A. (2011, August). *Hospital stays for children, 2009*. HCUP Statistical Brief #118. Rockville, MD: Agency for Healthcare Research and Quality. Retrieved October 10, 2014, from www.hcup-us.ahrq.gov/reports/statbriefs/sb118.pdf

GLOSSARY

AAI = Adult Attachment Interview

The adult attachment interview was developed by Professor Mary Main and her colleagues at University of California, Berkeley. The interview elicits an adult's narrative account of his/her childhood. The interview is rated for the extent to which the individual has successfully resolved past traumatic losses and/or abusive experiences. The coherence of the story is used to assess the adult's attachment style as either secure, dismissive of attachment relationships, or overly preoccupied with them. The AAI has been shown to be a reliable and valid measure of the degree to which adults have "come to terms with" their childhood history.

ABS = Alternating Bilateral Stimulation

Alternating bilateral stimulation refers to visual, auditory, or tactile stimuli that are provided in a rhythmic left-right pattern. Visual bilateral stimulation could involve a toy or hand or lights moving from left to right and back repeatedly to guide eye movement. Auditory bilateral stimulation could involve listening to tones, clicks, music, or other sounds that are delivered through headphones, alternating between the right and left sides of the head. Tactile stimulation could be provided by small buzzers that are held in the hands and buzz alternately between the right and left hands.

ACE = The Adverse Childhood Experiences (ACE) Study

The ACE study is ongoing collaborative research by Kaiser Permanente and the Centers for Disease Control. The researchers collected and analyzed the responses of 17,000 patient volunteers to routine health screening questionnaires. Data resulting from their participation reveal that childhood trauma greatly increases the risk of both mental and physical illness in adulthood. The co-principal investigators of the study are Robert F. Anda, MD, MS, with the CDC, and Vincent J. Felitti, MD, with Kaiser Permanente (http://acestudy.org/).

AIP = Adaptive Information Processing (AIP) Model

The AIP model postulates that everyone has an innate information processing system that integrates new experiences into existing memory networks. Memories of overwhelmingly distressing experiences remain unmetabolized and are stored in an isolated neural network in an excitatory state. These unprocessed memories are triggered by a variety of internal and external stimuli, resulting in inappropriate emotional, cognitive, and behavioral reactions. EMDR therapy, based on the AIP model, involves accessing the dysfunctionally stored memory; connecting it with "adaptive," useful information; and activating the information processing system to metabolize the memory (Shapiro & Solomon, 2008). Children do not have the "adult perspective" and often need assistance, in the form of information and reassurance, in order to process distressing memories to adaptive resolution.

Attachment

Attachment is one specific aspect of the relationship between a child and a parent; its purpose being to make a child safe, secure, and protected. Early interactions shape neurological patterns in the brain and establish a template for how the child will relate to others.

Secure Attachment—The securely attached child uses the primary caregiver as a secure base from which to explore and, when necessary, as a haven of safety and a source of comfort.

Earned Secure Attachment—Children (and adults) are capable of changing the attachment style that served them as infants and young children. Earned secure attachment can be gained through a strong, healthy relationship with an attuned caregiver, as well as through therapy with an attuned, skilled therapist.

Insecure Attachment:

ambivalent or anxious resistant—Children may exhibit ambivalent attachment by becoming very distressed when a parent leaves. The child cannot depend on the parent or caregiver to be there when he/she is in need. Ambivalent attachment is used to describe a child who is beyond the age of normal separation anxiety.

insecure-avoidant—Children may exhibit avoidant attachment by avoiding parents or caregivers or treating strangers and well-known adults with the same regard. Avoidant attachment may be a response to chronic neglect of essential needs or feelings.

insecure-disorganized—Children who experienced inconsistent behavior from parents who are a source of both comfort and fear may exhibit disorganized attachment. The confusion may result in a child who alternately expresses needs and resists help.

216

Attunement

Literally, "attunement" means to bring into a harmonious or responsive relationship. Parents become attuned to their child by learning what the child's nonverbal signals mean as well as verbal communication and then responding with appropriate tone, intensity, information, and comforting.

Bonding

Bonding typically refers to the process of attachment that develops between parents and children, romantic partners, or close friends. This bond is characterized by affection and trust.

Cognitive Interweave

A cognitive interweave refers to information provided by the therapist during EMDR processing. The interweave usually explains something relating to safety, responsibility, control, and choices.

Critical Incident

Critical incident refers to any single experience that is traumatic.

Desensitization

Desensitization is the process of taking the distress or charge off of a traumatic memory. After desensitization, the memory moves from current memory to past memory so that the event feels "over."

Dissociation

Dissociation refers to a range of psychological states that allows a person to tolerate stressors that may be as mild as overstimulation or as severe as painful physical abuse.

The degree of dissociation may be mild and normal, as in daydreaming. Dissociation may be moderate, as when a child feels far away and may not be clearly aware of what is actually happening around him/her. Dissociation may be severe, as may occur when an overwhelming experience is so physically or emotionally painful that the child separates so completely from his/her normal, integrated self that he/she feels that separate selves hold the terrible thoughts, feelings, and memories.

In this book, "dissociation" refers to the moderate to severe end of the spectrum in which the traumatized child may be "absent" or detach from a traumatic event or reminder of the traumatic event. Dissociation can be regarded as a psychological form of "hiding" from real or perceived danger and may correspond to the "freeze" and "shield" response that may be a reaction to a terrifying situation.

EMDR = Eye Movement Desensitization and Reprocessing

Eye Movement Desensitization and Reprocessing therapy, introduced by Francine Shapiro, PhD, in 1987, is an evidence-based psychotherapy method for treating trauma. EMDR is now being used in about 100 countries to treat posttraumatic stress disorder and a variety of mental health conditions. EMDR has been sufficiently researched and has been endorsed and highly recommended for treatment of trauma by the World Health Organization (2013), the California Evidence-Based Clearinghouse for Child Welfare (2010), the International Society for Traumatic Stress Studies (2008), the American Psychiatric Association (2004), the Department of Veterans Affairs and Department of Defense (2004, 2010), and the UK's National Institute for Clinical Excellence (2005).

The World Health Organization compared EMDR with cognitive behavioral therapy (CBT), another recommended method for treating PTSD in children, adolescents, and adults: Trauma-focused CBT and EMDR are the only psychotherapies recommended for children, adolescents, and adults with PTSD. "Like CBT with a trauma focus, EMDR therapy aims to reduce subjective distress and strengthen adaptive cognitions related to the traumatic event. Unlike CBT with a trauma focus, EMDR does not involve (a) detailed descriptions of the event, (b) direct challenging of beliefs, (c) extended exposure, or (d) homework" (World Health Organization, 2013, p. 1).

Float Back

When a person recalls a recent incident that felt upsetting and induced distorted or negative beliefs, a therapist may encourage the person to "float back," or remember an earlier experience when he or she felt the same way. Specifically, the therapist may ask the person to picture the image of the recent event along with sensory information, to think the negative self-belief that goes with it, to notice the emotion it evokes, and then to focus on the physical sensation. Then the therapist will invite the person to "focus on the physical sensation and allow your mind to float back to a time when you had the exact same physical sensation." Desensitizing and reprocessing earlier memories may result in more generalized clearing of distress.

Marschak Interaction Method

The Marschak Interaction Method (MIM) is a structured technique for observing and assessing the overall quality and nature of relationships between caregiver and child. It consists of a series of simple tasks designed to elicit behaviors in four primary dimensions in order to evaluate the caregiver's capacity to:

• Set limits and provide an appropriately ordered environment (Structure).

- Engage the child in interaction while being attuned to the child's state (Engagement).
- Meet the child's needs for attention, soothing, and care (Nurture).
- Support and encourage the child's efforts to achieve at a developmentally appropriate level (Challenge).
- Evaluate the child's ability to respond to the caregiver's efforts.

Mindfulness/Meditation

One of the goals of therapy is for a person to be more present—that is, to notice himself/herself and his/her environment as they are in the present. Mindfulness can help the individual to experience the safety of the present unencumbered by painful memories of old traumatic experiences or worries about the future. Meditation focuses on the breath to anchor a person to the here and now.

Narrative

A narrative is a constructive format that describes a sequence of nonfictional or fictional events. The word derives from the Latin verb *narrare*, meaning "to tell," and is related to the adjective *gnarus*, meaning "knowing" or "skilled."

The word "story" may be used as a synonym of "narrative." It can also be used to refer to the sequence of events described in a narrative.

Narrative Therapy

Narrative therapy is a form of psychotherapy that was initially developed during the 1970s and 1980s, largely by Australian Michael White and David Epston of New Zealand. A narrative approach views problems as separate from people and assumes that people have many strengths and resources.

Negative Cognition

A negative cognition is a self-referencing negative belief that is false, negative, irrational, and/or distorted—for example, "I am bad" or "I am unlovable."

Nonverbal Cues

Nonverbal cues refer to facial expressions and postures that convey emotions.

Object Constancy

Object constancy is the understanding that objects continue to exist even when they cannot be seen, heard, or touched. Children who have had a change of primary caregivers during the first two years of life may not develop the belief that their primary caregiver is thinking about them, protecting them, or loving them when they are out of sight. Much attachment work focuses on establishing a sense of object constancy.

Peek-a-boo and hide-and-seek are favorite games that test object constancy. The implicit messages in these games are "There you are," "I'm delighted to see you!" and "You were meant to be." The games give an opportunity for the parent or caregiver to generate excitement and then to encourage release of energy followed by calming. Repetition of this cycle reinforces the child's emerging ability to regulate his/her emotional states.

Positive Cognition

A positive cognition is a self-referencing positive belief that is true, useful, and self-enhancing—for example, "I am lovable," "Now I can stand up for myself," and "It's over."

Posttraumatic Symptoms

Many children who do not meet all criteria for PTSD exhibit dysfunctional behaviors that are the result of exposure to a traumatic situation. These children may have been "traumatized" by a situation or media that felt threatening even though the child was actually safe. Parents may bring children to therapy because they have posttraumatic symptoms such as aggression, anxiety, or unusual, disturbing behaviors.

Reprocessing

Reprocessing refers to the phase of EMDR processing that involves changing negative cognitions to positive beliefs about the self that are true, useful, and self-enhancing.

Resource Installation and Cultivating Positive Emotions

Resource installation refers to the process of strengthening positive emotions by applying alternating bilateral stimulation while the person is remembering or imagining positive experiences.

Resources

Resources are personal qualities, positive experiences, spiritual beliefs, interests, skills, favorite books and music, connections with nature, and supportive people.

SUDS = Subjective Units of Distress Scale

The Subjective Units of Distress Scale was developed by Wolpe (Shapiro & Maxfield, 2002; Puffer, Greenwald, & Elrod, 1998).

It is a scale from 0 to 10 that is used to measure the intensity of the feeling of distress, with zero being calm, relaxed, and neutral and 10 being the most distressed imaginable.

Target

A target refers to a focus for EMDR processing. A target may be a specific moment in a critical incident that represents the worst part of the experience, a thought that is distorted, an emotional response that is way too strong for a given situation, or a physical sensation that represents a distressing memory.

Theraplay

Theraplay is a child and family therapy that has as its goal enhancing and building attachment, self-esteem, trust in others, and joyful engagement. The principles underlying Theraplay are that, in healthy relationships, there should be natural patterns of playful, healthy interaction between parent and child. The goal of Theraplay is a changed view of the self as worthy and lovable and of relationships as positive and rewarding. It is one type of play therapy that can be used with children.

Trauma

A trauma is defined as any experience that undermines the sense of safety and well-being and gives false, negative, irrational, or distorted beliefs about the self or the world. Traumatic experiences rupture trust. Memories of traumatic experiences are stored as visual images with accompanying sensory information, a negative cognition, a feeling or affect, and a physical sensation.

VoC = Validity of Cognition

The Validity of Cognition scale is an individualized measure of beliefs developed by Shapiro (1989). How deeply the person believes his/her positive cognition is measured using the VoC scale. The goal is for the person to accept the full truth of his/her positive self-statement at a level of seven (completely true).

APPENDIX

Developmental Trauma Disorder

Described by Bessel A. van der Kolk, MD.

A. Exposure.

- Multiple or chronic exposure to one or more forms of developmentally adverse interpersonal trauma (e.g., abandonment, betrayal, physical assaults, sexual assaults, threats to bodily integrity, coercive practices, emotional abuse, witnessing violence and death).
- Subjective experience (e.g., rage, betrayal, fear, resignation, defeat, shame).

B. Triggered pattern of repeated dysregulation in response to trauma cues. Dysregulation (high or low) in presence of cues. Changes persist and do not return to baseline; not reduced in intensity by conscious awareness.

- Affective.
- Somatic (e.g., physiological, motoric, medical).
- Behavioral (e.g., reenactment, cutting).
- Cognitive (e.g., thinking that it is happening again, confusion, dissociation, depersonalization).
- Relational (e.g., clinging, oppositional, distrustful, compliant).
- Self-attribution (e.g., self-hate, blame).

C. Persistently altered attributions and expectancies.

- Negative self-attribution.
- Distrust of protective caretaker.
- Loss of expectancy of protection by others.
- Loss of trust in social agencies to protect.

- Lack of recourse to social justice/retribution.
- Inevitability of future victimization.

D. Functional impairment.

Posttraumatic Stress Disorder (PTSD) in Young Children

Posttraumatic stress disorder, or PTSD, is diagnosed after a person experiences symptoms for at least one month following a traumatic event. The disorder is characterized by three main types of symptoms:

- Re-experiencing the trauma through intrusive, distressing recollections of the event, flashbacks, and nightmares.
- Emotional numbness and avoidance of places, people, and activities that are reminders of the trauma.
- Increased arousal such as difficulty sleeping and concentrating, feeling jumpy, and being easily irritated and angered.

Diagnosis criteria that apply specifically to children younger than age six include the following:

- Exposure to actual or threatened death, serious injury, or sexual violation.
- Direct experience.
- Witnessing the events as they occurred to others, especially primary caregivers. (Note: Does not include events witnessed only in electronic media, television, movies, or pictures.)
- Learning that the traumatic events occurred to a parent or caregiving figure.

The presence of one or more of the following:

- Spontaneous or cued recurrent, involuntary, and intrusive distressing memories of the traumatic events. (Note: Spontaneous and intrusive memories may not necessarily appear distressing and may be expressed as play reenactment.)
- Recurrent distressing dreams related to the content and/or feeling of the traumatic events. (Note: It may not be possible to ascertain that the frightening content is related to the traumatic event.)
- Reactions as if the traumatic events are recurring; the most extreme being a complete loss of awareness of present surroundings. (Note: Such trauma-specific reenactment may occur in play.)

- Intense or prolonged psychological distress at exposure to internal or external cues.
- Marked physiological reactions to reminders of the traumatic events.

One of the following related to traumatic events:

- Persistent avoidance of activities, places, or physical reminders.
- People, conversations, or interpersonal situations that arouse recollections.
- Diminished interest or participation in significant activities such as play.
- Socially withdrawn behavior.
- Persistent reduction in expression of positive emotions.

Two or more of the following:

- Irritable, angry, or aggressive behavior, including extreme temper tantrums.
- Hypervigilance.
- Exaggerated startle response.
- Problems with concentration.
- Difficulty falling or staying asleep or restless sleep.

Eight Phases of EMDR With Children

1. Client History

Meet with parents alone first to learn about presenting complaints and trauma history.

Ask about birth, early experiences, illness, injury, separation, loss, or other upsets. Ask about medications.

Begin to connect presenting symptoms with identified trauma.

Be sure to learn about child's strengths, resources, play interests, style of meeting developmental challenges, school performance, and relationships with parents, siblings, friends, and other caregivers.

Ask parents for negative cognitions they think their child may have, and ask them about positive cognitions they would like for their child.

Explain EMDR to the parents and obtain consent.

If the child is preverbal, experienced trauma while preverbal, or is trauma-avoidant, consider using a storytelling approach. (This will involve meeting alone with the parents another time to help them write the story. I decide whether to have the story-writing session after I have met the child.)

Tips for Success

Meet both parents. Each parent has a valuable perspective and role.

Get lots of information about the child and family. Much trauma is not identified as trauma by parents.

Talk with teachers or other caregivers or therapists to learn how the child behaves in various settings.

2. *Client Preparation*

Meet the child with the parents.

Identify your office as a "safe place" where "you can play whatever you want but nothing and nobody gets hurt for real."

Notice whether the child makes eye contact with you and caregivers.

Notice the child's developmental level.

Notice the child's mood, choice of toys, activities and conversation, and themes of play.

Notice whether the child has repetitive play.

Ask the child and the parents what they would like to "go easier" for their family.

Explain about trauma and EMDR in a way that is developmentally appropriate.

Get to know the child by observing, talking, and playing.

Encourage and teach methods of calming and self-soothing to parents and child (e.g., safe place and safe person).

Tip for Success

Children do only what they want to do.

Learn what the child is motivated to change. Make friends with the child and elicit his/her cooperation and involvement in helping things be easier for him/her. Remember, the goal of EMDR is for the child and family to have more fun every day.

3. *Assessment*

Assess the developmental level of the child. Many children who have been traumatized display coping strategies that were "stuck" at the time of the trauma.

Assess the cognitive capability of the child. Developmentally disabled patients can be treated with EMDR, but do not expect that targeting the image representing the worst part of the incident will clear the symptoms. The traumatic memories must be targeted "frame by frame."

Determine the degree of dissociation if present.

Get to know the child well enough to determine whether you can basically use the adult protocol or whether you need to modify it by integrating EMDR into play, sand tray work, art therapy, or storytelling.

Assess the child's readiness to desensitize and reprocess traumatic memories. Ask the child about the upsetting memory, and ask whether it would be OK to get over it and erase some of the upset. If the child is reluctant to "get over it and erase the upset," there is a good reason. Wait until the child agrees that he/she is ready (although you may be able to work through the whole trauma without ever talking about it—for example, by treating the teddy bear). Nothing will happen unless you have cooperation.

In a child three years or older, you may ask about images, feelings, and SUD rating. I recommend that you not ask a child for a negative cognition. (You may ask, "When you remember what happened, what do you think about yourself now?" but don't be surprised if the child cannot respond.) You may suggest a menu of positive cognitions and ask which ones the child likes.

Determine the best way to deliver alternating bilateral stimulation (ABS). Introduce the child to the ABS aspect of EMDR in a positive way.

Start by offering different modalities of ABS with a range of enjoyable memories. For example, try auditory tones while remembering a fun time; try hand tapping while remembering the feeling of being loved by someone; try following fingers or lights while remembering a success experience; try various tones via headphones while remembering a learning experience. Let the child choose which modality he/she likes best.

Consider whether to have a parent present during sessions.

Ask teachers and parents to report any "triggers" they notice.

Tips for Success

You can help a child feel safe only if he/she *is* safe.

Children can relax and feel secure only if their parents feel relaxed. Assess the parents' degree of trauma resolution and treat or refer the parents if necessary.

Assess readiness for rapid processing. Avoid abreaction by following the child's comfort level. The worst that can happen while doing EMDR is that the child may stop and refuse to continue desensitization and reprocessing.

4. Desensitization

Ask the child to choose "Stop" and "Go" signals. Remember "Stop" means stop!

Children under five years old usually cannot follow past mid-line, so auditory or tactile stimulation might be a better choice than eye movement for delivering alternating bilateral stimulations. Some young children like to look at the lights (usually at top speed), and connecting headphones to the eye scan machine for synchronized ABS will ensure that they receive a therapeutic effect.

Young children (under about eight years old) do not spontaneously process associated memories (usefulness of history, parents' story for the child, and encouraging child to remember other times when they felt "that way").

- Adults who were traumatized as young children process in much the same way as young children.
- Desensitize until SUD = 0 or hands together. You may need to use educational interweave or imaginal interweave in order to desensitize the memory.
- Abreactions in children are rare, but "that happened a long, long time ago," followed by "Where are you right now?" are useful lines to remember.
- "Looping" in children sometimes occurs because children do not have the "adult perspective." To resolve stuck points, two types of interweaves are more valuable than questions about responsibility, choices, or safety.

Educational Interweave

Offer information or a perspective that will help with trauma resolution.

For example, teach the child that mistreatment is not acceptable even if the perpetrator gives a gift or praise. Teach the child to use a strong voice to say "stop" or to call for help or to phone 911, etc.

Imaginal Interweave

Ask the child to imagine something that might have been helpful at the time of the trauma.

For example, "Can you imagine a yummy medicine that could make the yucky medicine taste better?"

"Can you imagine what you would tell your 'baby self' in the orphanage about how life turned out with your forever family?"

Tips for Success

Even though this is sometimes scary work for the child, do what you can to make it feel as safe and enjoyable as possible. Using metaphors can make the experience more palatable. For example, you may offer to help the doll get over an upsetting memory by having a unicorn, superhero, or figure of the child's choice dance on his hands. Children may need only a very few minutes of ABS.

5. Installation

For all young children and most school-aged children, you will have to provide the positive cognition. Remember that children do not have an "adult perspective," so the adult (you) will have to supply the adult perspective.

You may need to add educational or imaginal interweaves so that processing can come to "adaptive resolution."

Shapiro's (2001) Adaptive Information Processing model posits that EMDR facilitates the accessing and processing of traumatic memories and other adverse life experiences to bring these to an adaptive resolution. After successful treatment with EMDR, affective distress is relieved, negative beliefs are reformulated, and physiological arousal is reduced. In adolescents, you may need to teach judgment or problem solving before a positive cognition can feel true.

Young children will not be able to give a validity of cognition.

Tips for Success

Assess the child's appearance to determine whether it appears that complete resolution with SUD rating of zero has been achieved. Occasionally a child will say that the SUD rating is zero in order to please you. They know "zero" is the response you want. Check your results.

6. Body Scan

After the positive cognition is strengthened, ask the child to revisit the target memory. Then ask, "Is there any place in your body that still holds upset (or feels tense) when you remember what happened?" If so, ask the child to notice the tension and continue ABS until there is no longer a physical sensation associated with the memory. Sometimes it helps for the child to put his/her hand on the tense spot.

7. Closure

If there is still distress at the end of the session, help the child put the remaining upset in a container (literally or metaphorically) and reassure him/her that you will work on it together next time to continue erasing the upsetting feelings. Remind the child of a safe place or butterfly hug or whatever self-soothing the child enjoys.

Ask parents to notice (and keep a log) of continuing triggers and behavioral disturbances and to report by phone prior to the next visit.

8. Reevaluation

Recheck your work with the child and the parent. How has life improved? What is still a problem? Recognize that when symptoms have subsided and life has returned to normal, no one will be excited about the child's behavior anymore. Even parents may not recognize that the EMDR contributed to the improvements, and it's OK for you to point out the possibility that EMDR made a difference!

Use ABS to install future template.

INDEX

unfairness 88; stealing 190;
transition problems 21
Child Maltreatment Report 113
choices, age appropriate 16
clinical judgment 37
closure of incomplete session 229
cognitions 163–4, 173, 175;
transitional 176; umbrella 28; *see
also* negative cognitions; positive
cognitions
cognitive behavioral therapy
(CBT) 218
cognitive interweave 27, 175, 217;
educational 99, 163–4, 171
comfort 119
complex trauma 92, 104, 109, 141,
205; approaches 97; principles
of treating children with 87, 99,
113–14
confusion 86, 97, 169; definition 28,
effect on learning 54, 111; medical
trauma and 35; understanding 110,
173, 174
Connected Child, The (Karyn
Purvis) 13
connection 15; parenting for 158
container 229
control 122, 128, 130, 149; need
for 53; parents 77, 147; *see also*
challenging behaviors
cooperation 8, 104, 227; games 11,
147–9; precursors to 15
coping strategies 176
cortisol 204
critical incidents 174, 177, 217
cuddling 13, 141

danger 172
death of a parent 48, 80, 90; fear
of 132
desensitization 20, 23, 43, 78, 227;
definition 217; phase 19, 26,
227–8; systematic 43; as a video 28
"detachment" therapy 35, 195–7
developmental considerations 96;
delay 96, 100, 103, 115; directive
205; disabilities 103; egocentricity
28; level 226
developmental trauma disorder
15, 223
Diagnostic and Statistical Manual of
Mental Disorders (DSM-5) 14–15

DID *see* dissociative identity disorder
dissociation 128, 131; approach
109, 172, 114; definition of 217;
indications of 110, 112; *see also*
dissociative identity disorder
dissociative identity disorder 110
divorce 185
dreams 52, 224
dual attention 112
dyadic resourcing (Philip
Manfield) 151
dysregulation 223

eating disorder 39
educational interweave 27, 28, 99,
108, 228
egocentricity 108, 169, 174
EMDR 15, 26, 114; and AIP 215;
comparison with CBT 218;
eight phases of 225; eight-phase
protocol 25, 26; endorsements 218;
indications for 18; preparation for
16; principles 20; young children
19, 25
emotional dysregulation 14
Epston, David 219
Erikson, Erik 15
eye contact 30, 33, 147, 149, 159

face painting 149
facial expressions 219
fault 174
fear of: abandonment 104; being
restrained 97, 103; blood draw 102;
breezes 130; closet 99, 114; crowds
111; food 105, 127; knocking on
the door 107; mechanical sounds
125; open window 125; toilets
17, 22–3; transitions 129; the
unexpected 87, 106
float back 174, 218
foster parents 204
"four-section method" 100, 114; *see
also* artwork and EMDR

games: hide and seek 120; "I spy"
157; peek-a-boo 130; *see also*
games for cooperation
games for cooperation: animal cracker
147; bubble 148; lollypop 149–50
glossary 215
grief therapy 90

CPSIA information can be obtained
at www.ICGtesting.com
Printed in the USA
LVHW081051271122
734078LV00023B/1280